Fatherless

© 2021 by TGS International, a wholly owned subsidiary of Christian Aid Ministries, Berlin, Ohio.

All rights reserved. No part of this book may be reproduced or stored in any retrieval system, in any form or by any means, electronic or mechanical, without written permission from the publisher except for brief quotations embodied in critical articles and reviews.

ISBN: 978-1-950791-86-6

Cover and text layout design: Kristi Yoder

Printed in the USA

Published by:
TGS International
P.O. Box 355
Berlin, Ohio 44610 USA
Phone: 330.893.4828
Fax: 330.893.2305
www.tgsinternational.com

Fatherless

Harold R. Troyer

I delivered the poor that cried,
and the fatherless,
and him that had none to help him.
Job 29:12

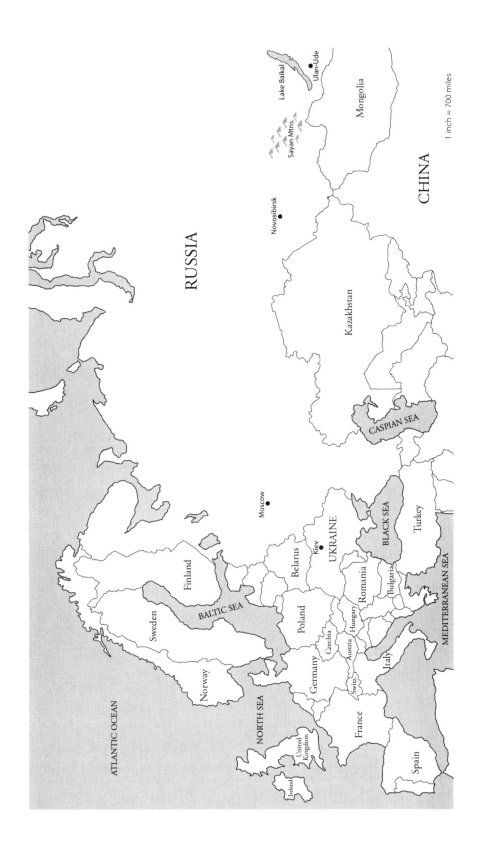

Map of Kiev Area

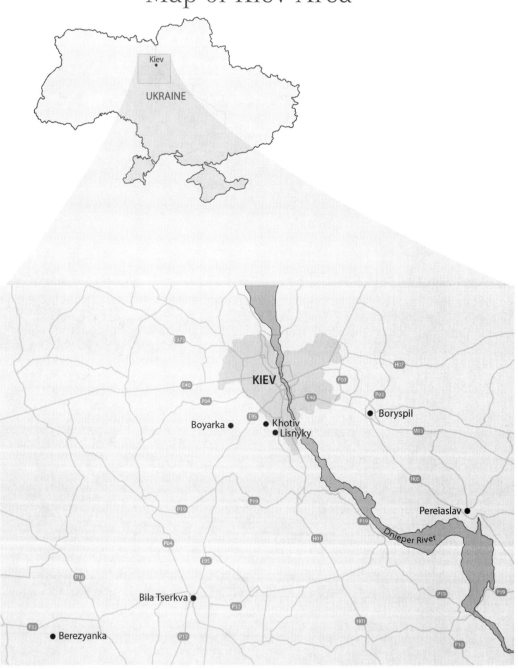

1 inch = 20 miles

Table of Contents

1. Fatherless 9
2. Troubled Roots 15
3. Raised by the Government 25
4. Another Failed Attempt 35
5. God Under the Stairs 45
6. Building the USSR 51
7. Born in Siberia 59
8. Not Without My Daughter 67
9. Back to Ukraine 77
10. Place to Place 87
11. Improvements 103
12. What's Yours Is Mine 111
13. The Americans 119
14. Shtundists or Orthodox? 127
15. The Food Parcel 135

16.	Mama's Story	141
17.	Orphanage Life	147
18.	A Sudden Death	155
19.	Spain	167
20.	Adoption?	175
21.	The New House	179
22.	Keep Climbing	189
23.	Black Sea Summer	195
24.	New Desires	201
25.	The Struggle	207
26.	Friendships	213
27.	Sewing College	219
28.	Cross-Cultural Relationship	229
29.	Engaged	235
30.	Crushed	241
31.	Bible Camp	251
32.	The Visa	255
33.	A New World	265
34.	An Understanding Heart	275
35.	Married Twice	281
36.	Immigration	297
37.	Godly Seed	305
	Epilogue	311
	About the Author	317

Fatherless

1995

The girl's large brown eyes were pleading. She held out her hand as worshipers shuffled toward the stately church to make their confessions and pay their tithes. She watched for friendly-looking newcomers and stepped in front of them.

"Sir, can you please give me some money for bread?" the girl pleaded. "I have no papa. Please?"

"Here, little girl." A wealthy-looking businessman stuffed a bill into her outstretched hand.

"Thank you, sir!"

The warm breezes of spring had replaced the Ukrainian winter's brutal cold and snowfall, and the village cows were now herded to the fields outside the villages to graze during the day. Flocks of goats went with the cow herds to forage through the tangled brush along the open meadows. The villagers, enjoying the warmth of longer days to work in the fields and gardens, called back and forth to each other as they plowed and worked the rich soil.

In the city of Kiev, Ukraine, workers cleaned the streets and sidewalks, picking up trash and bottles exposed by the melting snow. Employees washed large storefront windows that had been stained by the blowing snow and the splashing water and dirt during the spring thaw.

In the southern part of the city, the sweet fragrance of lilacs filled the grounds around the Demiivska Orthodox Cathedral. With quiet whispers and bowed heads, worshipers moved in and out of the gold-domed church. Positioned just outside the exterior doors stood an eleven-year-old girl with tangled hair and dirt-smudged cheeks. She wore red pants and a torn brown jacket. Her name was Larissa.

"Ma'am, please give me money for bread," Larissa begged.

"No, I can't give you money." The middle-aged lady in a dark maroon overcoat stopped beside her. "But you do look hungry, so I'll buy you some bread. Here, come with me."

As Larissa followed the lady across the road to a small store, the aroma of fresh food made her realize how ravenously hungry she was.

"Give me a fresh roll," the woman told the clerk. She placed some money on the counter.

After receiving the bread, Larissa darted out of the store and gulped down the roll. She returned to the church and continued to beg, her pockets slowly filling with coins and bills. During a lull when few people were arriving, she stepped behind a nearby lilac bush to survey her gains. A small smile played across her pinched features. *This has been a good day,* she thought. *I will keep begging for a few more minutes.*

Automobiles zoomed along the street, and a trolley bus screeched to a halt at a nearby station filled with people. A young mother ambled by with a stroller, her young son skipping along beside her. Pigeons squawked and fluttered around the church janitor as he threw a few sunflower seeds to them. Larissa stepped forward as a fashionably dressed lady made her way to the church.

"Ma'am, a few kopeks, please?" She held out her hand. "I'm hungry."

"Here, girl," said the woman, giving her a gentle smile. "Take this." She thrust some bills into Larissa's hand. "Go get something warm to eat. You probably have some siblings somewhere too."

"Thank you," murmured Larissa.

A tall man strode off the street and up to the church.

"Sir, please. Could you give me money for bread?" Larissa dropped her eyes.

"I will show you what I can give you." The tall man grabbed her arm. "You know better than begging in front of the church. I will take you to jail."

Larissa struggled to get free.

"Ha. You will go to jail, little girl, until I can find your mother."

Larissa continued to twist and turn. A tearing sound came from her jacket.

"You are pretty strong for a young one." The man grabbed Larissa's other hand as she swung at him. Pigeons squawked and fluttered wildly out of their way.

The man had a crushing hold on Larissa's arm as he dragged her along. She tried to jerk away, but he was too powerful. As they left the church grounds and crossed the street, Larissa had an idea. She would show him.

She bent and bit his hand. Hard.

He shouted in pain and let go.

Off like a shot, Larissa darted around buildings and through alleyways. She could hear the man running close behind her. She rounded an apartment building and dashed across another street. The driver of a large truck honked the horn and slammed on the brakes to avoid hitting the fleeing girl.

Larissa threw herself behind a few dumpsters beside the street. She peered between them, trying to ignore the sour, rotten smell of decaying garbage. She wrinkled her nose and pinched it to keep from sneezing.

I hope he doesn't come over to this side, she thought. She could see the tall man across the street looking bewildered. *Sorry, sir,* she grinned to herself. *I didn't want to hurt you, but I had to do something!*

She watched to see if the man would follow her. She was breathing hard, but she knew if she had to she could probably outrun him and outsmart him. She was thankful her little brother Maxim hadn't been with her today.

The tall man scowled as he scanned the street. The girl had disappeared into Kiev's smoggy air. He turned away, and Larissa sighed with relief as she watched him go. She saw him rubbing his wrist as he disappeared around the corner.

Shadows lengthened as Larissa trudged between the high-rise apartments. A black cat hissed and slunk back into an alleyway. Above her, a woman was hanging out her wash on a balcony. For a moment, she paused to watch the lone girl below her before turning back to her duties.

At the bus station, Larissa hurried to find the bus to her hometown of Lisnyky. As usual, she found a crowd of people waiting. The sun slipped below the horizon and temperatures dropped as Larissa shivered and stood in line for a ticket.

Finally, after nearly thirty minutes, the bus arrived. It was packed with people, and Larissa had to squeeze in between two grandmothers. The bus was filled with villagers, including a few she knew. Larissa hunkered down, trying to stay inconspicuous. At least she could get warmed up now.

"You by yourself?" asked a villager. "Where's your mama?"

Larissa shrugged. "Probably at work," she replied, looking away.

"You're not carrying anything," the woman pressed. "Where were you?"

Larissa ignored the woman for a moment. This was Ana's wealthy mother. Ana was in her grade at Lisnyky Elementary School and had made fun of her for not having a papa like the other children. Larissa felt her cheeks grow warm as she remembered the taunting she had received.

"I was in the city," she finally replied, looking out the window to avoid the woman's probing eyes. She thrust her hands into her pockets and felt the money. *It isn't my fault I don't have a papa,* she sighed. *I will ask Mama again why my papa doesn't live with us like other children's papas. Why are we so different?*

As the bus rumbled its way through Lisnyky and slowed for the station, Larissa stood and moved to the aisle. She jumped off the bus with a few other villagers, trudged across the street, and entered a little store. *Now's my chance to get some ice cream,* she thought.

"Give me an ice cream bar," Larissa instructed the storekeeper, pointing to the one she wanted.

"Where did you get your money?" The storekeeper raised his shaggy eyebrows. "You're Nadia's daughter, aren't you? I know she doesn't have money for ice cream." He glared at her. "Did you steal it?"

Larissa ignored the question and continued to point at the bar. He could think what he wanted. But Alexander the storekeeper was right. They barely had enough money for necessities, let alone ice cream. *I hope he doesn't say anything to Mama.* She took the ice cream and stepped outside. As she meandered along the street savoring the cold treat, she pulled her threadbare jacket closer to her shivering body. The ice cream was delicious, but it didn't help her get any warmer.

Larissa mused on her day. Even though her pockets were full of money, she hated begging. Her heart clenched tightly and tears filled her brown eyes as she thought about her papa. Mama had helped her write a letter to him when she was in third grade. Why hadn't he written back? *I wish my papa would come live with Mama. Then we'd have lots of money, and I wouldn't have to go begging. We would have plenty to eat and lots of ice cream.*

2

Troubled Roots

1963

Yakov pounded on the doorframe. He had arrived in Lisnyky at the small village house built by his father. Rings of smoke curled from the chimney, and the door stood wide open. He hoped his sister Maria was at home—but too often she wasn't. With all the snow, the seven-mile walk from his home in Kiev had taken nearly four hours, and he didn't have time to waste.

"Maria! Ma-r-i-a! Are you home?" He peered through the doorway. As his eyes adjusted to the darkness, he could see she was not there, but what *was* there enraged him. Two men sat with their backs to the brick stove, one smoking and the other pouring a glass of vodka. They stared back, glassy-eyed and unconcerned.

"What are you doing here?" Yakov shouted at the two men. "Get out!"

He grabbed a stick beside the door and charged into the house. The men attempted to dodge his blows and staggered out the door with Yakov brandishing the long stick behind them.

"Go!" Yakov shouted. "And don't come back!"

They will probably hide in the bushes until I leave. The thought angered him even more. His sister and her men were never a good combination. He stopped to catch his breath and calm his nerves. *I need to tell Maria to stay clear of these men.* He snorted. *But it probably won't help.*

An orange-and-white cat rubbed against the corner of the house, arching its back as Yakov turned back to close the door. *I wonder where she could be.*

Yakov sighed. This was disgusting. While he and Marusia worked hard to care for her baby, Maria roamed at will.

He called again. As the cold wind penetrated his olive-green overcoat, he pulled it closer, shivering. *Where could Maria be on a cold day like this?* Well, there was nothing to do about it. Snow crunched under his boots as he reluctantly started for home.

Suddenly he stopped in his tracks as a thought came to his mind. *I know what.* He rubbed his smoothly shaved chin with the back of his hand. *I'll talk to Greesha and her sister Olga. They're neighbors and my cousins anyway. They can give Maria a message when she comes home—if she ever does.*

Before he could change his mind, he walked up the dirt lane to Greesha and Olga's house. Maybe they would know something of Maria's whereabouts. A scrawny dog barked and lunged on his leash as Yakov banged on the gate.

"Who's there?"

Tiny Olga finally shoved open the door, and the wind banged it against the wall.

"Oh, it's you." She wrinkled her nose. "Looking for Maria, are you?"

"Yes," replied Yakov with a scowl. "I wanted to ask her something important. I should ask her in person, but I want to get back home before too late. Could you or Greesha tell Maria that my wife and I want to adopt her daughter?" His voice softened. "Marusia is too old to have any more children, so we'd like to adopt baby Nadia."

"I'll tell her," answered Olga, with a kinder glint in her eye. She wiped her hands on her stained but clean apron. "We'll give her your message."

Yakov hurried back the way he had come. He didn't bother following the road, for he could save thirty minutes by going through the forests and fields. This part of Ukraine was mostly flat or slightly rolling and had some forested areas. Most of the wildlife in the forests had been harvested for food, and only wild boars were still plentiful. He hoped he wouldn't meet one. He had experienced enough worries for one day.

The snow in the forest was still fluffy, for the sun hadn't melted it during the day. After walking for several hours, Yakov stopped to rest. A gust of wind knocked off a shower of snow from a branch above, scaring a sleeping owl who flapped his groggy way deeper into the silent forest.

It's too bad Maria has to be this way, he mused. She had kept company with a man named Valera for the last year or so, and although they had never married, they now had a baby. Yakov doubted that Maria would care for her child. He groaned. If only his sister would stay away from men. He brushed a branch to the side and plowed on.

The cold shadows of evening embraced the city of Kiev when Yakov finally arrived home to his simple Ukrainian duplex. He and his wife Marusia and their daughter Natasha lived in one apartment while his wife's brother Niko and his family occupied the other. Right now, Marusia's mother, Varvara, was also living with them.

After Yakov had hung up his overcoat and pulled off his boots, he put on his slippers and pushed through the door. Marusia was standing at the kitchen stove stirring a pot of borscht.[1] She turned when the door swung open.

"Are you tired?" she asked.

"Of course," he answered a bit shortly. "Make me a cup of hot tea, please." Yakov sat on a creaking chair and scooted closer to the rickety table.

"What did your sister say?"

"Nothing. She wasn't there. I asked Greesha and Olga, but they haven't seen her for a few days. I left a message with them that we would like to adopt Nadia." Yakov shifted his feet impatiently and rubbed his hands together for better circulation.

Marusia poured black tea concentrate into a mug, filled the mug with boiling water, and handed it to her husband. She set a sugar bowl within his reach. The bowl was cracked, but Yakov had glued it back together.

Hot tea was a vital part of life in the cold, dreary climate of north-central Ukraine. Just a few hundred years earlier, tea had been available only to the upper nobility, as it had taken a year or more to transport it from the Far East by camel caravans. But now the railway had drastically cut the transport time, making tea affordable for everyone.

A cry came from the living room where the baby lay in Varvara's arms. Baby Nadia had been so quiet that Yakov had not noticed her. He had been so upset with Maria that he had forgotten the reason for his trek that day.

Yakov got up to see why the baby was crying. She definitely had a powerful cry for a little baby. Maybe she would be a good singer. He would make sure she joined the Orthodox choir when she was old enough. Varvara sang quietly to the baby and looked up as Yakov

---

[1] A sour soup very popular in Russia and Ukraine, usually made with beets.

came near.

Five-year-old Natasha sat quietly beside her grandmother. "Hi, Papa," she said. Her brown eyes sparkled as she leaned toward the baby. She wanted to keep this baby as much as her parents did.

"Nadia is okay. She's just hungry," Varvara responded to Yakov's worried look. "She is strong and will make you a good daughter if Maria lets you adopt her. I'm sorry you didn't get to talk to her today."

The simple light fixture fastened to the whitewashed ceiling cast a shimmering light over the room. Heavy blankets stretched from one wall to the other to help insulate the rooms from the frigid cold sweeping across the western Eurasian Steppe. Window drapes moved slightly at the moan of the wind, and a slight draft reached the room where the baby snuggled down, toasty and warm in Varvara's embrace.

"Could you stoke the fire, Yakov?" asked Marusia. "I'm cold."

Getting to his feet, Yakov walked to the sitting room. The large stove, built of clay bricks, had an oblong bottom chamber for the long sticks of wood. A larger back allowed the heat and smoke to travel up and down through vertical chambers to collect and conserve the heat. The stove was not really hot, and sometimes on cold winter nights one of them would nestle down and sleep right on top of it.

After Yakov added some wood, he returned to the table to finish his tea and eat the borscht and buttered bread Marusia had prepared. He finished his meal with some cold fish out of a small tin can.

"Do you have any idea where Maria went?" asked Marusia as she mopped the kitchen floor.

"No. Hard telling. Probably ran off with some man." He shrugged. "I would be surprised if she wants the baby. She didn't want it when they were released from the hospital."

The night passed, but Yakov did not sleep well. He tossed and turned as he thought about his sister and her baby. Well, he decided, if his sister Maria wouldn't care for her baby, he and Marusia would.

Maria swung open the door to her house. Her hands were red from the cold, but she finally managed to find the light switch. A rat scuttled into a hole in the floor to escape the light.

"Crazy rat!" she hollered. She stuffed straw and sticks into the stove and tried to strike a match. As the damp match crumbled, she swore, then tried again. This time it sizzled into a flame. She pushed the match into the dry straw, and soon it began to burn. As the fire crackled, she rubbed her hands together, warming them. Dragging her straw mattress closer to the large brick stove, Maria crawled onto the mattress and soon fell asleep.

Loud pounding on the door awakened her. She blinked and looked around the room in the dim light coming from the dirty windows. The pounding shook the house again.

"Maria! Ma-r-i-a!"

Maria crawled out from under her blankets, her hair standing out like a scarecrow's. She leaped for the door. *Who could it be?* She unlocked the door and swung it open.

"Time to get up, Maria," said Olga. "The early bird drinks the dew."

"Who cares about dew? I want to sleep." Maria rubbed her red eyes.

"I have a message for you. Your brother Yakov was here a few days ago looking for you. He and Marusia want to adopt baby Nadia. You need to let him know what you think." Olga turned to leave. "You should let them know soon, Maria."

Maria slammed the door and locked it. *I sure don't want to take care of that baby. I am going to sleep for a while yet, then I'll go see Yakov and Marusia.* She added some more wood to the fire and crawled back into her straw bed.

Later that morning Maria roused herself and got dressed. She dipped some water out of the bucket on the table and took a gulp.

Ugh! She spat half a mouthful onto the floor in disgust. *It tastes like rats have been swimming in it.* Grimacing, she grabbed a wrinkled apple out of the box along the wall and took a bite. Today she would have to buy some food at the market after her trip to Yakov's house. She grabbed her hoe. Her eyes gleamed as her troubled mind whirled. *This should take care of Yakov and Marusia.*

As Maria walked through the snow-covered fields and forests, she thought about her baby. *Why should I let my brother raise her? If I don't want to raise the baby, I don't want him to raise her either. Maybe I should just get rid of the baby too.*

Yakov splashed water over his face. Marusia was in the kitchen banging her pots and pans again. He wished she would be quieter. He liked a calm, relaxing atmosphere, like the St. Volodymyr's Cathedral where he worked as a janitor.

"Good morning, Marusia," Yakov greeted his wife as he entered the kitchen. He sat down at the table. A bowl of steaming potatoes, a plate of fried eggs, and a few pieces of salo[2] caused his stomach to growl.

"Do you think your sister will ever show up?" asked Marusia, flopping a loaf of bread onto the table and hacking off a few large pieces.

"Who knows?" Yakov reached for a piece of bread.

After they had eaten, Marusia gathered up the dishes. "I need to go to the market today to buy some milk for the baby. I also need some clothes for her."

"Sounds good," replied Yakov. "Thank you for the tasty breakfast. I need to be on my way to work." He grabbed his bag, some hand tools, and his work clothes before heading out to catch the trolley.

---

[2] Cured pork fat. So popular in Ukraine that over 99% of the men know how to prepare it!

From the forest, Maria watched her brother's house for movement. The house was modest by Ukrainian standards, with white wood siding and gray asbestos tile roofing. Both sides of the duplex appeared deserted. However, the stick that was normally propped against the door to signal the housekeeper's absence was lying next to the steps.

An evil gleam appeared in her eye as she finally spotted her sister-in-law Marusia standing beside the snowy street talking to a neighbor. Maria crept along in the shadows, closing the distance between her and her prey. She jumped and swore as a rabbit exploded from almost under her feet.

When she was directly across the road from the two women, Maria broke out of the forest and charged across the road, swinging the hoe.

Marusia looked up in shock. She screamed and raised her hands to ward off the flailing hoe. The bags she was carrying and the container of milk flew from her hands.

"Here! Come in here!" shouted Vera, a neighbor, as she shoved open her gate.

As Marusia quickly darted into the courtyard, Vera slammed the gate and latched it. Unable to enter, Maria cursed and swung her hoe at the gate. It clanged and bounced off. Dropping the hoe, Maria turned and ran for Yakov and Marusia's house. She tried the latch on the front door, then slowly opened it and stepped inside. As she pushed open the entry door that led into the house, she could hear someone singing softly. She tiptoed further and peered into the next room. There was Marusia's mother holding baby Nadia. Maria crept forward. The aged woman looked up in surprise.

Suddenly Maria darted forward and tried to grab the baby. The older woman turned away, but the younger and much stronger woman soon overpowered her. Wrenching the baby away, she hollered, "You cannot have my baby! No one can. Not Yakov either." She grabbed the baby by the neck and started squeezing. Varvara tried to tear the choking baby away from her. The tussling and thumping of the two struggling women and the screams of the baby aroused the occupants of the next apartment, and Marusia's brother Niko came running.

"What's going on?" he demanded, pushing his way into his sister's apartment. The two women were wrestling, and the baby was screaming at the top of her lungs.

"Help me!" cried Varvara when she saw Niko. "Get this mad woman out of here! She's trying to kill the baby!"

Marusia had followed Niko into the room. Together the three of them wrenched the red-faced, screaming baby from the swearing woman. Then they wrestled the fighting woman to the floor and sat on her to keep her down.

"We have her under control," Niko panted. "Call the police."

The police soon arrived and handcuffed the young mother. Once her arms were fastened behind her back, Maria became a totally different person and calmly sat down in a chair. Her face still flushed from the fight, she grinned at the police.

Raised by the Government

1963-1970

The clacking of wheels and the swaying motion of the train soothed Yakov. "We should be getting close to the orphanage," he said, glancing at Marusia, who was holding baby Nadia. Beside her sat her mother Varvara.

The frozen white landscape, now sporting some bare spots, flashed past the small frosted window. Soon the snowdrops, the earliest flowers, would be pushing up through the snow, telling the world that spring was just around the corner. The long, dreary winters made spring a welcome time of year.

Yakov pondered the events of the last few weeks and sighed. With Maria so adamantly opposed to adoption, he had pursued a different plan for baby Nadia. At an appointment with a local official, he had secured permission to put the baby into a government orphanage. This way she would at least be protected and have a decent place to live.

"My sister has proven that she cannot care for her baby," Yakov had told the woman minister. "My wife and I would like to get a referral to place her in the Boyarka Baby Orphanage. My sister is mentally incapable and has tried to take the baby's life. She even attacked my wife because we were caring for the baby."

He smirked as he recalled the minister's consternation at seeing Maria with her hands tied behind her back.

"Loose her," the minister had ordered. "Such a beautiful young mother standing there so calm and innocent. It's a pity."

Yakov had tried to explain, but to no avail. With no guards around, Yakov knew it wasn't safe.

"You don't need a referral for this baby," the minister continued. "This mother can take care of her own child. Am I right, madam?"

She nodded at Maria.

Nadia's mother, Maria.

Maria looked at the minister with a slight grin as Yakov untied her hands. Suddenly, without warning, she had grabbed the chair she was leaning against and swung it at the minister. The minister ducked, but the chair had caught her off guard, and she crashed backward to the floor. Swearing quietly, she rose to her feet. Immediately Maria reached for another chair, but Yakov had grabbed her in a crushing hold.

Another official had called the police while Yakov held Maria down. The minister wiped her forehead with her handkerchief and sat back down at the table.

"Here are your permits," she said as with a flourish she signed two documents. One was to place the baby in the orphanage and the other to send the unpredictable mother to the hospital. The police had soon arrived to take Maria to a mental hospital.

Yakov's thoughts were interrupted by an announcement.

"Approaching the Boyarka Station," called the conductor. Yakov nudged Marusia slightly. She had dozed off in the rhythmic sway of the train as she held Nadia. They pulled their coats tighter and moved toward the opening doors. Varvara followed.

The Boyarka Baby Orphanage hummed with children three years old and younger. Some toddled along the tile hallways and others crawled on the large carpet in the main room. A few of the older children pattered around, touching objects out of curiosity. Younger ones not yet able to crawl lay in their cribs along the walls. Caretaker Elena reached out to help a little boy trying to stand next to a chair.

"Here, you little rabbit,[1] she said. "Let me help you." She wiped his dripping nose with her apron as he stood looking at her with his piercing, dark-brown eyes. Elena's heart twisted as she thought about her own son who had died at birth. He had been her only son. Her boyfriend had left her after he had heard she was expecting a child. Her heart still hurt as she thought of how unfair life seemed. Tenderly she picked up the little boy and cuddled him close. How she loved these little children. Maybe the pain she had experienced gave her something in common with these little tykes.

Just then she heard pounding on the orphanage door. Setting the

---

[1] In Ukraine, parents or caretakers often call little children endearing names such as "Zaika," which means "little rabbit."

little boy down, she walked to the front. Oleg, their director, arrived at the front door at the same time.

"This may be our new arrival," said Oleg as he opened the door cautiously.

Before them stood a tall, powerful man and a small woman holding a little bundle. Behind them stood an elderly woman.

"Who are you?" asked Oleg sharply. "What do you need?"

"We brought a baby and a referral signed by the Minister of the Presidium," replied the man. "I am sure you were notified."

"Just making sure you were authentic," replied Oleg. "Never can tell what people will pull on us these days. Sometimes they drop off their children just for good riddance. Come in."

The big man stepped inside the orphanage and pulled off his fur hat. Thrusting out his hand, he introduced himself. "My name is Yakov."

"Is this your wife?" asked Oleg. He nodded toward the little woman with the bundle.

"Yes, Marusia, and her mother Varvara."

"Welcome. Can we see the baby? She's nearing two months; am I right?" Oleg nodded to Elena, who took the bundle and pulled back the blankets. The baby blinked at the sudden rush of light.

"It looks like her name is Nadezhda," said Oleg, peering at the referral.

"Yes," replied Yakov. "We call her Nadia."

"She looks healthy," said Elena. "Would you like a little tour of the place to see where Nadia will be living?"

"Yes, of course."

Later, as the three adults left the orphanage grounds, Yakov stopped momentarily to look back, heartsick at the thought of leaving baby Nadia behind. It had not been an easy decision, but he knew the government funded this orphanage and would have the resources to support Nadia well. But he would miss her. He and Marusia had become attached to Nadia, and even now his stomach was tied in knots at the thought of letting her go.

Elena smiled as she watched little Nadia run along the walkway. The sun was shining warmly, and Elena could smell the scent of lilacs in the afternoon breeze. She had taken several of the children outside for fresh air. A couple years had passed since Nadia's uncle had brought her to the baby orphanage, and Nadia was now a healthy two-year-old. She would soon be leaving for another orphanage.

Uncle Yakov and Marusia, years later, with a young grandson.

"What is it?" Elena asked, looking in the direction Nadia was pointing.

"Butterfly." Nadia hopped toward the fluttering insect. Just as she reached the butterfly, it fluttered away. Nadia stopped and scowled as it zoomed overhead.

Elena laughed softly. "You missed it, Nadia. You need a butterfly net. Here, let me fetch you one." She stepped into an outdoor building close by and retrieved a small, ancient net. The other two-year-olds crowded close.

"Let me show you how to use it." Elena scanned the grounds in search of another butterfly. "Let's go find one," she told the youngsters. It wasn't long before Nadia pointed to a butterfly fluttering nearby.

"Good. Now I will show you how to use this net." Elena crept close to the jittery insect. Just as the butterfly lifted to fly away, Elena swung her net and caught it.

Nadia squealed and held out her hand. "Want it." She giggled as she took the tiny butterfly and held it in her hands. As she opened her hands to get a closer peek, out zoomed the butterfly.

"Oh, you lost your butterfly, Nadia." Elena brushed the hair out of Nadia's face. She loved the little children.

"Why don't we look for one more, and then we will head inside for supper."

Supper that evening consisted of rye bread and buckwheat soup and a small cookie. The toddlers and young children sat at tables in the dining hall while the cooks and caretakers brought the food. Even though there wasn't a large variety, the babies and toddlers usually had enough to eat.

Elena enjoyed her work with the children except for one thing—the parting. After several years of nurturing them, loving them, and pouring out her heart for them, they would outgrow the baby orphanage and would have to leave. She sighed. Such was life.

The sun peeked through the oak trees along the eastern edge of the orphanage grounds near Bila Tserkva, where Nadia had been transferred to when she was three years old. An almost imperceptible air current pushed the morning fog across the grounds, through the fencerows, and into the wheat field to the west. Fruit hung heavy on the apple and pear trees, and the chestnut trees were dropping their nuts. The dry, dusty smell of summer filled the air.

Children were lined up in straight rows outside the whitewashed orphanage, waiting for the caretakers and teachers to organize them into groups.

Seven-year-old Nadia stood at attention with her fellow comrades, waiting for instructions. She scanned the orphanage grounds for any signs of life. She loved the outdoors and nature. Her eyes caught sight of a sparrow. It was only a small bird, but it brought her joy.

I wonder what the next orphanage will be like, Nadia wondered. She couldn't remember the baby orphanage very well, but Uncle Yakov had told her about it. She had lived there until she was three years old, then she had been transferred to this orphanage in Bila Tserkva. Now, at the age of seven, she was once again being transferred to a new orphanage.

A large, dust-covered work truck rumbled up. Its rugged appearance spoke of its multiple uses and the many miles it had traveled.

The driver climbed out of the cab and handed a few documents to the orphanage director. After a minute of scanning the papers, the director signed them and handed them back. He spoke a minute with the truck driver, then turned to the caretakers and teachers.

"Anya and Luda, you will be riding along with the children."

The children carried only a few personal items as they climbed onto the back of the flatbed truck. Some of the children held onto the ribbed metal sides while others squatted down until the entire truck bed was filled. Caretakers Anya and Luda sat at the back since there was no tailgate. Nadia sat close to her friend Svetlana, who was also seven years old.

"Are you afraid, Svetlana?" asked Nadia, snuggling close. Svetlana was a petite girl with golden hair and a thin face.

"Yes, but we will stay together. We shouldn't talk too much, or the caretakers won't like it." Svetlana jerked her head toward the back of the thundering truck.

As the large truck bounced through a pothole, the truck bed slammed down with a jarring crunch. The girls clung to each other as they bounced along.

After a couple hours they arrived at a small plaza on the outskirts of Kiev and stopped for a short break. The plaza had two gas pumps, a small store, and a little restaurant. The children piled off to stretch their legs. Some looked longingly at a circus across the road.

Once everyone was loaded again, the truck roared out of the plaza to continue the journey. The girls again clung to each other, trying to sit as securely as possible on the shuddering truck bed. An hour and a half passed quickly as they traveled southeast toward the small, ancient city of Pereiaslav, along the Dnieper River about sixty miles southeast of Kiev.

The truck pulled off the street and stopped at a gate in a swirl of dust and smoke. Impatiently the driver revved the engine and honked the horn. A short, trim man strode out and opened the gate. The truck roared in and parked next to the orphanage.

At a cue from Anya and Luda, the children jumped down one by one from the truck bed and stood at attention. The man who had opened the gate introduced himself.

"My name is Constantine, and I am the director of the Pereiaslav Orphanage," he said. "We will be showing you your rooms in a few minutes."

The children did not have long to wait. A small, elderly woman with a warm smile called them to follow her. The boys were taken to the second floor, and the girls were shown to the third.

This orphanage felt new and strange to Nadia. *I want to go home,* she thought. *But where is home? Why doesn't Mama want me?* She shivered.

Nadia bent over her copybook, trying to draw the letter her teacher had written on the chalkboard. It was Friday, a week since they had arrived. The first day of school had been on Tuesday. Her marks so far were poor, and her teacher had slapped her fingers with a ruler and reprimanded her severely.

She sighed as she looked up from her work. Out of the corner of her eye she noticed a movement. It caught her attention and she stared. A spider was crawling across the wall.

Teacher Katerina saw her distraction. "Nadia, get to work!" Her sharp voice quickly brought Nadia's focus back to her lessons. Nadia sighed, squirming on the hard seat as she continued her writing lesson.

The room was full of first graders in black-and-white uniforms, all writing in their copybooks. Two students sat at each desk. The teacher strode between the students, pointing out their mistakes and slapping their fingers with a ruler. The spider continued to crawl across the wall.

Can anyone ever please her? Nadia thought despairingly. She erased the letter and tried again. The class seemed to last forever. A little girl at the front of the class began to cry as Katerina scolded her. Finally the teacher announced loudly that it was break time.

Nadia saw Svetlana waving at her. "Let's go outside for a minute."

"Sure," replied Nadia. They headed down the hall hand in hand.

"What do you think of this place?" asked Svetlana as they stepped outside and squatted on the school steps. A bit of old concrete crumbled off the edge of the step below her foot.

"There are so many bigger boys and girls," replied Nadia. "It's not the same as the other orphanage where all the children were our age or younger. It's kind of scary."

"Let's stay close together," murmured Svetlana.

"Yes," agreed Nadia.

A raven swooped above them and glided across the grounds into the nearby orchard. Its caw had an ominous tone.

Returning to the classroom, Nadia looked at her fingers. Red welts marked where the ruler had hit them. She would have to find a way to do better, or soon her fingers wouldn't be able to hold the pencil. Her teacher had said the USSR deserved better.

Another Failed Attempt

1971

"No, you may not have your daughter," replied the director as he faced Maria. "I have the records in front of me, and it is clear that you need a permit from the hospital." His eyes flashed with the determination of one who knew how to use his authority. Constantine had been raised during the Communist era and had been toughened to think logically and with little emotion.

"Do you understand?" he asked Maria sternly. Pulling his navy handkerchief from his pocket, he wiped his forehead. The day was unusually warm and muggy for May in central Ukraine. "Come back only when you have a permit signed by the doctor." Again he wiped his forehead.

Maria had tried to persuade the director to let Nadia go home with her. She had even brought along a beautiful, life-sized doll and a baby carriage, hoping to show them how much she cared for Nadia. But the director was not swayed.

"We still have two more weeks of school," he continued. "Come back after May 15 with your permit, and you can take Nadia home with you." He stood and walked to the office door. "I will talk to you in two weeks."

With nothing else left to do, Maria grabbed her bags and clomped out of the orphanage. Stepping outside, she gave the main door an extra hard slam.

What a beautiful gift, thought eight-year-old Nadia. She felt warm inside. *Maybe Mama does care about me.* She had never seen such a big doll. It looked so real, and there was even a carriage to go with it. Nadia pushed the carriage along the dirt paths between the buildings. Some of her classmates watched her.

"Look at her," the girls murmured to each other. "Nadia thinks she is special."

"She is pretending to be a mother." The girls' jealousy of Nadia's gift was obvious.

That afternoon after Maria had left, caretaker Ekaterina approached Nadia. She scowled, and her face seemed even more twisted than usual.

"You are playing too much with your doll all by yourself," she said. "We must play together. Our founding father Lenin wants us to be united and to work and play together as one. I must take the baby and the carriage away from you. I will put them in the basement on the top shelf in the toy room."

She grabbed the little carriage and the doll and carried them away. Nadia watched her go in horror. Ekaterina's stout figure seemed to ooze jealousy and hatred. The day of happiness had ended. Fighting tears, Nadia turned and fled to her room.

Nadia sat in a circle with her classmates as they played Drop the Hanky. As Nadia sat and waited for her turn to grab the red cloth and run around the group, she thought about the words of her teacher: "We must be united." Lenin had said it, so it must be good. She felt torn between wanting her doll back and wanting to please Lenin.

Nadia fingered the little badge on her chest. It was a ruby-colored, five-point star badge with a portrait of Vladimir Lenin in his childhood. It indicated that she was a Little Octobrist.

She had received the badge this past autumn when they had celebrated the anniversary of the 1917 October Revolution. Nadia was determined to prove that she could be the best Octobrist ever. She would amount to something. Then she would be able to join the Pioneers, the next level after the Octobrists.

Children in the Soviet Union were expected to be a member of the Pioneers between the ages of nine and fourteen. But to join, they needed to achieve good grades in school. The Pioneers were taught social skills and could go to special, publicly funded summer camps.

But that's not until next year, thought Nadia. *This summer I will be at home with Mama. She will soon come to get me.*

But May 15 came and went, and Mama did not appear. *I wonder where she is,* thought Nadia as two more weeks passed. The exams had been completed and school was out for the summer. The children eagerly awaited summer camp.

Camp offered a welcome vacation for the orphanage children. The camp was often close to a river where the children could bathe and swim during the hot, sultry days of summer.

Excitedly the children packed their clothes and belongings. They looked forward to all the fun they would be having. This year they were going to the little village of Tashan along the Supiy River, about a forty-minute drive from the orphanage.

Since Maria had not come to take her daughter home, the orphanage director decided that Nadia would go along to the camp with the other children. Nadia was excited to accompany them but still wondered where her mother was. Quickly they piled on the orphanage bus and were soon bouncing along on the dirt road toward camp.

"Nadia. Na-d-i-a." Someone was calling her. She splashed to the river's edge and climbed out.

"Where are you going?" called Svetlana. She was swimming a short distance from the riverbank with a few other girls. A breeze rippled the water.

"The director called me," shouted Nadia over her shoulder. She walked back to the camp. The trees next to the camp swayed and danced in the gusty wind.

"Your mama is here," said the camp director. "She has come to take you home. So get your things together immediately." Nadia could see the orphanage bus parked in front of the camp. Sure enough, Mama stepped out of the bus.

"Come, Nadia. Let's go home," said Mama.

Good! Mama has come to get me, thought Nadia. *Her clothes are extra clean today. She is pretty.*

Nadia's thoughts whirled with excitement as she ran to get her belongings. Quickly grabbing her clothes, she stuffed them into an old leather bag. Spotting an uneaten apple from last night's snack, she put that into her bag too.

The director spoke with the bus driver, then motioned for Nadia to climb on. Happily she settled down beside Mama, overjoyed that she had come to get her. A cloud of dust rose into the air as they headed back toward the orphanage.

When they pulled up to the orphanage, Nadia grabbed her bag and followed Mama. A few doves jerked up their heads and watched them momentarily before resuming their search for grain and seeds in the dirt and gravel nearby.

"You may go with your mama," the director told her. "She has promised to care for you and will bring you back later this summer."

Nadia walked beside Mama. It was dark as they trudged from the little village of Khotiv to their hometown of Lisnyky. At this time there was no public transportation from Khotiv to Lisnyky, so they had to walk. As they passed through the outskirts of Khotiv, they heard a drunkard coughing a deep, rasping cough. All they could see of him was the tip of his cigarette glowing in the dark.

The night was pitch black by the time they reached their little house in Lisnyky. As they opened the door and stepped inside, Nadia stared in surprise. A man was sitting there.

"This is Ivan," said Mama. "He lives with me."

"Hi, Nadia. I am your mama's man. How are you?" His eyes were red, but he seemed friendly and kind. His light-brown hair wasn't combed.

Is this my papa? wondered Nadia. Maybe it was, but she was afraid to ask. Instead, she turned her attention to a gray cat rubbing against her legs. It arched its back as she stroked its soft fur, and she could feel the vibrations as it purred contentedly. She relaxed as she watched Mama prepare something to eat. After a silent meal with Ivan and Mama, it was time for bed.

The next morning Ivan, Maria, and Nadia walked across the village to a little garden plot. The sun peeked across the treetops, and the morning was still cool.

"Nadia, I want you to pick these strawberries," said Mama, pointing at the ground. "After we fill a couple of baskets with strawberries, we will take them to the market."

"Where are the strawberries?" asked Nadia as she began walking through the garden. She was excited. She had never seen strawberries before.

"No! No! You foolish girl!" screamed Maria. "You are stepping on the strawberries." She grabbed her hoe and began to beat Nadia with the handle.

In terror, Nadia raised her hands to ward off the blows.

"Get off the strawberries! I will teach you!" Maria swung her hoe again.

"Maria!" Ivan yelled. "Stop!"

"Stop beating the little girl!" shouted a neighbor man as he and his wife came running.

Maria put down her hoe and stared.

"Maria," the neighbor continued sternly, "if you don't stop hurting your daughter, we will call the police."

Maria paled and dropped her hoe. "Please, no," she begged. "I will stop."

Nadia cowered in terror and rubbed her arms where the blows had hit her. *Why is Mama so angry?* Fear gripped her heart.

Maria beckoned to Nadia. She dropped to her knees and pulled back the strawberry plants, but Nadia kept her distance. She didn't want to be hit again.

"See, Nadia," Mama said sweetly. "See the red berries. Pick only the red ones. The red strawberries are ripe. You may eat one once in a while."

Maria and Nadia got to work while Ivan sat and watched. As

Nadia picked strawberries and even ate a few, she kept a wary eye on Mama. *Is she going to hit me again? Why did she do that?* Her heart still pounded.

"Now we'll take them to Kiev to sell," said Mama when their baskets were full. "I can usually get a good price for them at the market there."

They carried their baskets of strawberries to Khotiv and then caught a bus for Kiev. There were many exciting sights in the city. The buses, trams, and cars zoomed up and down the streets while pedestrians walked along the sidewalks.

At the market, the strawberries sold quickly. Most customers complimented them on the taste.

"Your strawberries have a good flavor and are sweet," said one customer. "They are better than most."

Mama bought a loaf of fresh bread and some kolbasa[1] before they caught the tram back to the bus stop. When they arrived home, Nadia felt tired and sleepy. It had been a long day. After eating the bread and kolbasa, she climbed up onto the long clay stove body and curled into the comforter. In a few minutes she was fast asleep.

The next day Mama showed Nadia how to wash clothes. They drew water from the neighbor's well and poured it into a large basin. They soaked the clothes in soapy water, then brought them up one piece at a time and rubbed them on a washboard propped against the side. The slow, hard work made Nadia's hands sore. After she finished scrubbing each piece, she rinsed it carefully.

As she washed the clothes, Nadia thought about the garden. Picking strawberries had been better than washing clothes. *But why did Mama get so angry?*

The next day they were off to the garden again to pick strawberries. This time Nadia knew what strawberries were. They picked until their

---

[1] Russian sausage/bologna used primarily as an inexpensive cold cut for sandwiches.

two baskets were full, then they were ready to set off for the market. Since Ivan had left for the day, they were alone.

"Let's go," grinned Mama. They picked up their baskets and started for Khotiv. This time they took a shortcut through the forests and the fields. Sunshine glinted through the clouds, and a few birds were singing.

Mama and Nadia crested a ridge and began their descent. Ahead of them was a dump. Nadia was puzzled. *Why are we going through the dump? Why didn't we stay on the road?*

"Set your basket here," said Mama. "Right here beside mine." She pointed to the ground. A raven was walking through the dump looking for something to eat, and Nadia could smell the awful stench of decaying garbage.

Suddenly Mama grabbed Nadia. "Now I can kill you! I can do it right here, and no one will ever know." She grinned as she began to beat Nadia.

"Now you can't get away," she hissed. "There are no neighbors around to see me this time." She grabbed Nadia and tried to wrestle her to the ground.

"Mama! No! Let me go!" Nadia screamed as she struggled frantically to get loose.

"No, you will not get away. You crushed my strawberry plants, so I will kill you." Maria clasped her hands tightly around Nadia's neck.

Struggling to breathe, Nadia kicked and fought to get away. Everything swam before her eyes as she fell to the ground and slipped from her mother's grasp.

Trying to catch her breath, Nadia heard shouts and pounding feet.

"Get out of here! Leave the girl alone!" a voice shouted. A pair of hands gently lifted her up. They brushed back her hair and tenderly felt for any broken bones. Nadia looked up into two concerned faces. Her entire body shook convulsively with fear.

The big man picked her up and carried her. It felt good to be in his strong arms. She heard the woman who was with him speak.

"Fedor, we should probably take her to her uncle Yakov in Kiev, don't you think?"

"Yes, Ulyana. We can take her to our home for the night and take her to him tomorrow."

"Where is Mama?" Nadia asked fearfully.

"She ran into the forest."

Nadia closed her eyes. *Why did Mama want to kill me?* She was glad the big man and his wife had seen what was happening. *But where is Mama? Why was she so angry again?* Nadia felt hot tears running down her cheeks. Would her mother never love her?

Marusia hugged Nadia as Fedor told them what had happened. Nadia listened quietly.

"We were passing by the dump when we saw Maria beating her," Fedor began. "If we hadn't rescued her, I don't know what would have happened. We kept her at our house for the night, but now we will leave her with you."

"I will take care of her." Yakov clenched and unclenched his fists. His neck was red. "Maria has proven again that she cannot be trusted."

"It was an act of God that you were there at the time," murmured Marusia.

5

God Under the Stairs

1972

*A*steady rain had been falling all day. Now, as the girls dressed for bed, the temperature had dropped and the rain had changed to snow. The heavy, wet snow clung to branches and stuck to buildings. Nadia looked around her at the twenty-two beds lined up in straight rows in their room on the third floor. Several light bulbs dangled from the ceiling, giving just enough light to dress. The room was getting chilly as the snow swirled and danced outside.

The laughter and voices of a few boys and girls defying the curfew could be heard in the hall. They would be soundly scolded if they were caught out too late, but usually they managed to scurry off to bed if a caretaker came to investigate. Nadia lay quietly in her bed listening to the voices.

Why don't I have a papa like other children do? Why doesn't Mama like me? When Mama had visited her this winter with Uncle Yakov, she had seemed extra nice. Thankfully, Uncle Yakov had promised to come again when he could get off work.

As Nadia lay in the darkness trying to sleep, she thought about the doll and the carriage her mama had given her. She had not seen the doll since Ekaterina had taken it away. Life didn't seem fair. Why were some people so mean?

When Nadia awoke, the snow was still falling, and everything was covered with a thick layer. Nadia joined the other girls as they peered out the dorm windows at the white world.

Below them, they could see Urie, the groundskeeper, shoveling the walkways. His dark brown parka was white with snow. He straightened to relax a moment and adjusted his fur hat to a more comfortable position before continuing his work.

"It'll be a good day to have a snowball fight," commented one of the girls as she tucked in the comforter around her mattress. Quickly the girls continued their morning ritual of making their cot-sized beds, brushing their teeth, and getting dressed for school.

"Come on, everyone," called Anya. "Breakfast will soon be ready." Chattering, the girls headed for the cafeteria.

Breakfast this morning consisted of fried eggs, cooked buckwheat, and a few bits of salo. The children jostled each other as they excitedly discussed playing in the snow at recess. After breakfast was over, they headed for their classrooms.

Nadia was now in third grade. Although she studied hard, her grades were still low. It seemed no matter how hard she tried, she could not improve them. She would have to tell Uncle Yakov about her marks. He would know what to do. At least it was for Lenin's USSR that she was suffering.

She glanced out the large window at the falling snow. It looked so beautiful and clean. *If only my life could be more like that snow.*

"Barbar Nadezhda, you are wanted in the assembly hall." Director Constantine stood at the door of the classroom and motioned to her. *What is this all about?* Nadia wondered as she pushed up her glasses. Her heart pounded. Maybe Uncle Yakov had come to see her.

Sure enough, Uncle Yakov rose from a chair in the hall and gave her a big hug. It was so good to see him. It seemed like ages since he had come.

"How is it going, Nadia?" he asked. They were alone in the auditorium. She poured out the story of her low grades and how her teachers grew impatient with her. He listened patiently.

"Well," he said, "I'm sorry to hear this, but I have something that might help." He picked up his bag and opened it.

"Here," he said as he dropped something into Nadia's hand. It was a little silver cross necklace. "Let me show you how to put it on." Carefully he placed the trinket around her neck.

"Be sure no one sees this," Yakov warned. "If any teacher or caretaker sees it, they will take it away and trash it. The USSR is opposed to any teaching about God or anything that reminds us of Jesus or God."

"I also copied the Lord's Prayer for you," he said, handing Nadia a piece of neatly folded paper. "And here is a second prayer I copied for you. It's from an old Orthodox prayer book." Yakov spent a few minutes teaching Nadia how to say the Lord's Prayer, then he also read the second prayer with her.

"Now, when you can find a quiet spot, take the cross and kiss it," he said. "Then quote the Lord's Prayer. Tell God about your problems, and He can help you. Ask Him to help your grades improve, and who knows, they might."

Nadia's eyes beamed with wonder as she listened to her uncle. Her heart beat fast with hope. As Yakov rose to leave, the floor creaked under his weight. He was a big man with a big heart. He gave Nadia another big hug.

"Be good," he said. "Work hard, and don't forget your cross. I need to catch the bus back to Kiev now."

With new hope, Nadia fairly flew back to her class. She stopped momentarily on the stairs and looked around for anyone who might be spying on her. Then she pulled out the cross and kissed it. The silver felt cool to her lips. She would have to find a hiding place to read her prayers.

When Nadia reached her class, the pupils were streaming out the door. Class had just been dismissed for recess. "Barbar Nadezhda, let me show you your lesson," called Teacher Katerina.

Nadia could hear her classmates grabbing their coats and heading outside, but she followed her teacher's instructions and wrote down the page numbers. As soon as she was free, she rushed out to join the others in the snow. Snowballs flew, and the boys and girls dodged and ran. What laughter, what fun! All too soon the next class bell sounded.

As Nadia walked to her class the next morning, she noticed a space under the concrete stairs where rags were often stored. *I'll check out that space the first chance I get,* she thought. *Maybe I could squeeze in under those stairs to pray.*

The next day as Nadia entered the school building after first recess, she made sure she was the last one up the stairs. Listening for footsteps but hearing none, she crawled under the stairs among the boxes of rags. Quickly she pulled out her little cross and kissed it. Then she unfolded the pieces of paper. Just enough light glinted under the stairs to read the prayers.

When she was done reading the prayers, she added a little prayer of her own. "I need better grades, God. If you are real, make my grades better." She listened, her heart pounding. Uncle Yakov had said the government did not want anyone to pray. What was wrong with praying?

Before she crawled out from under the stairs, she paused. Hearing no one, she scooted from her hiding place, scrambled up the stairs, and ran for her classroom.

The weeks turned into months, and spring flowers replaced the snow and ice. As often as possible, Nadia visited her secret hiding place. Slowly her grades improved, and her teacher's abusive remarks and knocks diminished. She worked harder and prayed that she would be promoted from an Octobrist to a Pioneer. The celebrations would be held in May.

"Strive to be a hero like Volodia Dubinin," Teacher Katerina had instructed. "He was brave in his resistance in Kerch. As a thirteen-year-old Pioneer, he led the USSR soldiers through the catacombs of Kerch in their resistance of the German Nazis. Let him be your pattern of excellence. He gave his life for the cause." She wiped the sweat from her brow.

All the nine-year-olds sat erect. Nadia listened with fear and excitement.

6

Building the USSR

1982

A stiff wind scattered the leaves along the cobblestone street as eighteen-year-old Nadia and her friend Irina approached the train station in Kiev. They had just left the trolley bus, and the sidewalk was full of other travelers.

"Are you sure you have your passport?" asked Nadia. Late summer clouds floated lazily across the sky.

"Yes, it's in my purse," Irina smiled. "And I suppose you have the money?"

"Yes," Nadia replied. "I made sure of that."

It had been ten years since Nadia's mother had tried to kill her. Nadia had been in several orphanages since then. Eventually she had graduated from the government school orphanages and had begun to provide for herself. She had been promoted from a Pioneer to a Komsomol[1], of which she was proud. Her last job at the sewing factory had paid well, but she was young and wanted adventure, so why not travel to Siberia?

Nadia at the Kiev Zoo, 18 years old.

It had all started with an announcement by their director. "There are a couple of projects in far eastern Siberia close to Ulan-Ude," the director had said. "One project is the construction of a railroad that President Brezhnev has called the construction project of the century. Another is the construction of a massive airport in Ulan-Ude. If you would like to be part of promoting our great country, let me know in the next month, and we will register your name and begin the process. There will be groups leaving in a couple months for both of these areas."

Cheers arose, and hats were thrown into the air as the hundreds of employees began discussing the adventure and the opportunity to serve their country. The government would buy train tickets for anyone who wanted to go and would also pay a good wage for their contribution, making the offer even more attractive.

Those who had volunteered to go needed to undergo physicals and checkups to be pronounced healthy and fit for the rugged work ahead. Nadia was sent to a specialist to see if her eyes would pass the test. After the doctor had approved her eyes, she was cleared to go. The next few days had been busy with packing her belongings and buying additional items for the trip. She had also visited Uncle Yakov to say goodbye.

"Do you have your cross along, Nadia?" Uncle Yakov had asked. Nadia had winced inwardly. In recent years, she had hardly ever thought about the little silver necklace. She didn't really think she needed it anymore. She was now a tough Komsomol headed for Siberia. She had a purpose bigger than herself to live for. She would live and die without regrets.

"I'll take it along," Nadia had replied evenly.

As the train chugged its way out of Kiev, Nadia peered out the window. She could see the Motherland Monument in the distance, sunlight glinting off the steel coat. As they crossed the Dnieper River, she spotted anglers out on boats for an evening catch.

Since Irina had made a mistake on a coat she had sewn, the sewing factory had withheld her last paycheck. Nadia had then offered to pay for her ticket, knowing the government would reimburse them when they got to Siberia. Since Nadia had to make her money stretch for both girls, she was limited to buying the cheapest train tickets. But she was glad her friend had waited to travel with her instead of going with the other forty-eight Komsomols who had left earlier. Nadia's doctor appointment had delayed their departure, but now they were finally on their way.

The cheap tickets Nadia was forced to buy did not provide any blankets or pillows for the trip. All they had was a seat in the open area of the car. The compartments were reserved for those who could afford them. The train swayed as it chugged its way northward.

Nadia slipped on her jacket and scooted down with her head against the window. Irina slid in beside her. She smelled of smoke.

"I think I'll take a walk through the train," Irina said, blowing the last bit of smoke through her nose.

"Please don't blow smoke around me." Nadia wrinkled her nose. "It makes me sick."

When Nadia awoke the next morning after a restless night, the train still chugged northward, and sunshine poured in the window. Beside her, Irina snored loudly. Nadia pulled back the curtain and tied it. She grabbed the window frame as the train lurched and swayed. Along the tracks stood forests of birch, aspen, and gray alder, as well as a few cedars. The seemingly endless forests had a tint of autumn colors.

It was almost noon before the train approached Moscow, the capital city of Russia. Nadia and Irina disembarked and stood for a moment to gaze at the hundreds of passengers moving between the trains and the station.

"Wow, so many people," observed Irina.

"I hope they are not all going on our train," replied Nadia. She picked up her suitcase. "Come on. Let's go."

At the ticket counter, Nadia asked what it would cost for two tickets to Ulan-Ude. As she expected, they were too expensive. Thankfully she had enough money to pay for tickets to Novosibirsk, which was over halfway. Perhaps she could find her friend Svetlana who had been sent to Novosibirsk to work as a construction engineer. Svetlana had sent her a letter after she had arrived in Novosibirsk, and Nadia still had the address. She would look her up.

After receiving their departure time and directions on how to find the train, the two girls moved away to find a seat in the huge building. A station attendant chasing a stray dog rushed past them.

Nadia's stomach growled as she caught a whiff of food. Someone near her had opened a bag and was eating lunch. Maybe she could buy a couple small rolls for herself and Irina. She found a vendor and bought two raspberry Danishes and two cups of hot tea. The Danishes were delicious, even though they were mostly bread. The black tea sweetened with sugar tasted delightful.

"Why are you so kind to me?" Irina asked. "First you buy my tickets, and now you buy food for me. You're a good friend." She smiled.

"Well, I suppose if I was the one who needed something, I would be glad if someone helped me," Nadia replied. She took another small sip of hot tea. She wanted to make it last as long as possible. "And I didn't want to travel by myself. So I suppose there are several reasons."

Nadia threw her plastic cup to the skinny dog that had returned to the station. It chewed on the cup and licked the sticky inside. She could count its ribs.

"What are we going to do when we get to Novosibirsk?"

"My friend Svetlana lives there, and I have her address. We will find her and see if we can borrow some money from her. She had straight A's in school and was sent to an institute to study engineering. Later the government sent her to Novosibirsk."

"You think she will help us?"

"I think so."

That night Nadia again tried to sleep as Irina left their car. Around her, other passengers stretched out as best they could on the immovable seats. She hoped Irina would not get into any trouble. As usual, Nadia didn't sleep very well.

Nadia and Irina cheered as their train approached the station in Novosibirsk. They had traveled for almost three days and were ready to return to solid ground.

"I hope we can find Svetlana," murmured Nadia, looking at the envelope. "We need to find someone on the street and ask where this is."

"Hello, sir. Can you tell us how to get to this address?"

The middle-aged man looked at the paper and frowned. "No, I can't," he replied. He lowered his head and hurried away.

"Well, let's try someone else." Nadia spotted a woman bent over her cart as she pushed it along the street.

"Hello, Madame. Can you tell us where this address is?" asked Nadia. The woman pushed back her scarf to reveal a wrinkled face. Her bony finger traced the address.

"I think it's close by," she said as she turned to hurry on her way.

The fifth person they asked finally told them which bus to take to reach the street where Svetlana lived.

"I hope we can find her place before dark," Irina said despairingly.

The street lamps were just flickering on when they reached the address on a dormitory downtown.

"I think this is the place," said Nadia. They spoke with the manager of the dormitory.

"Yes," she said, "Svetlana Chumakova does live here."

When Nadia knocked on the door of Svetlana's room, she heard her friend's voice from inside. Nadia knocked again and the door swung open.

"Nadia! What are you doing here? You're over two thousand miles from home!" The two friends embraced each other.

"And who is this?" Svetlana gave Irina a hug. "A friend?"

As the two friends caught up on each other's lives, Nadia explained their predicament to Svetlana.

"I don't have much money on hand myself," replied Svetlana. "But I can ask some of my friends here at the dormitory, and then you can send the money from Ulan-Ude when the government reimburses you."

That evening the girls enjoyed a big meal provided by Svetlana. After the delicious meal, they laughed and talked until well past midnight. When the girls finally stretched out to sleep, only a few hours remained until morning.

The next morning Svetlana accompanied them to the train station and bought the tickets for the remainder of their journey to Ulan-Ude. Nadia and Irina waved from their train window as the train slowly started on its way. The sound of a whistle floated back from the locomotive and smoke drifted past the window as the train rounded a corner and Svetlana disappeared from view.

They still had over a thousand miles left on the trip, and Nadia was tired. Tired because she had not slept much the last few nights. Tired of traveling. Tired of smelling cigarette smoke. It would be at least two more days before they arrived in Ulan-Ude.

That night Irina invited Nadia to accompany her to the conductors' room.

"Let's have some fun," she said. Nadia hesitated.

"Come on," coaxed Irina. "They'll likely have some food and wine again. Let's go."

At the thought of food, Nadia couldn't resist. She was already feeling hungry, and there wasn't much money left.

The two young conductors seemed to enjoy the company of the girls—and the girls enjoyed their company too. It was late when Nadia decided to return to her seat. The younger conductor had drunk more wine than was good for him and was scooting up against her.

"I'm tired," said Nadia, getting to her feet. "I think I'll get some rest."

She headed back to their car, stepping over the legs of a passenger who was sleeping next to the aisle. The train chugged farther east, jerking and swaying through the Sayan Mountains bordering the Central Siberian Plateau.

On the afternoon of the third day they approached a large body of water that Nadia assumed was Lake Baikal. She had studied about this lake in school and knew it was a tourist attraction.

Just then the door slid open and Irina stepped into the room. She pointed to the lake.

"See that water? That's Lake Baikal. They tell me this is the deepest freshwater lake in the world. It is four hundred miles long, fifty miles wide, and a mile deep. It has almost one-fourth of all the fresh water in the world." She plopped onto her seat.

"Wow!" Nadia replied. "Where did you learn all that?" Then, gazing out the window, she added, "It's nice too."

As they passed alongside the water, Nadia could see a heron at the water's edge. A few minutes later three ducks winged by the train window. Since they were passing Lake Baikal, Nadia supposed they were not far from Ulan-Ude. Maybe they would arrive in another hour or two.

She was right. About an hour later, the city of Ulan-Ude loomed into view. Nadia rose to stand by the window as the outskirts of the city slid by.

What could she expect in this place so far from home? She was disturbed at how much time Irina spent with the young men on the train. She had hoped Irina would stay with her. Fear suddenly gripped Nadia. She felt alone in a big world.

Born in Siberia

1983-1984

Nadia dipped her paintbrush into the can and then applied the paint with gentle, sweeping strokes across the stuccoed interior wall surface. She was careful to keep the paint from touching the metal window frame.

It was now late spring and the snowdrifts were almost gone. Flowers were peeking out, and the temperatures were rising to a more comfortable level. Nadia could see Lake Baikal from where she was working. Her group had been transferred from the airport project in Ulan-Ude to a small railroad town two hours away, right next to the lake. They were helping with the construction of a new hospital.

Nadia's group had been sent here in March and were living at a local hostel. The rooms were clean and the food delicious. Andre Zaikova, a native Buryat Siberian, had also come out on the train a few days later and was staying at the hostel.

Nadia and Andre had met each other at a New Year's party and had been seeing each other regularly since then. They got along well. She had been afraid she wouldn't be able to see Andre at this new jobsite, but now he also had a room at the hostel. He was able to pick up odd jobs in town to get some income.

Nadia and Andre.

"Could you also paint around this window?" asked Alosha, the ruddy foreman, as he pointed to a window across the room. "You do a great job of doing it without getting paint on the frame."

"Sure," said Nadia. She stepped down from her ladder and moved it across the room.

She definitely enjoyed painting better than plastering. She didn't like the smell, but it was easier than lifting heavy loads of cement.

Nadia was happy to be a part of the united effort to build a great nation, a great USSR. She was punctual and faithful at her job and was making a good wage. She tried her best to please the foreman at her work and received sporadic praise.

Her mind wandered to Andre and their hopes to get married soon. He had been required to register with the military and could be called to duty anytime. She hoped she wouldn't lose him, as she found herself depending on him more and more for support and leadership. After almost four months of spending time together, she was greatly enjoying their relationship.

That evening after supper Nadia and Andre took a walk along the lake. The sun had disappeared over the Sayan Mountains to the west of the lake and the shadows were lengthening. A few Baikal seals slid across the ice and disappeared through an open hole.

"Alosha says we will be transferred back to Ulan-Ude the last of April," said Nadia. "On May 1 and 2, we will be off work for Labor Day."

"That sounds great. May 2 is my birthday, so we could have a party at my parents' house," Andre suggested. "Also, if you move back to Ulan-Ude, that means I get to move back home." He grinned, then sobered.

"I would like for you to meet my parents," he continued. "Perhaps you can come for an evening dinner on May 1." He stopped to pull out a cigarette and light it.

"That would be good," Nadia said. "I need to meet your parents."

They decided that Andre would take the train back to Ulan-Ude a few days before Nadia's group was to return. Nadia waved until the train disappeared from sight. She knew if she wanted to marry Andre, she would have to meet his parents and learn to know them.

Saturday morning found Nadia and her group traveling back to Ulan-Ude. They would be working at the airport again after the Labor Day vacation.

The next day seemed longer than usual as Nadia prepared for the evening dinner at Andre's house. Andre planned to come to her house, then they would ride to his parents' place together.

A few minutes before five o'clock, Nadia grabbed her light jacket, smoothed down her skirt, and nervously tripped down the stairs. She didn't have long to wait. Here he came—tall and handsome. She loved to watch him walk.

"Ready?" he asked with a smile.

"Ready." She slipped her arm into his as they walked to the station to catch the trolley car.

Nadia watched her manners carefully as Andre introduced her to his parents and his brother. She waited until Andre's mother Lyubov pointed out a seat for her.

"It's about time we got to see you," said Lyubov. "We have heard a lot about you. It sounds like you are an angel." She didn't smile as a hum of laughter rippled through the family.

"Let's sit down and eat." Andre's father Nikolai waved everyone to the table loaded with food. Nadia could smell fried fish. She hoped it was salmon from Lake Baikal, since that was her favorite.

Andre's only brother Alex and his wife Olya had also been invited for the evening. Alex was three years older than Andre and had been married for several years. *They sure know how to talk,* thought Nadia as she reached for another piece of fish.

"So what do you think will happen now that President Brezhnev has died and Andropov has been elected?" asked Andre. He poured himself another glass of vodka.

"Brezhnev was a strong leader, although I think his decision to invade Afghanistan was foolish," replied Nikolai.

"I don't really care who the leader is," said Alex as he reached for another helping. "As long as I have a job, food to eat, and some wine once in a while, who cares?"

"Well, it could make a difference in your job. And maybe even in your food and drink," laughed Nikolai. "Depending on who leads this country, we could be without jobs and have to go hungry."

Nadia smiled to herself. She enjoyed hearing or reading news about politics. She too had been distressed at the news that President Brezhnev had died. And she also wondered what kind of leader Yuri Andropov would be.

It was Saturday, February 18, 1984—nine months after the wedding. When Andre had received sudden notice that he would have to leave for the army on May 20, they had quickly decided to get married before he left. The wedding was planned for May 19, the day before Andre left for the army. It turned out to be a beautiful day.

Now, as Nadia gazed out the hospital window, she wished with all her heart that Andre could be with her. It was a bitter cold day, with snow blasting the city during the morning hours. This only added to the drifts of snow deposited earlier after weeks and weeks of winter. Fifty-mile-per-hour winds roared out of the northeast, whistling eerily around the five-story Ulan-Ude hospital.

Nadia gasped as another contraction hit her. *So this is what it is like to have a baby?* Whatever was happening was coming oftener and harder. She motioned to the nurse who had come into the room to check on her.

"Shall I call the doctor?" asked the nurse.

"Please."

The doctor soon came into the birthing room to check on Nadia. She was a Buryat woman and very gentle.

"We should soon see your baby," she said with a smile.

A few hours later a tired mama was helped to a room to join seven other mothers who had recently given birth. Their babies had been taken to be washed and then wrapped in warm cotton wraps. These tightly wound wraps would help the babies feel warm and secure. The doctor had wrapped a string around each baby's wrist with the mother's name on a small slip of stiff paper. Nurses gave the babies small bottles of milk and changed their cloth diapers every three hours or so. After three days, Nadia was finally allowed to hold her tiny daughter.

Nadia smiled with delight. She was sure Andre would be happy, and her in-laws would be happy too. She would name her baby Larissa. The baby squirmed, sucked, and fell asleep in Nadia's arms.

The other mothers had advised her to make the baby nurse as long as possible and not let her fall asleep. Otherwise, the baby would wake up soon and be hungry.

"Pinch her nose shut. That way she will wake up and open her mouth to suck in air," the mothers had told her. "Then she will latch on again."

After fifteen minutes, the nurse returned to take baby Larissa back to the nursery. Sometimes babies wailed for more milk, but no nurse came to comfort them or feed them. The babies had to learn the schedule of nursing every three hours.

The hospital staff was accommodating and tried their best to teach Nadia how to take care of Larissa. After a week of rest and plenty of checkups on both mama and baby, they were released to go home.

"You may go home on Friday," the doctor told Nadia. "Your mother-in-law has made arrangements to take you home that day."

Nadia experienced mixed feelings about leaving the hospital since she knew that once she was at home she would need to work hard. Not only would she have to take care of Larissa, she would have to keep the house warm, wash their clothes, and prepare all the meals. At least here at the hospital they took good care of her and it was warm. Two things she wouldn't miss though were all the crying babies and the smell of antiseptic.

Around ten o'clock Friday morning the nurses came to tell Nadia to prepare to leave. They helped her find her few articles of clothing and her purse. They wrapped baby Larissa in more wraps and blankets and helped Nadia dress warmly in her overcoat and boots.

When Nadia walked into the lobby, Nikolai and Lyubov were waiting for her. Nikolai embraced Nadia carefully and pulled back the blanket enough to see the baby. Lyubov pushed close to see.

"Looks like a beautiful Zaikova girl," Lyubov commented loudly. "Glad she looks like us instead of like you."

Lyubov's spiteful words were spoken so loudly that the receptionist stared at them, and the people sitting around the room looked up. Nadia pushed the blanket back over the baby's head. She wanted to leave as quickly as possible.

Nikolai seemed to understand and pushed open the door. Nadia and Lyubov followed him out to the large company gas truck.

When they arrived home, Nikolai helped Nadia to the ground. The truck cab had been crowded with the four of them, but at least she didn't need to ride buses and the trolley car to get home.

The next day Andre's brother Alex and his wife Olya came to see baby Larissa. Even though they had been married for several years, they did not have any children yet. Olya held Larissa wistfully and watched her small movements.

Lyubov and Nikolai, with Lyubov holding baby Larissa.

The day Nadia arrived home, Lyubov telegrammed the military base where Andre was stationed to request a few days' leave for her son. A telegram soon came back refusing Lyubov's request.

"I guess I'll have to go and bring him back myself," Lyubov muttered angrily as she packed her bag. The next morning she said goodbye to Nadia and stamped out of the house.

For the next few days, since Nikolai was often gone, Nadia was alone with Larissa much of the time. Nikolai kindly brought wood into the house and stacked it whenever he was at home. This saved her a trip out into the bitter Siberian cold.

About a week later, as Nadia was changing Larissa's diaper, she heard voices outside the house. She quickly pinned the cloth and wrapped the baby tightly. As she peered out the front door, she was delighted to see Lyubov—and even more delighted and surprised to see Andre with her.

It was so good to see him again after nine months of missing him. Lyubov had personally spoken to the general, who had then granted Andre a leave to see his newborn daughter.

Andre proudly held Larissa. He lugged firewood and kept the stove going. He brought in water from the well house up the street. He even helped Nadia with the washing. Nadia wished it would never end. It was so much fun to eat meals together, to laugh together, and to listen to his stories from camp.

The only problem was Lyubov, who seemed to resent the attention Andre gave Nadia and Larissa. *Why is she jealous?* Nadia wondered. *I am his wife. Maybe it is the mother instinct.*

"Aren't you glad I brought my son home from camp?" asked Lyubov as Nadia gave Andre a parting hug. Nadia clung to Andre until she knew she had to let him go. His train would be leaving soon, and he must not be late.

Two months passed, with Nadia working hard to carry wood from the woodlot. She dressed warmly while the baby slept and went out into the frigid weather to bring wood to the house. The first week Lyubov helped, but soon the novelty wore off and she was often drunk or sleeping. Nadia carried only a few sticks of wood at a time since she didn't want to overdo herself.

With the temperature dipping to forty or fifty degrees below zero, Nadia washed the clothing indoors. She still needed to walk down the street to the well house to fetch water. By the time she returned, ice had formed a crust in the pails of water. After unwrapping her layers of clothes, she poured the water into a large kettle on the brick stove.

Nadia looked forward to spring and warmer weather since it would greatly lessen her workload. Baby Larissa was growing rapidly and needed much attention.

8

Not Without My Daughter

1984-1986

One evening when Nadia returned to the house after going on a walk along the forest path, she reached up to open the door. It seemed stuck, so she pulled harder. *What? It's locked. What's going on?* She knocked on the door loudly. There was no answer, so she started pounding on the door.

"Stop banging on the door!" Lyubov hollered.

Desperate now, Nadia tried to force the door open. *Where is Nikolai?* she thought desperately. *I know he's at home.*

At that moment Lyubov yanked the door open and shouted, "What do you want?" She came charging out the door with Nikolai behind her. Nadia could see that they had both been drinking.

Nikolai pushed Nadia back. "Go back to Ukraine," he slurred. "Go."

"I want my baby." Nadia tried to push past them to reach the door.

"No!" Lyubov screamed. "Larissa is our girl. I take care of her, so I get to keep her. Go!"

In the struggle, Lyubov slipped on the snow and fell. Nadia had almost reached the door when Nikolai swung his arm and hit her from the side. She staggered and fell against the house.

What? A shock ran through her. *Nikolai hit me!* Never had he done anything like this before. Before she had time to react, he swung again and hit Nadia a glancing blow on the shoulder. Terrified now, she ran for the gate and then out onto the street. She could still hear her in-laws yelling at her.

Nadia's knees were shaking as she staggered toward the neighbors. What should she do? She was too embarrassed to ask for help, so she sat down on the bench in front of their house. Tears ran down her cheeks as she wept.

It was nearly dark, so Nadia curled up on the bench and pulled her coat tightly around herself and slept. After a few hours she awoke from the cold. She walked back and forth to warm up, then lay down again and slept until early morning.

Nadia sat up when she heard a door bang. It was their neighbor, Volodia.

"Nadia!" he said in surprise. "What are you doing here?"

When Nadia started telling her story, he beckoned her to the house. "Come inside where it's warm. Then you can tell Tamara and me what's going on."

"We should call the police," responded Volodia after they listened to Nadia's story.

When the police officer showed up, he listened carefully as Nadia detailed what had happened. "I'll go check it out," he said with a grin.

After impatiently waiting for over an hour to hear back from the police, Nadia decided to walk across the yard and peer through the fence. The sight made her angry. There was Nikolai and the policeman sitting outside the house laughing and drinking vodka together.

That night Volodia and Tamara insisted that Nadia sleep at their house. It was difficult for Nadia to sleep and not worry about Larissa. The next day she went to the city to visit her friend Yana, who was studying to be a lawyer.

Yana welcomed Nadia. "You may stay here as long as you need to," she said. "My husband and I will help you all we can. Somehow you need to get your daughter back."

Yana decided to accompany Nadia to seek help from the army general at the camp in Ulan-Ude. Since Andre was serving in the army, the general would likely try to help.

"I understand your predicament perfectly," the general said. His uniform was spotless and his boots shone like mirrors. His chiseled face had the appearance of strength. "I have a daughter who was staying with my son-in-law's family. They also kicked her out of their house." He spoke kindly. "I will instruct the Komsomol laborer dormitories to find you a room within two days."

Nadia thanked the general profusely and shook his hand. Tears filled her eyes. "I am indebted to you," she said.

"I will also call three soldiers and two police to go with you to get your daughter and belongings," the general continued. "Wait in the lobby until you are notified."

When the soldiers and the police arrived, they accompanied Nadia and Yana to Nikolai and Lyubov's house. After they knocked, Lyubov opened the door with a surprised look on her face. Then her countenance darkened.

"What do you need?" she barked.

"We have been sent by the general with orders to retrieve Nadezhda Zaikova's daughter Larissa and any or all personal belongings of the mother and daughter." The soldier moved toward the door. Lyubov began to close it, but the soldier stuck his foot in to keep it from latching. He pushed the door open and beckoned to the others to follow.

"Get out of my house!" Lyubov yelled, cursing the soldiers. They paid no heed to her and stepped inside. Two soldiers guarded the angry woman while Yana and Nadia went in search of Larissa. They found her awake in her crib. Yana held Larissa while Nadia quickly gathered all her clothes and a few other possessions.

Nadia could hear the soldiers chuckling and saying something about a bear in the kitchen. She hoped Lyubov would be smart enough not to do anything rash. Even though Lyubov's actions had hurt her deeply, she didn't want to see her mother-in-law go to prison for something worse.

The police and soldiers took Nadia back to Yana's apartment, where she would stay until the general found an apartment for her.

Nadia sat holding baby Larissa, who was sleeping quietly. How wonderful it felt to have her daughter in her arms again! Unlike her own mother, who had disowned her soon after she was born, Nadia wanted to raise her daughter and teach her well. She did not want to ever be parted from her.

She sighed and turned from the window where her eyes had stopped seeing the traffic as she reminisced. She was so glad for this apartment to live in. It was small, but it would have to do until Andre came home.

As she gazed out the window again, she decided to take advantage of the nice weather and go out for a walk with Larissa. After a refreshing stroll to a nearby store where she bought some crackers for Larissa, she headed back for her apartment. The manager saw her enter the building and called for her.

"Nadezhda, you have a piece of mail." She stepped out of her office to hand it to Nadia. "Out for a stroll?"

"Yes. Fresh air. My baby needs fresh air, you know."

Nadia took Larissa into her arm as she folded the baby carriage. Larissa wriggled slightly, but Nadia held her close as she reached the top of the stairs and made her way to her apartment.

After putting Larissa on a blanket on the floor with some toys, Nadia opened the letter. It was from Andre.

Nadia caught her breath. She couldn't believe what she was reading.

> *I can no longer trust you because I have found out that you are going out with other men and leaving Larissa at home with my mother.*

Nadia immediately knew that Lyubov must be feeding Andre this untruth. She continued reading the letter.

> *Mama says you are not a responsible mother for our daughter and that she should care for Larissa.*

Nadia's eyes widened. How could Lyubov write such things to Andre? *She knows I work hard to care and provide for Larissa. She knows I'm not out running around.*

There was only one thing to do. She would write back to Andre and explain the truth about the whole situation. She would write how Nikolai and Lyubov had locked her out of the house, and how they in their drunken stupor had beaten her. She would write every detail so he would know the facts.

The next day Nadia felt better as she returned from mailing her letter. She took Larissa to the park for a stroll and spent some time enjoying the beautiful fall day. Now six months old, Larissa greatly enjoyed the walks in the park with her mother. Nadia watched a small gray-brown bird with a white underbody flit through an evergreen bush.

As she pushed the stroller along the gravel paths, she contemplated her life. She wished she had more money to buy clothing for herself and Larissa. She also wished she could get some meat—especially fish. She usually bought only the cheapest food since she received only fifty rubles[1] per month. For the first two months after Larissa's birth, the government had given her five hundred rubles each month, but now it was down to fifty. This was not enough to buy even the necessities, so Nadia knew she would have to go back to work.

Nadia was glad for the room provided for her in the dormitory, but she worried about the moisture. Their room was at the top corner of the building. As the roof lacked adequate overhang, water and snow ran off the roof and down the walls, creating a damp wall. Larissa seemed to be sick quite often, and Nadia blamed it on the cool, damp living quarters. Perhaps she could obtain a drier room elsewhere in the building.

Quite frequently at night the husband and wife in the room next to them became drunk and would argue and fight. As they tussled around, banging against the walls, plaster sometimes fell off the wall in Nadia's apartment.

Nadia talked to another couple that was affected by these nightly disturbances. "I think we should report this," they agreed. "Not only are they disturbing the peace, they are also damaging the apartment."

"Yes," said Nadia, "it's hard to sleep when there is so much noise. Even Larissa wakes up and cries because of it."

After the surrounding families reported the fighting and damage, the offending couple was moved out of the apartment. After a week had passed, Nadia asked for and received permission from the manager to move into the vacant apartment since it was drier than hers.

---

[1] The ruble is the basic Russian monetary unit. The kopek is a coin equal to 1/100 of a ruble. After the Soviet Union fell and Ukraine became an independent country in 1991, the ruble was phased out and replaced with the Ukrainian kupon.

The new apartment was also warmer, and Larissa's health soon improved. Nadia asked the manager for cement, and then using her skill at this work, she stuccoed the damaged spots in the apartment.

A few months passed, but no more letters came from Andre. Finally, at the advice of her friend Yana, Nadia wrote to the army general.

"When you send your letter, you should also include the letter Andre wrote to you," Yana had advised her. "Tell the general that Andre is paying more attention to his mother than to his own wife. Perhaps the general will talk to him about it."

It was nearly two weeks before Nadia received a response to her plea. The letter came in an official envelope from the camp where her husband was serving. The general was sympathetic in his reply and said he had talked to Andre. He had explained to him that although a son needs to honor his parents, his first priority should be building a relationship with his wife.

During the next year, Nadia wrote Andre as often as she could with her demanding job and baby girl. Andre also wrote back several times.

Nadia was in for a surprise one August day in 1985 when a knock sounded on the apartment door. When she opened it, there stood Andre. With a big smile he engulfed her in a bear hug.

"Andre!"

"Did you tell your mother you are home?" Nadia asked as she helped him take off his boots.

"No, I didn't tell anyone."

Nadia quickly prepared a hot meal at the dormitory kitchen, and brought it back to their room. They talked over their meal and caught up on each other's lives. They didn't bring up the letter of accusation. Andre had completed his military duty and was at home to stay.

This is how marriage is supposed to be, thought Nadia as she watched her husband play with Larissa. Nadia still worked at the airport during the day, often doing painting and stucco work. Andre would take Larissa to the daycare center while he looked for work. On the way home from her job, Nadia picked up Larissa and brought her home. Then she would go to the public kitchen in the dormitory and make supper for the three of them.

Eighteen-month-old Larissa could now toddle around the room and loved when Andre crawled after her growling like a bear. Desperately she would try to climb up onto her chair. But just before she made it, Andre would grab her and pretend to eat her. She would scream, and then it was all over as she snuggled into his strong arms.

Nadia smiled as she watched the two. She hoped that between her job and Andre's job, when he found one, they could save enough money to buy or build their own house.

It was not to be.

Three weeks after Andre returned from the army, he staggered into their apartment one evening. Nadia took one horrified look and saw that he was drunk.

"Who have you been running around with?" Andre shouted at Nadia. He ignored Larissa, even when she toddled to him and grabbed his legs. "I met my mama today and she said you have been with other men." He slapped Nadia's face. "Tell me about it."

Nadia backed away. "I have done no such thing. Why have you been drinking?"

"It's none of your business. Just tell me the truth." Andre stopped to get his breath. "Tell me, or I'll beat you!"

"I work. And I take care of our daughter—that's what I do." Nadia backed away, but Andre moved closer. His breath smelled like the homemade brew his mother made.

Andre slapped at her again, but she ducked and his hand hit the closet. He swore as he held his hand. His eyes were glazed and distant. "I had a good woman in the army when I first got there . . ." His voice trailed off. He jerked as if he were waking up from a dream. "I need to lie down."

Nadia tried to sort through her thoughts as she mulled Andre's confession and his accusations. Why would Andre's mother turn him against her? Nadia knew that when Andre was drunk he didn't realize what he was doing, but she couldn't live with that. She would have to be firm with him. He had also revealed a relationship with a woman at the army camp. What did he mean?

A few days later Andre came home from looking for a job. Nadia heard him fumble to unlock the door. He swore as he dropped his keys. Nadia's heart sank. *He's probably drunk again.* Sure enough, his breath smelled heavily of drink as he towered over her.

"I heard you were out with another man." He pointed an accusing finger at her. "Mama said she saw you with him."

Nadia stood her ground. "I was not with another man. You are the only man I have ever been with. You are the one who is guilty. The last time you were drunk, you said you had another woman at the army camp."

"What?"

"Yes, the last time you came home drunk, you said you had another woman while you were serving at the army camp."

"How dare you accuse me?" Andre clenched his fist and swung. Nadia screamed and ran for the door. Andre lunged for her but missed.

"Help!" Nadia shouted. A few doors in the main hallway popped open at her cries. Two men from neighboring apartments soon appeared.

"What's wrong?" one of them asked.

Before Nadia could reply, Andre staggered out and attacked her again, but this time the two men caught him. They forced him down the hall and out the door.

Nadia was trembling as she closed the door and locked it. Now what should she do? Her husband was losing his mind. She knew it was because of his mother and the brew he was drinking. She picked up Larissa, who had been playing with her doll but had begun to cry. Nadia held her daughter close as she thought about her own mother's attempt to kill her when she had been a little girl. Now it was her husband who was attacking her. Why could she never experience the love she wanted? She remembered the Lord's Prayer Uncle Yakov had taught her. As she recited it, she began to feel a bit more peaceful.

Nadia wondered when Andre would return. No doubt when he sobered up, he would be ashamed of how he had acted. That was the way it always worked.

A few days passed with Nadia working extra hard at her job to erase the memory of Andre and his drinking. What should she do with him? She supposed she would have to accept the fact that he wasn't perfect. She wasn't either.

She would try to make her marriage work and accept him if he came back and apologized. Her heart resisted the idea, but she knew it was the right thing to do.

Back to Ukraine

1985-1986

It was three weeks before Andre showed up. He was sober and knocked quietly before coming in. Since it was Sunday morning, Nadia had the day off.

"Nadia, may I come in?" Andre called, pushing the door open.

Nadia stirred from her seat. She had been reading the news from the day before.

"Yes, come in."

Andre stood quietly. "What are you reading?"

"Politics. Why?"

"Can we talk?"

"I think we can both talk," said Nadia with a nervous laugh.

"I am sorry about going home and listening to Mama's stories and getting drunk. I want to come back and try to do better."

"Okay. But please, Andre, don't drink. And please believe me—I have not been running around. As far as what happened at the army camp, I guess it happened, and it's in the past."

Andre shifted from one foot to the other.

"I'll try to do better," he said.

Nadia got up and they embraced. It wasn't a romantic embrace, just a forgiving one. They would both work hard to make a good home.

Soon after Andre returned, they decided to go to the taiga forests to harvest Siberian pine nuts. Since Andre had been going to the forests each year, he knew the best areas for harvesting nuts. Andre asked his mother if she could watch Larissa for a few days, and she agreed.

Nadia was glad Lyubov didn't raise a fuss about watching Larissa since she and her mother-in-law were still not on the best of terms. *But really,* she thought, *Nikolai and Lyubov should be happy to see Larissa since they almost never visit us.*

Andre asked his friend Bogdan to go along to help gather the cones. The two men drove their motorcycles with Nadia sitting behind Andre, holding on for dear life as they roared deep into the forest. They rode along narrow trails and up rugged terrain to reach the areas where there were tall Siberian pines with an abundance of pine cones.

Andre and Bogdan climbed the trees, while Nadia stayed on the ground. Andre picked the pine cones and threw them into the bag on his back. When the bag was full, he handed it down to Bogdan with a long pole and a hook. Bogdan then handed it on down to Nadia, who stacked the bags around their camp.

The Siberian pines could grow up to 150 feet tall, depending on the forest conditions. Most of the trees they climbed, however, were only around eighty or ninety feet tall.

It was dangerous work, but all three enjoyed the fresh forest air and the great outdoors. At night they built a fire to roast the strips of meat they had brought along and to keep any unwanted beasts at bay. As they watched the fire, ate their meal, and told stories, life seemed good once more. Somewhere across a ridge a wolf howled.

Nadia shivered and added another stick to the fire. The flames sprang to life and licked up the new wood, pushing back the darkness. Beyond the treetops, the stars popped out to say goodnight as two of them slid into their sleeping bags while one stood guard. For their safety, they needed to keep the fire burning.

One morning there were giant bear tracks around their camp. Nadia shivered as they stared at the tracks.

"I fell asleep during my watch this morning," confessed Andre. "It's a good thing he ate his supper before coming to visit us." He grinned, but they all realized it wasn't funny.

That day Nadia extracted the nuts from the cones while the two men picked more cones. After they had filled several bags with shelled nuts, they decided to call it quits.

That week Andre brought home good news. A local company needed an excavator and had agreed to give him the job. With two incomes, they could finally begin saving money for the future.

But before Andre could begin his job as an excavator, he heard about another job opportunity that would pay him a higher wage—being a truck driver. However, he would first need to go to school to get his license.

"I think the driving job would be better," advised Nadia. "Your father and brother both do this too."

"Yes, I would get paid better for driving truck," agreed Andre.

The decision made, Andre began attending driving school to get his license. Every morning Nadia got up early to pack their lunches and dress Larissa. Afterwards she would take Larissa to the daycare center before going to her job.

When Larissa fell ill with pneumonia, the daycare center advised

Nadia to place her in the hospital until she recovered. Since Larissa was still too young to be alone at the hospital, Nadia needed to take off work to stay with her.

At the hospital, food was provided for Larissa as a patient but not for Nadia. *Now what am I going to do?* she wondered.

"Why aren't you eating?" asked a young woman who slept in the bed next to hers.

"I don't have food or a way to get any," replied Nadia. She was uncomfortable with the pointed question. "I need to stay here with my daughter, and I have no one to bring me food."

"Here, take some of mine," offered the young woman, who had introduced herself as Ella.

Nadia graciously accepted the cooked buckwheat and meatballs and thanked the young woman profusely. She guessed that the older couple who had brought Ella food that day must have been her parents.

Soon Ella and Nadia became acquainted and shared their life stories with each other. Every day Ella insisted that Nadia take some of her food. One day she made an offer to Nadia.

"Why don't you run home to see your husband and make yourself a hot meal?" she suggested. "I can watch Larissa for an hour or two."

Nadia was eager to taste some of her own cooking and to change into some clean clothes, so she accepted Ella's offer. She let the nurses know where she was going before she left. Humming to herself, she walked the streets toward home.

As she topped the stairway that led to her apartment room, she could hear voices.

The door to her apartment was unlocked and standing open a crack. She could smell cigarette smoke and hear Andre's voice. There were other voices too. Nadia knocked gently.

"Next!" Andre boomed from inside.

Nadia stepped inside. Andre, Bogdan, and two young girls were seated at the table drinking vodka and playing cards.

"Why are you here drinking and smoking in my apartment?" Nadia asked, raising her voice. "You do not belong here. And you, Andre," she said accusingly, "why can't you come visit us at the hospital and bring me some food?"

Nadia scanned the room. She grabbed the mop standing in the corner of the kitchen and ran at the four who were by now scurrying for the door. Andre swung his hand to catch the mop but missed and hit Nadia. Her glasses flew off, but she kept swinging her mop.

Nadia was devastated. *Why does life have to be this way? Isn't Andre serious about our marriage?* Nadia sat on a chair and leaned against the table with her head in her hands. Great sobs of grief shook her body as she gave way to waves of weeping and tears. She lost track of time as she sat there, but finally she roused herself. She needed to get back to the hospital—and she hadn't done anything she had planned.

One thing was sure. This was the end. She would never forgive Andre. She couldn't make herself use his name. He didn't value her or their marriage. She would divorce him.

Nadia stood in line to buy tickets at the train station, her bags beside her on the concrete and Larissa clinging to her skirt. It had been over four years since she and Irina had rolled into this same station when they first arrived in Ulan-Ude. They had been full of dreams about building the USSR and finding fulfillment and purpose in a cause bigger than themselves. Now she was leaving with a little girl and a broken heart.

When it was her turn to buy tickets, Nadia stepped forward. She was thankful to learn that their train would be leaving shortly. Picking up her bags and calling Larissa, she headed for the platform to find the train.

Quickly Nadia boarded the train and found their assigned room. After stuffing her bags under the seat and drawing Larissa close, she sat back to sort through her confused thoughts.

A few minutes later a conductor came by to check on the passengers before stepping back to the doorway and waving approval. Nadia felt the car jerk forward an inch, then another. Larissa looked at her and pointed out the window. Snow was falling steadily.

As evening approached, the train passed the southern edge of Lake Baikal and headed for the Sayan Mountains. Nadia placed Larissa on the couchette across from her and tucked her in with pillows and a blanket the conductor had provided. After Larissa had fallen asleep, Nadia lay back and tried to relax.

Her mind began to spin. *How could Andre do this to me? How could he just bring another woman into my apartment as soon as I was gone?* She hung her head as great silent tears slid down her cheeks. *Doesn't he love me at all?*

And that was not all. A neighbor had informed her that another woman was now living with Andre at Nikolai's house. Nadia put her hand to her head. Why was life so hard? So unfair? Overcome with grief, she buried her face in the pillow as the tears continued to fall.

As the morning sun glinted off the moving train, Nadia stirred. She got up and scraped the frosty window with her fingernails. Outside, a cold wind blew drifts of snow across the track, but it wasn't enough to hinder the chugging train. Hearing her mother scrape the window, Larissa awakened. She scooted off the seat and wrapped her arms around her mother.

"Hi, little one," said Nadia, scooping her up in her arms. "How are you? Shall we go find something to eat?"

After combing Larissa's hair, Nadia poured a little water out of a bottle to wash her face and hands. She grabbed her purse, locked the door behind them, and led Larissa toward the dining car. Cigarette smoke lingered in the hall.

When Nadia reached the dining car, it was full of hungry travelers, and she had to wait. A young fellow ahead of her was looking over the menu. He muttered something under his breath and left the car.

It's no wonder he didn't get any breakfast, thought Nadia. Everything was expensive. She chose an egg for herself and one for Larissa. She also got a piece of bread and some black tea for herself and a cup of milk for Larissa. After paying for the meal, Nadia found an empty booth where she could see forward as well as out the side windows.

After breakfast, Nadia stood by the window in her train car and watched the passing landscape. She could see the snow-covered forests. Occasionally she saw small meadows surrounded by shrubs and birch trees. A little village slid by. She noticed a single horse pulling a wagon along the snow-hardened street, the driver hunched over from the cold. The village appeared to be almost dead except for the smoke curling up from the houses.

Watching the countryside slide by gave Nadia ample time to think. She thought of the little cross Uncle Yakov had given her. *Is there a God who knows everything about me? If so, where is He? How can I learn more about Him?*

After Nadia had been kicked out of Nikolai's house, she had heard over the radio of the beautiful Buddhist temple and had gone to see if perhaps God was there. She had been appalled at the hideous faces and had noticed there were no icons. She didn't feel comfortable and hadn't stayed long. She did not think God was there.

At least the icons at the St. Volodymyr's Cathedral in Kiev were nice to look at. She remembered going there once out of curiosity and watching worshipers making the sign of the cross and kissing the icons and images of Jesus and Mary. However, when Uncle Yakov, who worked as a groundskeeper at the church, had seen her, he had rebuked her.

"Go find a skirt to wear before you come again, Nadia," he had said gruffly. It had been the first time he had ever been rough with her, and it was only because she had been wearing pants in the cathedral.

Nadia sighed. She turned to see Larissa playing with the doll her grandmother Lyubov had given her. Larissa was almost three years old now, but still far too young to understand the significance of this trip. She didn't know that she would likely never see her father again. The doll was all she thought about at the moment.

After five days of travel, the train approached Moscow. There was excitement in the air as passengers leaned against the windows and watched the approaching city. Some were looking forward to being at home; others just wanted to get off the train.

Situated on the banks of the Moskva River, this huge city had many bridges. Skyscrapers and high-rise apartments with twinkling lights could be seen as they approached. As they entered the suburbs, row upon row of dirty gray houses appeared. A light covering of snow made the ground look clean and covered some of the garbage along the back streets.

When the train came to a stop, Nadia gathered her bags and guided Larissa to the door. The hallway was crowded with people pushing for the exit.

After buying tickets to go on to Kiev, Nadia asked where she could send a telegram. She wanted to inform Uncle Yakov that she was coming. Perhaps he could meet her somewhere. Nadia bought a couple of hot potato pirozhki[1] for herself and Larissa. The food here was cheaper and tastier than it had been on the train.

As Nadia sipped her hot tea, her mind again tumbled over with thoughts of a God she didn't know. She recalled the prayers her uncle had taught her and how she had prayed that her grades would

---

[1] Baked or fried boat-shaped buns with a variety of fillings.

improve and they had. Maybe there was a God out there somewhere. She now repeated the Lord's Prayer in her mind and felt comforted by the familiar words.

As she waited, her thoughts went to her father Valera. She had met him only once, when she was fourteen years old, and it was not a good memory.

Nadia remembered how she had received a letter from her father's first wife, Galina. Galina had found out through Uncle Yakov that her husband Valera had a daughter living at an orphanage. This angered Galina so much that she eventually divorced Valera. In her letter, Galina invited Nadia to come visit her. During the visit, Galina had taken Nadia to meet her father.

Nadia had found her father a man who could not be trusted, and her reminiscing troubled her. She quickly stood up and grabbed her bags. She held Larissa tightly as she headed for the train.

That night as the train whistle blew and the cars jerked into motion, Nadia huddled on the seat with Larissa in her arms. This would be the last leg of their journey.

As she relaxed on the seat, Nadia curled Larissa's brunette hair around her fingers as she rocked her to sleep. *Kiev. It will be so good to see Kiev again. It will be a homecoming for someone with no place to call home.*

Place to Place

1987-1989

The day was gray and dreary as Nadia left the Kiev city office. The dreariness seemed even more depressing since she couldn't obtain the documents she wanted. An old bus lumbered by, mingling the smell of diesel smoke with the falling snowflakes. Her boots crunched on the ice and snow that hadn't been completely cleaned from the sidewalks.

As she walked along the street, she thought of all the problems she had experienced since returning from Ulan-Ude. She had been told that if she would fill out all the necessary paperwork, the city would give her an apartment and a monthly wage in exchange for cleaning leaves, shoveling snow, picking up trash, and other work on the streets of Kiev.

But now she had spent all her money, plus some she had borrowed from Yakov, and she still didn't have the job.

Uncle Yakov had allowed her to move in with them, but Marusia was complaining, so Nadia knew she had to find another place to live. Nadia hoped her uncle hadn't told Marusia that she had borrowed money from him. She would really be upset then.

That reminded her. She needed to get home soon. The later it got, the unhappier Marusia would be.

Maybe she could go see her good friend Svetlana, who was back from Novosibirsk. Svetlana was now a practicing lawyer in Kiev and might have some good advice for her.

"I am sorry," Svetlana told her the next day when they met. "I am not sure what to tell you. If you did what they told you and you still don't have the job, I would recommend looking for something else. Why don't we go for a walk while we talk about some options?"

Svetlana, Larissa, and Nadia, from left to right.

Thankfully, after about a week Nadia did find a new place for her and Larissa to stay—at her great-aunt Efrosinya's place. Before she had gone to Siberia, she had often stayed at Efrosinya's dormitory room. The government had later given Efrosinya a small apartment, so there was a bit more room this time. It was still barely big enough, but Nadia found security in having a place to live with the elderly woman.

She also found a job at a daycare center within walking distance from the apartment and could take Larissa along. Nadia worked as a janitor and groundskeeper. Her job included clearing the snow off the walkways and steps. It was a cold, messy job during the winter, and her feet and legs were often cold and wet. However, it was a job that brought some income, and she was able to repay Uncle Yakov the money she had borrowed. She was also able to buy some vegetables and bread, and occasionally meat. She bought store milk for Larissa, although she did wish she could get fresh milk. *Oh well,* she thought, *at least it's milk, even if it is probably diluted with water.*

Working at the daycare center during the spring and summer was much easier than in winter. Nadia especially enjoyed the spring months with the warmer weather and the blooming trees. It was relaxing to walk home through the scents, sights, and sounds of spring.

Nadia and Larissa enjoyed living with "Grandma," as they called Efrosinya. Although the small apartment didn't really feel like home, it was a place to stay, and Nadia felt grateful.

About a year after they moved in with Efrosinya, she suddenly became sick and after several weeks she died. *I knew she would die sometime,* Nadia thought as she wiped away a tear. *I just didn't think it would be this soon.*

Now what? Nadia sat on the sofa and drew Larissa close as she pondered the future. Would they get kicked out of the apartment? She hoped the government would not find out and make her leave.

Soon after her great-aunt's death, Nadia found a better-paying job at a filming studio. She would start cleaning at three o'clock in the afternoon and sometimes worked until ten o'clock. Since she didn't start her work until afternoon, she often brought Larissa with her.

"My name is Pavel Petrovich." The young fellow introduced himself to Nadia with a smile. Uncle Yakov shifted his weight and nodded.

"He is Marusia's nephew," Yakov told her. "He has a house here in Kiev."

The next few months sped by rapidly with Nadia and Pavel going out together on dates. Sometimes they took Larissa along, and sometimes they found a babysitter. Pavel had a dark complexion like Andre but was shorter. He wasn't as lighthearted as Andre had been but still laughed easily. His dark eyes crinkled almost shut when he laughed.

Sometimes they spent an evening at a bar to dance and drink. *Maybe he would be a good family man,* thought Nadia. *Why not?* She needed a good father for Larissa, and Pavel had a decent house. He was likeable, and he didn't seem like the kind of man who would run around on her. But she did want to be careful before she made up her mind.

One morning in the summer of 1988, Nadia heard hammering on the door of the apartment. Her heart sank. She could hear a tool prying at the lock; then more hammering. She had failed to appear in court a couple of times regarding Efrosinya's apartment. *Let them come and take it from me,* she had thought. Knowing she had no place to go, and that they would eventually force her out, she had pitched the letters into the trash and simply enjoyed each day she could stay.

From the sounds of the hammering at the door latch, she knew her time was up. Suddenly the door burst open, and two stout men strode in. Without looking at her, they headed into the back room. Soon they came out carrying the bed. Wordlessly they carried all the furniture out of the apartment and down to the street. Nadia quickly grabbed some bags and stuffed her belongings into them. Larissa wailed as she watched the men carrying everything outside.

"Mama, what are they doing?" She clung to her mother, her eyes wide with fear.

"We must move out," Nadia told her. She grabbed a stack of newspapers she had saved and threw them into a bag. She might need them to start a fire depending on where she ended up. She quickly ran to the neighbors and called Yakov to tell him what was happening. He probably wouldn't be at home, but Marusia could let him know. She was surprised to hear Yakov answer the phone.

"I'll be right over," he said. "I have today off anyway."

Nadia sat on the bed and waited for her uncle to arrive. It was embarrassing to have her possessions piled on the sidewalk. Larissa played with a branch that had fallen from one of the trees. *Now where?* Nadia thought of her uncle's faith in God and her own reliance on the government. But now the government was turning her out onto the street, and her uncle's God didn't seem to be showing up much either.

After she had waited several hours, a large truck rumbled up to the apartment buildings. A breeze flung a bit of dust along the street as the truck crunched to a halt. The truck doors sprang open, and Uncle Yakov and Pavel climbed down.

"We'll get you fixed up in no time," the driver said, coming around to greet her. He grabbed a small table and hoisted it onto the truck bed. He climbed up and pushed it forward. Uncle Yakov and Pavel loaded the furniture, and the driver stacked it tightly, securing it with ropes. Nadia had tried to pack their clothes the best she could in the bags she had grabbed.

The sun peeked through the clouds for a moment as they loaded the last of Nadia's things. After that, clouds drifted across the sky to hide the sun once more.

"We'll take you over to Lisnyky," said Uncle Yakov. "You are legally registered at your mother's house, so you have the right to live there. The bigger question is whether your mother will let you."

Maria grudgingly agreed to allow them to live in the back room, but she wasn't happy with the arrangement. She complained often about Nadia and Larissa living in her house, and at night she sang loudly until the wee hours of the morning.

After a couple weeks of enduring this misery, Nadia visited Uncle Yakov. She described the difficulty they were facing.

"I am not sure what I should do," Nadia said. "I think she is trying to make it miserable for us so we leave."

"Let's try to contact your father Valera," Uncle Yakov said. His voice was determined. "He should do something for you since you are his daughter."

"Do you think we should?" Nadia pulled Larissa close. It had been ten years since she had seen her father. "Is he safe?"

"I don't know. Probably just as safe as your mother." Uncle Yakov didn't smile. "I guess we will just have to find out. I know where he is living."

"When should we go?" Nadia asked.

"Now," Uncle Yakov replied with determination. "Let's go. Marusia can go along too."

Nadia was uneasy. She recalled the only time she had met her father and the creepy way he had acted.

After a forty-minute bus ride, they arrived at the last station. They would need to walk the rest of the way.

"Valera is married to his third wife, I think," Uncle Yakov said as they walked along the street in Kiev. "I found out that he is living at his wife's apartment. But since he is a registered invalid, he also has an apartment that the government gave him."

Maybe it would be all right to stay in one of his apartments, Nadia tried to reassure herself. *I hope he is at home.*

The wind was almost still and the clouds appeared sluggish. A few sparrows scratching in the soil along the sidewalk hopped behind a dumpster as the group neared. A bus horn sounded nearby.

"Here it is," Yakov announced, pointing to a tall apartment building. They ascended the steps to the apartment number and rang the doorbell. The door opened and a short, pudgy woman greeted them.

"Well, it's Yakov," said the woman. She had met him before at the St. Volodymyr's Cathedral where Valera also worked.

"Hello," said Yakov. "I would like to talk to Valera. May we come in?"

Without waiting for an answer, Yakov waved the women in and stepped in behind them.

"Have a seat while I get him," the woman replied. "He arrived home from church not long ago and is sleeping."

The group sat in the living area to wait. It wasn't long before Valera stepped into the room.

"What is this all about?" he asked. His face was marked with irritation.

"We have come to see if you can help us out." When Yakov spoke, his voice filled the room. He explained the problem Nadia was having with her mother and with finding a decent place to live.

"I know you have two apartments," Yakov finished. "Maybe you could allow your daughter to use one."

Valera's face flushed deeply. He stood to his feet and shouted, "She is not my daughter! I don't know what you are talking about. Get out!" He grabbed his cane and swung it at Yakov. "I said *get!*" he screamed. "Get out of my house!"

Nadia grabbed Larissa and headed for the door, tears filling her eyes. Marusia was close behind.

"I don't know the woman!" Valera shrieked. He kicked Yakov in the shins. "Go now!"

Yakov backed to the door, defending himself from the swinging cane.

"You know better!" Yakov bellowed. "Nadia is your daughter, and we can prove it to your wife if she wants to know more." He nodded to Valera's wife, who was still standing wide-eyed at the spectacle.

"He's a selfish man," Yakov fumed as they walked back to the bus stop.

"At least you tried." Nadia wiped her wet cheeks.

"Mama, why was that man screaming?" Larissa asked.

"He wasn't happy with us being there." Nadia stooped down to her daughter. "We will be all right. We have Uncle Yakov to help us."

Another week passed, and Nadia was still struggling with the living conditions in the back room of her mother's house. She had pleaded

Place to Place 93

with her mother to keep quiet at night, but her mother had only laughed.

The house was dirty, and several men came and went at their leisure. The house smelled of vodka and unwashed clothing. Nadia tried to clean up the back room they were using but became discouraged with the dust and smoke. At night, the drunken men would stagger around and fall onto the floor in the next room. Their drinking and laughter would wake Nadia, who then couldn't sleep for fear.

"Why don't you move to my house," suggested Pavel when Nadia told him of the stress. "I will give you a place to live, and we can get married."

Nadia didn't take long to make her decision. "Okay," she agreed. Hopefully this would be her last move and she could settle down to a peaceful home life.

>   Little red berry, red berry, red berry of mine!
>   In the garden there is a berry—little raspberry, raspberry of mine!
>   Ah, under the pine, the green one,
>   Lay me down to sleep,
>   Oh-swing, sway, Oh-swing, sway,
>   Lay me down to sleep.

Nadia groaned as she heard Pavel's sister Natalka singing loudly. She was drunk again. Nadia heard her stagger through the living room to get back to her room.

Larissa was beginning to whimper. Nadia groaned and sat up. She needed rest, not all this drama. Groping in the dark, she found Larissa's head and gently stroked her until the whimpers subsided.

The tiny bedroom was just next to the living room. She and Pavel, at least when he wasn't drunk, would sleep in the small bed and Larissa in a small bed of her own—a suitcase.

Nadia didn't want Larissa sleeping directly on the floor, so she had searched for something she could use as a bed. She had found a large suitcase that she had lined with a small blanket and clean rags.

>Oh-swing, sway, Oh-swing, sway,
>Lay me down to sleep . . .

Will Natalka ever quiet down? As the singing finally faded off, Nadia lay back down and pulled up her blanket. Wearily she closed her eyes. Now for some sleep . . .

Pavel's house was built in two sections, with Pavel and his sister Natalka living in one section and his half-sister Alexandra and her husband occupying the other.

The two apartments were not big by any means, but at least it was a place to stay. It was much better than living in constant fear of the drunken men who frequented her mother's house. And Pavel was usually kind to her, and he let her live here without paying rent.

Every afternoon Nadia cleaned at the studio. It was a good job, and she didn't mind the hours. Occasionally while she cleaned, cartoons were playing. Those were Larissa's favorite days. Nadia even managed to find ways for Larissa to help with the cleaning jobs, much to Larissa's delight.

Today, as usual, they worked six or seven hours before heading for home. They needed to walk approximately fifteen minutes to the Kiev Metro station, where they boarded the city train. After switching trains at one point, they disembarked in Osokorky, in the southeastern part of the city. By this time, darkness had fallen, and only the rays from a few lighted house windows lit the streets as Nadia and Larissa walked toward home.

Home was not exactly the right word for Pavel's house. Actually, Nadia had never had a place she could really call home. And now she wasn't sure what she wanted to do. She had discovered that Pavel was addicted to vodka and would drink for days after he got his paycheck. Although his wages as a crane driver were good, he couldn't avoid the bottle once he had money in his pocket.

If only he could kick his habit. Nadia worried that he would kill himself with drinking. She did like Pavel, but his weakness for vodka worried her. And she had another worry too. She suspected that she was expecting another child. What should she do? She didn't want to marry Pavel if he couldn't control his drinking habit, but where would she live if she didn't marry him?

Arriving at the house, they pushed into the entryway, and Nadia tried their apartment door. It was locked. Digging through her purse, she found the key and unlocked the heavy door. She led Larissa into the little room. Once again Pavel was not at home. Nadia was not surprised, but still disappointed. *He's probably lying in his aunt's barn after a drinking spree.* Nadia sat on the edge of the bed and sighed. It was nearly midnight again.

Days turned into weeks and weeks into months and soon it was winter again. Working at the studio wasn't as easy now that she was heavy with child, but she didn't complain. At least she had a job that paid decent money. She wasn't getting rich, but she could buy food and necessities.

In the wee hours of January 10, 1989, Nadia awoke with a start and felt her abdomen contracting. Dressing quickly, she went out to the kitchen and knocked on the other apartment where Pavel's half-sister Alexandra lived with her husband. When she had roused her sister-in-law, she asked her to call the ambulance.

"I need to go now," Nadia gasped as she leaned against the wall. "Can you please watch Larissa while I am gone? I guess we talked about this before."

"Sure, Nadia," said Alexandra. "Larissa will be fine with us. You go have your baby, and Larissa will be okay here. I will run to the store and call the ambulance." She stepped back into her apartment to grab her overcoat.

When the ambulance arrived, Nadia was fully dressed and had packed a bag with her belongings. The doctor and nurse helped her climb into the ambulance. She lay on the cot and made herself as comfortable as possible.

"You'll be all right," murmured the female doctor, patting her shoulder. "We'll be at the hospital soon. Just lie down and relax."

Relax? thought Nadia. *I wonder if she ever had a baby.* The woman was thin and had a white cap and a white apron. Her dark eyes were sober and unblinking.

Nadia winced as the ambulance bounced along the streets of Kiev. *The heater sure works well,* she thought ruefully. It was almost suffocating compared to the chilly house she had just left. *Oh well, at least I'm not freezing.* Outside, the wind howled and shook the ambulance as it continued toward its destination.

When they finally arrived at the hospital, Nadia was placed on a stretcher and wheeled to the elevator. The elevator screeched all the way up to the fifth floor where it stopped with a clunk. In the birthing room, she was helped onto the bed. The smell wasn't the best and brought back a flood of memories. She thought of her experiences in Siberia and her relationship with Andre. If only Andre had been faithful to her. If only this child could have been his. But wishing wouldn't change anything. This was her life.

Several hours later, a little boy was born to Nadia. As usual, it was a few days before Nadia could hold her baby. *He is so cute,* she thought. *His name will be Maxim.* He had a dark sheen of hair and a wide smile. He cooed and made gurgling noises as he wriggled in her arms. It had been a painful birth, and Nadia had a long recovery. When Tina, one of the nurses, brought Maxim to her for nursing on the second day, Nadia had no milk.

"I guess we will have to keep bottle-feeding him," said the nurse. She smiled and lifted Maxim and placed him back onto the cart.

"A young woman dropped off a package for you." The nurse handed Nadia the package. "She said her name was Alexandra."

Nadia took the package in surprise. She sat up and tore off the paper. Inside she found a note, a package of cookies, and a short length of kolbasa.

"Where's Nadia?" asked Yakov. He had stopped in at Pavel's house to check up on her. He had knocked on Pavel's door, and since there was no answer he had turned to the other apartment.

"She's at the hospital," Alexandra replied. "She had a little boy on the tenth."

"Where's Pavel?" asked Yakov, raising his eyebrows.

"Probably out in the barn drunk." Alexandra shrugged. "You could check."

Yakov strode out to the barn behind the house.

"Pavel," called Yakov. "Where are you? Pa-v-el!" His voice boomed into the little barn. He stepped inside, straining to see as his eyes adjusted to the dimness. There was a mound on the floor covered with an old blanket. Yakov yanked the blanket off the mound to reveal Pavel.

"Ugghh," Pavel groaned as he tried to get up. He slumped back onto the straw-strewn floor. The cow mooed quietly and turned to look over the stall.

"Pavel!" Yakov raised his voice. "Get up now! You have a son. Be a man."

"What?" Pavel struggled to a sitting position. "A son?"

"You should be ashamed of yourself. Nadia had a son. It's been ten days already."

Pavel tried to get to his feet.

"I need a shot of vodka," he said. He grabbed the stall and pulled himself up.

"You don't need vodka," snorted Yakov. "You need to get back to work like a man and leave the bottle alone." He glared at Pavel. "Go get presentable, and let's go see that son of yours." Yakov waited in the kitchen until Pavel had washed and shaved.

"I need a little bit of drink or I can't make it," stammered Pavel. His hands shook as he poured himself a swallow.

The two men left the shelter of the house and walked through the falling snow to get to the metro station. After a nearly two-hour trip, they arrived at the hospital. It was midday. The nurse showed them to Nadia's room.

"Why didn't you come sooner?" asked Nadia. "We have a son." She smiled. "You need to be more responsible now that you are a father."

Pavel held Maxim and grinned.

"I guess I need to become a real father," he said. "No more vodka." He laughed.

"You need to go to church and pray," said Yakov loudly. The baby began to cry at the booming sound.

"And you need to come back and take Nadia home," said Yakov.

"I'll be back in a couple days," Pavel promised.

After the two men left, Nadia lay back and tried to relax. She was thankful that Alexandra came every other day to bring her some meat and cheese or at least something fresh. It was better than the thin soup the hospital served to the patients.

The next day the doctor stopped by to see Nadia. He stood ramrod straight as he brushed back his thick shock of brown hair and cleared his throat.

"You've been here long enough. I heard your man was here to see you."

"Yes," Nadia replied. Fear welled up inside. "He said he would come again in a couple of days." Inside, she had her doubts. Would Pavel actually show up? A pang of fear and dread about the future shot through her.

"Okay," the doctor replied. "I'll give you two days, and if he doesn't show up, you'll have to find some other way home." With that, he was gone.

Nadia tried to prepare herself mentally to leave the hospital, but the thought overwhelmed her. What would it be like to live at Pavel's house and do all the work herself? Especially if Pavel was working—or drunk? At least here they took care of baby Maxim. At home she would need to care for Larissa too. She sighed. Life just seemed so hopeless.

The next day, after Pavel did not come, she was told to pack her belongings and be ready to leave the next morning. That night Nadia didn't sleep well as she thought about traveling in the frigid outdoors. She dreaded wading through the snow and riding public transportation with a baby and her bags.

"Here," said Tina the nurse. "Take this long overcoat. I have an extra one I can use, and you need it worse than I do."

It was cloudy and a few flurries teased Nadia as she left the hospital and headed for the metro station. Walking with her son in one arm and her bags in the other was slow work. The wind chill drove right through her overcoat and clothing. The low-lying clouds and spitting snow made the darkened city feel like sundown although it was only noon. She also felt cold in her heart.

After taking the train to Osokorky, Nadia had at least a fifteen-minute walk yet to Pavel's house. It would probably take a bit longer since she was so exhausted. Again, fear welled up in her heart. Could she cope? What would she do if Pavel refused to help? She gasped as a sharp pain knifed through her abdomen.

Walking along the streets of Osokorky, she could see a few women out getting water from their wells. *Likely to make lunch*, she thought. She wondered what she would eat when she got home. She dreamed of a table full of warm food—potatoes, canned tomatoes, fried fish, bread, and fresh compote.[1] That, and a loving husband. Tears threatened as she realized the impossibility of her dream. It would never happen as long as Pavel kept drinking.

---

[1] Cooked fruit drink.

When Nadia arrived at the house and entered the entryway and kitchen area, she could hear sounds from Alexandra's apartment. She knocked on the door.

When it opened, Alexandra exclaimed, "Nadia! Please come in. You poor woman! You must be tired." She took the bundle from Nadia's arms and helped her to a chair next to the small round table. "I'm so sorry you had to come alone."

"Larissa, your mama is home," Alexandra called into the sitting room where Larissa had been playing.

Larissa bounced into the dining area and hugged her mama.

Nadia pulled her close.

"Do you want to see your baby brother?" Alexandra asked. She knelt and pulled back the wraps to uncover the little boy. At that moment, he wriggled and let out a tiny cry.

"Ohhh," said Larissa, giggling. "He is so tiny."

"Here, Nadia." Alexandra handed the whimpering infant to his mama. "Could you hold him while I fix him a bottle and get you some hot borscht?"

Nadia sighed. It was so good to have a sister-in-law who cared.

"Have you seen Pavel?" Nadia asked after she had finished eating the borscht and fresh bread.

"I think I heard him over in your apartment this morning, but I don't know where he is now. Whenever you are ready, I will help you settle in." Alexandra washed the few bowls and spoons in a big pan on the counter and hung up her towel. "I'll go over and check if the stove is hot." With that she was gone.

When Alexandra returned, she continued her usual banter. Nadia found it so refreshing to be around her.

"Feel free to sit and rest for a while, or you may go over to your apartment at your leisure," Alexandra bubbled.

"Thank you," Nadia murmured, holding Maxim tightly.

"I heard at the hospital that Mikhail Gorbachev is pushing for more openness in the Soviet Union and is calling for economic reconstruction. Have you heard of this?" Nadia asked as she adjusted Maxim in her arms. She was finally warm again, and her abdomen wasn't throbbing with pain.

"I heard that elections are going on now for some offices," Alexandra replied. "That already sounds like more freedom to me."

"Hopefully it also means better living conditions and job opportunities," Nadia sighed.

Days turned into weeks, and then they ran together for Nadia. Since Pavel was usually gone, either at work or at a bar drinking, she had to carry the wood herself and keep the fire going. She also had to prepare meals for herself and Larissa—and for Pavel when he was sober. Sometimes she would walk to the store and buy a few items with the few rubles she was given by the government.

Pavel had become moody since he was fired from his job for drinking. He now didn't have money to purchase his drink, so he was becoming more and more irritable.

"Get out of my apartment!" he shouted one day. It was a cold day in March.

"I am tired of the crying baby and your complaining. Get out!"

Outside there was still snow on the ground. Pavel shoved Nadia and the baby out of the living room and into the unheated kitchen. Then he grabbed Larissa and pushed her into the kitchen with the others.

"Go with your mama!" he shouted. "You're not my daughter." Larissa stumbled and fell. She began to cry.

"Mama, what's Uncle Posha doing?"

"Pavel, you can't do this to me. I have two little children." Nadia slumped onto the wooden bench in the kitchen area and sobbed. Larissa leaned against her.

Nadia bowed her head and tried to say the prayer she had been taught by her uncle. "Our Father which art in heaven . . ."

11

Improvements

1989-1993

*A*fter enduring repeated bouts of Pavel's drunkenness, Nadia was ready to find another place to live. Finally, in August when Uncle Yakov visited her to see how she and the children were faring, she broke down and cried.

"Please," she sobbed, "take me away. Pavel is always drunk and beats me."

Uncle Yakov clenched his fists.

"Where is he? I should teach him a lesson."

"No," Nadia said, "just take us somewhere else."

"Okay, pack as much as you can, and I will carry it." Uncle Yakov held Maxim and Larissa while Nadia packed her belongings.

Uncle Yakov slung the bags over his broad shoulders, then hoisted

Maxim and headed out the door. Nadia and Larissa followed.

At least at Uncle Yakov's we will be safe, thought Nadia as they got on the bus.

"Mama, where are we going? Uncle Yakov's?" Larissa clapped her hands excitedly.

The next day Yakov rode the bus out to Lisnyky and cleaned the back room at Maria's house. To make it more livable, he cut a door from the opposite side to make a separate entrance and built a lean-to for use as an entryway and a room for cooking, washing, and storing wood. Then he built a small brick woodstove inside the living quarters. The stove could be used for cooking and baking and would serve as a heat source for winter days. He also laid up bricks to close the doorway leading from Maria's side of the house to Nadia's room.

Maria resisted the idea at first, but Uncle Yakov explained that legally this was also Nadia's residence. He also built a new lean-to on Maria's side to help appease her wrath.

Pavel, too, was not happy with this move. After he sobered up, he tried to find out where Nadia was living. When he discovered she was living back in Lisnyky, he stopped in one day.

"Please," he said, going down on his knees before Nadia, "I want you to move back to my house. I'm done with drink. I'll stay sober and take care of you. I'm sorry for everything that happened."

"No," Nadia replied, "I need to provide for my children. You almost never helped me. You didn't even help me when I was in the hospital. And not only that—you wasted some of my money on your drinking habit. You might as well go home."

This was not what Pavel wanted to hear. In a rage, he got up off his knees. Red-faced and swearing, he slammed the lean-to door behind him as he left the house. Nadia sat on the edge of the bed and wept. She had no desire to hurt him, but what else could she do? She would take no more chances.

The smell of cows and vegetable fodder permeated the air as Nadia worked inside the long brick barn. The cows stood munching their meal as the milkmaids milked them, and mice scurried along the brick walls looking for seeds. This was a collective farm in Khotiv.

The collective farms had been forced upon the people in the USSR in the early 1930s. Land, animals, and equipment had been taken from private farmers and landowners and had become the property of the government. The locals worked eight hours each day on these farms.

As Nadia cleaned the cows' udders and attached the milkers, she reflected on the last few years. She stepped back as the cow swatted with her tail.

Nadia had gone back to work at the studio when Maxim was eighteen months old. The money the government had given her while she was on maternity leave was not enough to provide food and clothes for the three of them.

Finally, in the fall of 1992, she decided it was too inconvenient to travel all the way to the studio each day with Larissa going to school in Lisnyky. After talking to neighbors and friends, she discovered the need for milkmaids at the collective farm in Khotiv. Nadia applied for the job and was accepted. She began work at the farm with apprehension since she had never worked on a farm before, but she was happy that it would be only about three miles from home.

A big KAMAZ dump truck came by around 5:30 every morning to pick her up for work. She climbed on with Maxim and joined the other women. She had been up earlier to dress the children and make something to eat. Larissa would leave the house later in the morning to walk to school. Nadia took Maxim along with her to the farm, and then later a driver from the farm would take her to the daycare center to drop him off.

Nadia worked on the farm that fall and winter. Her group of milkmaids was in charge of 150 cows, and Nadia helped milk and feed them each day. It was strenuous work for a mother of two children, but she loved the farm work and the smell and warmth of the barns. She would load her wheelbarrow with the vegetable fodder that had been brought from the city factories and wheel it to the cows to eat. Sometimes the workers made their own fodder from the beets and pumpkins they grew on the farm.

Unfortunately, the job didn't last long. That spring Nadia twisted her back while working and was hospitalized. The doctor was emphatic that she must not lift heavy loads. Nadia gave the doctor's instructions to the collective farm manager, and after some discussion, the manager transferred her to the fields to help plant and cultivate the crops. "You will need to do a lot of walking but no heavy lifting," he told her.

Sometimes Nadia rode behind the tractor on the planter to drop the seeds or seedlings into the rows. Other times she walked behind the tractor to cover up the seeds. And of course, as the tomatoes, cabbage, and sweet peppers grew, so did the weeds. There was always weeding to do. There were also fields of beets to weed and harvest.

One day over lunch hour, her field friends began talking about the bicycles sold at a sports store in Kiev. It was a dream of most of the workers to own a bike.

"I've heard that there is a waiting line every time a shipment arrives," a fellow worker informed them. "There are long lines, and if you don't get one, you need to sign a paper and wait for the next shipment."

"It wouldn't take me long to ride to work if I had a bike," Nadia dreamed aloud. "I could easily ride back and forth when the weather is warm."

That afternoon as Nadia worked, she imagined herself riding a new bike through Lisnyky. She would be a step up in the world. The more she thought about it, the more determined she became—she would own a bike! She would save every kupon she could.

Several months later Nadia had reached her goal—she had enough money to buy a bike. After hearing from her fellow workers when the next shipment was scheduled to arrive, she planned her trip.

What can I do with the children? she wondered. *Maybe Claudia could help me out.*

Nadia had learned to know Claudia during the time she was living with her great-aunt Efrosinya. Claudia was an elderly woman but still well able to take care of herself. Nadia was hopeful as she and her two children neared her apartment.

"Come in. Come in," Claudia beckoned, opening the door wide. She smothered Nadia in a warm embrace. "And you brought your children. I have not seen them for so long. My, how they have grown!"

It was good to meet Claudia again, but Nadia had another reason to be here. She had hoped her hostess would be at home.

"I have a question." Nadia cleared her throat.

"What is it, my dear?" Claudia strained forward in her seat.

"I would like to buy a bicycle at the sports store today. I found out how much they cost and have saved enough."

"Oh!" Claudia raised her eyebrows.

"And I need someone to watch the children while I'm gone. Would that be too much to ask?"

"Why, of course not. No problem at all! You go right ahead and take as long as you need. I'll get them something to eat and entertain them."

Excitedly Nadia left Claudia's house. She wasn't sure what to expect, but it would be good to get to the store as soon as possible. She walked at an almost undignified pace as she scurried along the streets. When she arrived, her heart sank when she saw the long line of people ahead of her. She stepped into line while a few more arrived behind her.

The morning dragged as Nadia waited for her turn. Every time she saw a new bicycle being wheeled out, she wondered if it was the last one. Would she have to wait for the next shipment? She hoped not. She pulled out her cross and kissed it. Maybe that would help. She also quoted the Lord's Prayer quietly.

Each time a person entered, the door was quickly closed. Finally it was Nadia's turn. Impatiently she waited. Then the door swung open again, and the man inside the store called out, "Next!" Quickly Nadia stepped inside.

"I am here to buy a bicycle," she told him.

"How would I have known?" the tall man said with a sarcastic grimace. "Everyone wants a bike. But you've got only two choices—and both of them are men's bikes. You have a choice of a blue one or a black one. Take your pick and be quick about it. Both cost the same—$170 kupons. They're the last two." He spit into a box behind the counter.

What should she do? Nadia examined the bikes. She had wanted a women's bike, but she didn't want to wait another couple months or more. It was no telling when the next shipment would come in.

"I'll take the blue one," she said as she handed the tall man $170 kupons. She grabbed the bicycle and started for the door.

"Wait a minute!" the storekeeper hollered at her. His eyes flashed. "I need to write up this receipt before you go."

After Nadia left the sports store, she pushed her bicycle back toward Claudia's apartment. She would show it to Claudia and the children before taking it to Lisnyky. This was a dream come true. A stiff breeze kicked up some dust along the street, and an empty plastic cup scuttled along the sidewalk.

After showing the new bicycle to Claudia and the children, Nadia headed for home. Since public transportation didn't allow bikes on board, she pushed it. She wanted to practice riding it at home first.

"The children can stay with me tonight," Claudia had said. "They'll be okay. You can take your bike home today, then come back on the bus tomorrow to get the children."

The next few weeks were delightful ones for Nadia as she learned to ride her new bike. Before long she was riding it everywhere. Larissa often rode behind her mother, and Maxim perched on the bar in front of her. They laughed and giggled. They thought it was great fun.

Some days Nadia rode her bicycle to work if she missed her normal ride or if she wanted to do some shopping at the store in Khotiv in the evening. Maxim sat on the crossbar and hung onto the handlebars.

As Nadia and her children rode through Lisnyky, the villagers would stop momentarily to watch them go.

Maxim with Nadia's bike.

12

What's Yours Is Mine

1994

"Larissa, it's time to get up."

Larissa stirred and pushed back her blanket. The light Mama had already switched on blinded her for an instant. She rubbed her eyes and looked out the window. Still dark. She groaned as she thought about working in the fields again. Her body still ached from the long day yesterday.

When the large KAMAZ truck rolled up to their street, Larissa and her mother were waiting. The fresh morning air whipped through Larissa's hair as she and her mother rode with the other village women toward Khotiv. Just before the road descended into the village, the driver turned off onto a dirt lane leading to the sugar beet field. They rumbled back through a wheat field, through a small forest, and finally reached the beet field.

Each of the women took a row of beets and began to hoe. Larissa joined them, slashing at the weeds and hoeing carefully so as not to touch the beet plants. The rich, black Ukrainian soil was soft, and the weeds came out quickly. Larissa loved the feeling of the cool soil pushing between her toes. She looked up for a moment to see if she could see the end of the field, but it curved out of sight.

As the sun climbed higher, the cool morning turned into a sultry haze. Sweat trickled down Larissa's face as she tried to keep up with the older, more experienced field hands. A raven's harsh call came from somewhere near the forest.

Larissa stopped to stretch her aching limbs. The beating sun rose steadily as the long line of workers worked their way across the field. Around midmorning, a car from the collective farm pulled up with a large metal container of water for the thirsty women.

After filling her own little container with water, Larissa went back to work beside her mother. Even though it was hot, she enjoyed the outdoors much more than a schoolroom and books. She was thankful it was summer vacation.

"If you help in the fields, they will pay me a little more," Mama had told her.

That evening after work, Pavel stopped by to talk with Nadia and see Maxim. He gave Larissa a hug and pulled Maxim onto his lap.

"How was your day, son?" he asked, giving him a piece of candy.

"Good," said Maxim with a grin as he popped the hard candy into his mouth.

Larissa always felt apprehensive when Pavel showed up, but today he didn't smell of drink. When he was sober, he was kind. He and Mama had walked out to the little garden patch behind the house. *I wish I had a papa who would always be kind. One who would live with us all the time,* Larissa thought with a sigh.

"I'll be back later tonight," grinned Pavel after talking for a while. He winked at Nadia. "What's mine is yours, right? That's what the USSR teaches us. What's theirs is ours. Together."

"Around dark," he smirked. "Be sure to have your sacks ready." With that he disappeared down the little dirt path.

That evening Larissa watched as her mother made soup. At her mother's request, she drew a bucket of water and then helped cut the vegetables. Soon the buckwheat soup was bubbling on the woodstove.

Larissa picked up her doll. "We will travel when you grow up. We can go together," she whispered to the doll.

"Oh, I forgot that we don't have any bread," said Nadia. "Larissa, could you run down to the village store and get a loaf?"

"Sure, Mama."

Larissa took the money her mother gave her and trudged down the dirt path. One of their hens squawked out of the way with a fluttering of wings. When Larissa reached the street, she saw two neighbor boys hanging over the fence, smirking at her as she walked along the street. She reached down for a clod of dirt, but when she stood up to aim, they had disappeared. She dropped the dirt and smiled to herself. They knew better than to mess with her.

At the store, Alexander stood up from the keg where he had been sitting and reading the news. He eyed her suspiciously as she scanned the shelf for the Ukrainian black bread her mother wanted. The shelves in the store always seemed to be nearly empty.

"Please give me a fresh loaf of black bread," Larissa told him, pointing to a loaf that looked new.

"All my bread is fresh," growled Alexander. He took the money Larissa handed to him, smoothed out the bills, and tucked them into his box. Larissa eyed the candy bars for a moment and wished she could buy one. But no, she would have to find a way to earn more money if she wanted ice cream or candy.

That night just after dark as Larissa was playing with her doll and her mother was reading a paper, she heard a quiet knock on the door. Five-year-old Maxim was already in bed where Nadia had tucked him in. He was snoring lightly.

"Come with me," said Mama quietly to Larissa as she grabbed a dark jacket. "Wear something dark."

When they stepped outside, Pavel was waiting with a flashlight. After making sure they had brought the sacks, he shoved the flashlight into his pocket. Noiselessly they walked through the darkness and out of the village. Only the waning moon provided a bit of light to guide them.

Soon after leaving the village, they left the main road and took a dirt path along the forest until they came to a large field of cabbage belonging to the collective farm. In the darkness, they could faintly see the long rows of maturing heads. Larissa watched as her mother and Pavel began to cut off large heads of cabbage.

"Put them in a sack," whispered her mother. Larissa's tongue and throat were dry from holding her breath. They were stealing cabbage! Fear welled up in her heart. *I hope we don't get caught!* She put the heads of cabbage into a sack as her mother and Pavel gave them to her. When the first sack was full, Pavel carried it across the field and took it a safe distance into the forest.

They worked in silence, but in the stillness of the night the peculiar sound of cutting cabbage seemed very loud. The last bag was nearly full when they heard a shout from the direction of the guard's hut.

"Run!" hissed Pavel. "I'll get this bag." Nadia and Larissa ran for the cover of the forest. As they disappeared into the forest, they heard a gunshot behind them.

"Ahh!" came a muffled scream.

"Oh, no," Nadia gasped. "I hope he didn't get shot." She was breathing heavily as she held Larissa close. Mother and daughter peered back the way they had just come. The moon threw a sliver of light across her mother's face and Larissa saw fear in her eyes.

Suddenly they heard someone running through the forest near them.

"Nadia! Larissa!" someone whispered loudly. It was Pavel. He had escaped.

"We are here," Nadia called back quietly.

When Pavel found them, they huddled together. Somewhere in the distance an owl hooted mournfully. Music from a nightclub in the village drifted on the night air.

"I left the bag right where we were working so the guard will not suspect that we got more," Pavel said. "I did get hit by something he shot, and it's painful." He swore under his breath.

The three waited an hour and listened until they were sure no one was near, then Pavel led them to where he had hidden the cabbage. Larissa's heart pounded as she followed her mother and Pavel. They hoisted the bags onto their shoulders and began their trek through the darkness toward home. Larissa felt better when they unlocked their lean-to and pushed inside. She was safe.

"Could you check what is burning a hole in my shoulder?" asked Pavel, wincing.

Nadia looked and found a chunk of salt buried just under his skin. Larissa watched her mother dig it out with a small knife.

"That guard was shooting salt at you!" Nadia laughed as she showed Pavel the piece of salt.

"It burns, but I guess it shouldn't get infected." Pavel tugged his shirt back on and stood to leave. "I think I'll sleep up in the attic on the straw. I don't feel like walking all the way back to Kiev yet tonight."

A few days after the eventful night in the cabbage patch, Larissa and Maxim joined Mama on a bus heading for Kiev. The bus was crammed full, and Russian music played over the loudspeaker. They were on their way to the market with their mother. They were taking one large bag of cabbages and two baskets of strawberries that Larissa had helped her mother pick the day before in their garden plot.

At the Demiivska market, Larissa and her mother searched for a spot among the many vendors. Since there were no more open spaces along the main walk, they settled for a shady spot along a side path.

The market was teeming with life. A grandma selling apples watched as Larissa and Nadia laid out a cloth next to the path and set the cabbage heads in neat rows. Other vendors stopped calling for a moment to turn and scrutinize the newcomers before returning to their peddling.

Larissa and Nadia soon joined the other vendors in calling attention to their goods. Nadia placed the baskets of strawberries next to the cabbages. Maxim sat cross-legged beside the cabbages.

"Buy our cabbage. Fresh cabbage," Larissa called out to folks walking by. She was wearing brown pants and a slinky white shirt. They were both comfortable and looked good. *I want to look good if I am helping Mama sell food,* she had thought. She had also combed her hair and used a headband to keep it in place.

"Buy our strawberries. Sweet strawberries. This way," Nadia called above the din.

A middle-aged man stopped to look. He glanced at the cabbage and then moved closer to the strawberries.

"Are they good?" He looked doubtful.

"Try one." Nadia pointed to a large red strawberry. As the man tasted the sweet and sour taste, his eyes brightened.

"How much for a kilogram?"[1]

Nadia told him and grabbed the measuring box. After she weighed

---

[1] One kilogram is approximately 2.2 pounds.

the strawberries, she carefully put them into a bag. As the man moved on his way, Larissa watched with delight as a woman stopped to look at their cabbages.

"Did you raise these?" The woman bent to feel a head of cabbage.

"Helped," Nadia mumbled. The woman looked at Nadia and grinned.

"I understand. How much do you want for a head?"

As the day progressed, Larissa's stomach ached. She was hungry.

"Mama, may I go buy a meat roll? I'm hungry." Larissa looked at her mother, who was arranging the strawberries neatly. It was important to make the products they were selling look the best.

"We need to save all the money we make to buy things we need at home. You'll have to wait to eat until we get home."

As the afternoon passed, Larissa decided to take a walk through the market. With Mama's permission, she and Maxim set out.

As they walked along, a tantalizing aroma filled the air. "I smell chicken!" Larissa told Maxim. "It's over this way." A vendor was carefully arranging grilled chicken drumsticks on a sturdy table. Beside the drumsticks lay some whole grilled chickens. A small grill oven also had a few chickens turning on the shafts, with oil dripping into a tray below. Larissa's mouth watered. She grabbed Maxim and whispered into his ear.

The two children pushed to the front of the line and up to the table. A few people murmured at them for cutting in front. Larissa pretended to check out the chicken while Maxim stooped and grabbed a whole chicken from a box under the table. Turning around, Maxim took off, with Larissa close behind.

Shouts arose from behind them as the owner's wife dashed after them in hot pursuit. Larissa and Maxim dodged among the crowds of people. Larissa glanced back in time to see a tall man step into the path of the chasing woman.

"Leave the children alone," said the man, whom Larissa recognized as a police officer from Khotiv. "They are likely hungry and need the food. Let me pay you for the damages."

Larissa could see the scowl on the woman's face soften as the tall man handed her a few bills. *Sorry,* Larissa thought, *but we really are hungry.* The two children found a quiet spot to eat the chicken and watch the crowds surge through the market.

By the time they had sold all the cabbages and strawberries, it was nearing sundown.

The next day was Sunday. After eating a piece of bread with a bit of jam they had bought at the market, Larissa and Maxim grabbed two sacks and walked across the village and out to the collective farm fields. In one field was a large stack of wheat straw that had been stacked up for use as bedding for the cows.

"Let's fill our sacks behind the straw stack so no one sees us from the road," suggested Larissa. "This straw will be good bedding for our chickens."

"Why does it matter if anyone sees us?" asked Maxim.

"Because they might think we are stealing it."

"Are we?" Maxim's face was wrinkled in question.

"You ask too many questions," scolded Larissa. "Just help me pull out this straw. Here, let me show you how to stuff it into the sack."

13

The Americans

1995

Kiev, Ukraine, was frozen. Although Eastern Europe was usually milder than Russia, a Siberian wind nicknamed "The Beast from the East" was racing across the Eurasian Steppe, bringing brutal cold and snowstorms.

As the temperature dropped, whirling snow covered the sprawling city. Pedestrians hunkered against the moaning winds while public transportation crept along the treacherous streets. A drunkard lay sprawled on the sidewalk, unaware of his slow burial.

Near an intersection along M Street stood a tall brick building with pine trees guarding its entrance. The trees bowed in the roaring winds. A red-faced janitor vainly tried to clear the sidewalks, while inside the five-story, brick school building the voices of teachers and students rose and fell. At a cafeteria sink, a young woman was filling a pail with water.

Nadia's bright brown eyes watched the water level rise in the pail. Her wavy brown hair swung around her shoulders as she lifted the pail with the ease of one accustomed to hard work. If she wasn't happy, then she was certainly carrying herself with a positive air. Nadia was glad for her new job at the school. Even though Communism had collapsed and Ukraine was now a separate country instead of part of the Soviet Union, local laws still required every able-bodied person to hold a job.

Nadia had attended this school, known as Number 236 School, in ninth grade. Now she was back as an employee, working in the cafeteria. She was thankful that Olga, the school director, had agreed to allow Larissa to attend the school. With her son Maxim attending the kindergarten school just up the street, her new job was working out well.

Nadia picked up the pail of hot water and then glanced out the kitchen window. Snowflakes whirled by, nearly blotting out the janitor, who was still shoveling snow. Her mind often whirled just like the snowflakes, and she grew weary of all the tasks she had to juggle just to survive. Life had so many ups and downs. Sometimes she felt positive and happy, but at other times she felt overwhelmed with the crushing reality of life.

She had experienced so many painful things since she had left this school nearly fifteen years ago. If only she could have had a father to protect her. Or at least a husband who loved her and provided for her. But wishing wouldn't change things. She knew there was only one thing to do—go on and make the best out of life she could.

Raising two children without a husband was difficult. But Andre was 2,500 miles to the east in Siberia, and Pavel had not panned out, so she did it alone. The Russian government required Andre to pay alimony, but it was only a small amount.

Every workday morning Nadia prepared Larissa and Maxim for the day. Then they walked together from the village of Lisnyky through the forests and fields to the school at the edge of Kiev.

One evening in January Nadia was finishing her work. A few workers were still cleaning their assigned rooms, and the head cook was working at her desk in the office next to the kitchen.

As soon as Nadia had finished cleaning up the deserted dining area, she dumped out the dirty water and switched off the lights. Thinking no one was around, she slipped back into the dark dining hall and knelt in the shadows. Her lips moved in a whispered prayer as she pulled out the cross and kissed it.

"God, will you hear me?" she prayed. "I need you to help me. I think you see me, but I just don't know."

Suddenly Nadia sensed someone nearby and looked up. Shura, another employee, was standing beside her.

"Nadia, are you a believer?"

"Yes." Nadia shifted uneasily, getting to her feet.

"Do you believe in God?" Shura continued.

"Yes, I believe in God." Nadia pulled out her cross. "See."

"But what kind of believer are you?" persisted Shura. "God is not in your little cross. He is in heaven. It is idolatry to kiss the cross."

Nadia tucked the cross back into its hiding place.

"Icons are also a form of idolatry," Shura whispered. "If you are interested in what I am talking about, come to church with me on Sunday. Our services are held in this building." She pointed upward. "In the assembly hall."

"Who is having services in the assembly hall?" Nadia asked as she moved closer. She wiped her sweaty palms on her apron. She could hear papers rustling in the nearby office. A chair moved.

"The Americans."

"Americans?"

"Yes. They are believers from America who have come to share the Gospel and to help the poor."

"Why Americans?" Nadia asked.

"Don't ask so many questions," Shura said impatiently. "Just come Sunday morning at 9:30, and you will see for yourself. It will be full. You will need to repent though—that's the important thing."

The rest of the week Nadia mulled over her conversation with Shura. Saturday finally arrived, and school dismissed early. Laughing and shouting, the children and youth streamed out of the building.

Larissa came running into the cafeteria just as Nadia picked up her bags to leave.

"Hi, Mama. Are we ready to go home?"

"Yes, dear. Let's go get Maxim at the daycare center." Nadia shouldered her bags.

Shura approached them as they left the building. "Will I see you tomorrow at our services?" she whispered to Nadia.

"I will see." Nadia shook her head. "I'd like to, but I have only one day a week to wash clothes for myself and my children. Sunday is my day to work at home."

Nadia was deep in thought as Larissa chattered about school and Maxim kicked through drifts of snow. As usual, they skirted Feofaniya Park before walking through the forest on a direct route home.

The next morning a stiff breeze sent heavy clouds scuttling across the sky. The wind whistled along the eaves of the little house, rattling the windowpanes. Nadia could see her breath as she stoked the fire. After pitching a few sticks of wood into the stove, she tucked the blankets more tightly around Larissa and Maxim. Soon the fire was crackling and the room felt warmer. As Nadia sat on the edge of her bed, she noticed the icons on the shelves in the special corner she had made for them.

At that moment, she made her decision—she would go to the American church. She hurriedly put on her warm clothes and overcoat. Donning her hat and gloves, she grabbed two pails and left the house. It was a five-minute walk to the public well. She used this water for bathing and washing their clothes and dishes.

Her pails filled, Nadia hurried back to the house and set the pails of water on the stove to heat. She then grabbed another pail and headed for a neighbor's well just across the street. This water was good for drinking and cooking and was much closer.

Nadia and her children bathed and dressed warmly. After eating leftover soup warmed on the stove, they were on their way. It was a two-hour walk to the American service in Kiev. When they finally approached the school, Nadia felt ill at ease and found herself perspiring. She saw a few vehicles parked outside and took her time as she climbed the stairs. They could hear children singing somewhere.

"Mama, why are you stopping so often? Let's go." Eleven-year-old Larissa looked at her mother in bewilderment and pulled Maxim by the hand.

When they stepped into the assembly hall, Nadia was surprised to find it full of people. She looked around for a place to sit, but could see no empty seats.

"Nadia." Shura materialized from the crowd and seized her by the arm. "Come with me. First, let's take the children to their Sunday school class." She led the children through a door to another room while Nadia followed.

"Come," said Shura, nearly dragging Nadia back to the auditorium, where a few seats were available close to the front.

A black-bearded man in a dark suit was speaking, and a young man beside him was interpreting the sermon into Russian. It was all so new and different that Nadia forgot to listen to what was being taught. When the two men sat down, everyone stood to sing a song.

Larissa and Maxim came bouncing back from Sunday school with coloring books and smiles. Maxim excitedly showed Nadia a handful of candy.

"Mama, look," Larissa whispered. She held a little box of crayons.

After the song, a white-haired man and the interpreter walked to the lectern. The white-haired man spoke of repentance and the need to be baptized. The interpreter repeated everything, but Nadia still couldn't understand what he meant by repentance. The man also spoke of the purpose God has for every person.

After the white-haired man had finished his sermon, he asked if anyone wanted to repent. There was that word again: *repent*. What did it mean?

"Nadia," Shura hissed. "You need to go forward and repent." She pushed Nadia, but Nadia blushed and resisted. At that point a young man moved forward to kneel, and the white-haired man asked him some questions. The young man choked up as he tried to speak, and Nadia thought she could see a tear glisten on his cheek. The young man prayed, and then the older man also prayed.

After the service, Shura clung to Nadia's arm. Some of the people kissed each other in greeting while most talked in little groups. The man with white hair came and extended his hand.

"My name is Edward Miller," he said, his face wrinkling into a smile.

The young translator also said hello and introduced himself.

"We are glad to see you here, and we welcome you back next Sunday," continued Edward as he bent to shake hands with Larissa and Maxim.

The pastor seemed to stare right into Nadia's soul. "As you work this week, remember the words of Jesus, 'Come unto me, all ye that labor and are heavy laden, and I will give you rest. Take my yoke upon you, and learn of me; for I am meek and lowly in heart: and ye shall find rest unto your souls.'"

As Nadia and her children traced their way homeward, Nadia could not stop thinking about the minister's words. Yes, she needed rest. Lots of it. She needed physical rest, and she also needed rest in other ways. Life had never been easy, and now with two children and no husband, it was not getting easier. *Rest—that's what I need. And what was that other word he talked about?*

Maxim suddenly slipped on a patch of ice, interrupting Nadia's thoughts. She helped him up and wiped his tears. Along the edge of a field, several crows strutted along.

What was I thinking? Oh, yes, the minister's words. What did he mean by a "purpose" in life? I'll have to go back and find out.

Shtundists or Orthodox?

1995

"You what?" Maria stared at Nadia. "You went to listen to the Americans?"

"Yes." Nadia showed her mother the Bible she had been given the second time she attended the services.

"See, here is proof. They give Bibles to people who need them."

"Free?" Maria's eyes widened.

"Do you want to see for yourself?" Nadia asked. "You can go along sometime."

"The sooner the better!" Maria's chortle was high-pitched. "Let me know when you're going again."

I shouldn't have told her about the American services, thought Nadia. *Now I have two people trying to force me to go.* Although their relationship wasn't always the best, Nadia and her mother did talk to each other occasionally.

During the next few weeks, Nadia thought much about the church services she had attended. There was so much she didn't understand. She would need to listen more closely to what the pastors said. Pastor Edward had told her about rest. He had said Jesus could give her rest. Her mind spun. *Can Jesus supply our other needs too?*

On a Sunday morning near the end of February, Nadia, Larissa, and Maxim trekked through the forest toward M Street once again. Snow was falling gently, and the only sounds were the packing of snow under their feet and the murmur of their voices.

Nadia with Larissa and Maxim.

They arrived at the service earlier than usual. A young man was speaking to the group, and the children were still sitting with their parents. Shura appeared out of the crowd to usher them to a few empty seats. By now, Nadia recognized some of the people.

Today the pastor spoke about the Holy Spirit and the Trinity. Nadia thought she knew what the Holy Spirit was, but the term *Trinity* meant nothing to her. She listened carefully.

At the end of the service, the young pastor gave an invitation for anyone to come forward to repent. A woman raised her hand. She went forward and stood while the pastor asked her some questions. Then she knelt and prayed.

After the service, as Nadia made her way to the back of the assembly hall, she was surprised to see Olga, the school director, standing there. Nadia flushed and tried to avoid eye contact, but it was no use.

Olga blocked her way.

"So you are coming to the American services too?" she grinned slyly. "Come with me."

Nadia and her two children followed Olga outside to the street. "Come to my apartment," Olga said, beckoning them to follow. "I don't live far from here."

"Why are you going to the American services?" Olga asked as they walked along. "Don't you know they are Shtundists?"

"I don't know much about them," answered Nadia.

Soon they were sitting at Olga's table. Olga set out plates of cookies and salad while the water heated for their tea.

"You must not go to those services. They don't use candles or icons for worship." Olga sipped her tea. "They are a sect from America. Actually, I haven't even told the government that they are renting the school hall." She chuckled. "I am just using the money to fix up our school."

"I know they are from America," Nadia replied, "but I didn't know they are a sect."

"Yes, they are," Olga nodded. "They are very similar to a group of people that used to live in southern Ukraine called Shtundists. They refused to go to war. Dressed funny. Just like these people. And they had no icons."

Nadia was quiet as she listened. What should she say? She wanted to go home and think.

"If you want to go to church, you need to go to the Orthodox church. They have icons, and God is there. At least that's what all the elderly people tell me. Actually, I don't know if there is a God." She spooned more salad onto their plates, and they ate in silence for a few minutes.

Nadia was deep in thought as they left the apartment and started the trek home. She was oblivious to the snow-covered sidewalks and the evergreen branches drooping with snow. Larissa and Maxim's playful banter seemed distant.

Nadia was scheduled to work a 24-hour shift the next day. She had recently been transferred from the cafeteria to being a school guard, and instead of working every day, she worked a 24-hour shift every few days. To prepare, she worked hard all that Sunday afternoon and evening cooking, washing, and cleaning. She usually packed enough clothes for herself and her children for the day and night. Larissa and Maxim would sleep at the school while she stayed up and watched the grounds. Maybe she would have an opportunity to ask Shura if the Americans were Shtundists.

As Nadia lay in bed that night, her mind raced, reviewing the past few months. She could hear the children's gentle breathing. On the other side of the wall, she could hear her mother talking with some men. Minutes ticked into hours until she finally fell asleep.

Nadia's chance to speak with Shura came the next afternoon when they found a few minutes alone. They met by the large window overlooking M Street.

"Director Olga saw me attending the services yesterday," Nadia informed her, watching Shura's reaction.

"What about it?" Shura shrugged. "She has seen me too, but I just avoid her. I don't think she cares what I do."

"She told me to come to her house for tea," Nadia continued. She watched as a run-down bus crammed with people moved along the street.

"What did she tell you? Stop coming or else?"

Nadia paused. "She referred to them as Shtundists. Ever hear of them?"

"Not much."

"She said the Americans are a sect, and we should stay away from them. She said there used to be some people in southern Ukraine that acted the same as these people. They didn't go to war, they had their services in homes or halls, and they were against icons."

"Humph, I wouldn't worry about her," said Shura, rubbing her nose. "Let her think what she wants."

"The services are becoming more interesting," Nadia said. "I really want to learn more."

"Be sure you come for the Easter service," Shura said as Nadia turned to go. "That is the grandest of all their events. There will be lots of food and gifts, and the children will sing songs and recite poems; maybe even some of the adults will too."

"Will there be music and dancing?" Nadia asked.

"No," Shura giggled. "Not these people. I don't think they even know how to dance. But they make up for it in giving. Just don't miss the service."

The next three days, Nadia worked at home. In the mornings after the children were sent to school, she fetched water from the village well. She could carry two pails, each holding three to four gallons. On the days she washed their clothes, she sometimes made up to fifteen trips for water, which she heated on her stove. While she rubbed the clothes on the washboard, she thought about the American services. Shura had said that the pastors would likely visit her sometime and that she needed to make a meal for them.

After she had emptied the dirty water from the large tub, she made another trip to the well. A neighbor standing next to his gate watched her go.

"Heretic!" he suddenly spat out.

Nadia stopped short. Now what was that all about?

"Heretic!" he called again before stepping back into his house.

As Nadia continued on her way, her thoughts were whirling. *Why did he call me a heretic? Has he heard that I have been attending the American services?* Her heart sank. *I don't need any more problems. It's hard enough just trying to survive.*

The next Sunday morning Nadia built up the fire to last until afternoon. She then helped the children dress for the cold walk, glad that winter would soon be over. She was tired of the snow and ice.

This morning the walk to the American services didn't seem as long as usual. By now, Nadia looked forward to gathering with her fellow Ukrainians. She enjoyed the Americans too, but she still didn't understand their language or their culture.

Ruthann, the young pastor's wife, greeted Nadia and the children with a smile. "Hello," she said. "How are you?"

"Good," responded Nadia. She had learned that young Pastor Bruce and his wife Ruthann and their family were from Canada. Edward and Sarah, the older pastor and his wife, were from the United States.

After the service, Bruce approached her. "Hello, Nadia," he said. "I am glad to see you again." His Russian was not bad, although he did have an accent.

"We have a used clothing room, and you are welcome to come this week to see if you can find some clothes for you or your children," Bruce offered.

"Any day?" Nadia asked.

"Yes," Bruce responded. "Usually someone will be there until five o'clock. It's within walking distance from here." He gave her directions and the room number for the clothing room.

"And if you or the children have medical needs, see Diane Roth." Bruce motioned toward a small, slim woman talking with Ruthann. "She's our nurse."

One day after work that week, Nadia took Larissa and Maxim and found the clothing room. It was exciting to pick through the piles of clothes and shoes and find things they could use.

That Saturday, Uncle Yakov came to Lisnyky to visit them. Nadia was hanging out the wash when he arrived. Larissa and Maxim were climbing trees.

"Nadia, what have you been doing?" Yakov's voice matched his large frame. He set his bulky sack on the ground. "Why are you going to strange services?" His voice sounded concerned. "I heard that you are going to an American church. You must not go there. You must come to our motherland church, the Orthodox church."

The veins stood out on his neck in agitation. "Stay away from that church, Nadia. They are heretics!"

Yakov bent to pick up the sack. His voice softened a little. "Here is some food, Nadia. I brought it from the church. The true church."

Nadia finished hanging up the clothes, then picked up the large sack of food. Larissa and Maxim climbed down from the mulberry tree where they had been playing.

"Uncle Yakov," Larissa called, "did you bring us some candy?"

"I came to help cut firewood." His voice was gruff. "Let's go to the forest and cut some wood to fill your lean-to."

Cutting wood with a crosscut saw and hauling it home on a makeshift cart wasn't easy—but at least it didn't cost money. By the time darkness fell, the lean-to was full and Uncle Yakov was on his way home. Spring was just around the corner, and soon they would need a fire in the stove only for cooking and if it got extra chilly at night.

15

The Food Parcel

1995

"You may play outside while I'm in class," Nadia told Larissa and Maxim. The tall brick apartment building on M Street loomed above them. Cherry tree blossoms filled the air with fragrance while tulips danced in the evening breeze. Birds flitted here and there, carrying grass and sticks to build their nests.

It was Tuesday evening, and Nadia had come for instruction class. She had been coming for several weeks now. Something drew her to these people—to their teaching and lifestyle.

The class began with everyone standing while the pastor led in prayer. The interpreter would repeat the pastor's words in Russian. They had been studying about salvation and how God sent His Son Jesus to be the Savior of the world. When Bruce spoke of restitution,

Nadia was convicted. She remembered the many times she had wronged others. How could she go back and make those things right?

She raised her hand.

"Yes, Nadia?" Bruce said. Heads turned in her direction.

"What should we do if we stole a cabbage from someone at the market but don't remember whose it was?"

"Well, first we must acknowledge that what we did was sin," Bruce explained. "Then we should try to find the person we stole from to return what we took. God knows our heart, and He knows how repentant we are and how hard we try to make restitution." Bruce paused. "Does that answer your question?"

"Yes," Nadia nodded. She loved to ask questions, especially since the answers were reasonable and logical. The pastors often turned to the Scriptures and read a verse or two to show God's thoughts on the topic.

Nadia still couldn't grasp why these Americans cared about her and her fellow Ukrainians. Why would they spend time and energy to come across the ocean to help them? What did it matter to them?

Nadia began kneeling with her children in the evening to pray before they went to bed. She taught them to kneel with their bodies erect so they didn't drift off to sleep while they prayed.

"When we pray, we should pray in Jesus' name," Nadia told them. "The Bible says if we ask anything in His name, He will do it."

Knock, knock, knock. Someone was tapping on the door. "Nadia! Nadia!"

It sounded like Natasha, a woman in her instruction class.

"What do you want?" Nadia called.

"Open up. We brought you some food and gifts."

Quickly Nadia opened the door. There, smiling and holding bags and boxes, stood not only Natasha, but also Edward and Sarah Miller and several others.

"Come in," Nadia beckoned. Larissa and Maxim squirmed with excitement as the visitors ducked into the one-room lean-to. Some of the visitors sat on the two small beds while the others stood. Nadia and the children peered into the bags and boxes. They found big bags of flour and buckwheat and sugar, jugs of oil, boxes of cereal, and some canned chicken. Tears filled Nadia's eyes. She gave Sarah a big hug and a kiss.

"Thank you so much," she said, shaking Edward's hand.

"In the name of Christ," Edward replied as he handed candy to the children.

After the visitors left, Nadia knelt with Larissa and Maxim to thank God for the food. They also quoted the Lord's Prayer together.

"Mama," said Larissa as they looked through the boxes and bags, "this is like Christmas."

"I like the candy!" Maxim exclaimed. With a big grin he popped another piece into his mouth.

Nadia, Maxim, and Larissa, with Edward and Sarah Miller.

"God heard our prayers," Nadia answered.

Larissa looked at the colorful boxes of cereal. "I can hardly wait to open these," she told her mother.

On Nadia's next day of work at the school, Shura approached her with a smile. "I heard that our group surprised you." She giggled. "Didn't I tell you they know how to give?"

The Food Parcel

"I just never expected that," said Nadia. "But I need to go ring the buzzer for recess. Talk to you later."

"What did you think about all that food?" Natasha asked Nadia as they headed home from church the next Sunday.

"That was really a big blessing, wasn't it?" said Peter Kuzmich, a driver for the mission. He applied the brakes as they rounded the corner and descended into Khotiv.

"Yes, that's right," agreed Peter's wife, Katya. "You should really be thankful."

Nadia didn't know what to say. Of course she was thankful for what they had brought. She had never before had that much food at one time. It would last her for weeks, or maybe months if she was careful.

"I am thankful," Nadia said, recovering her wits and tongue. She was quiet.

"Sometime the Americans will want to come to your house for a meal," Natasha said. "They have been to our place, and we made them a large table of food."

"Yes," Katya laughed. "If you make your meal soon, you could use some of the food the Americans brought you."

Nadia didn't respond. She watched the landscape slide by.

Across this land of deep, rich topsoil, millions of little sprouts of barley and corn created a sheen of green. In other fields, large expanses of waving winter wheat planted the previous autumn were nearing maturity and would soon be harvested. Though the country was still poor, villagers were nurturing their crops in hopes of a plentiful and nourishing harvest.

That evening Nadia decided to visit her friend Alla, a next-door neighbor. Alla loved to cook, so maybe she could help her plan a meal for the Americans.

"That shouldn't be a problem at all," Alla said. "You could make varenyky[1] from strawberries since they are in season."

"I didn't think about that," Nadia replied. "That's a good idea."

"Or you could serve borscht and a big bowl of fresh strawberries. If the strawberries are over, you could serve varenyky made from sour cherries. They will soon be ripe."

"I'm sure glad I asked you," Nadia laughed. "You're a much better cook than I am."

"I know what—I'll help you!" Alla laughed merrily. "I'll help you make the meal, then I'll disappear before your guests arrive. They'll think you're an excellent cook, and nobody will be the wiser."

"Thank you so much," Nadia said as she rose to leave. "I really appreciate your help."

The next Sunday when Nadia invited the Americans, Edward accepted with a big smile. They planned to come one evening late in the week. When the day arrived, Alla was there to help as she had promised.

First Alla helped Nadia make a big kettle of borscht over an open fire. Then they prepared fresh strawberries and set a small table under the apricot tree. Larissa swept the dirt path up to the house and picked up the branches and trash. Finally they were ready. When they heard the van arrive, Alla disappeared.

Nadia and the children welcomed the visitors, which included Edward, Sarah, and Diane, as well as an interpreter and a driver. Nadia was nervous, but their fellowship under the tree went well, and the guests seemed to love the meal.

"We would like to give you a box of food each month," Edward said, wiping his mouth. "A nonprofit organization from America called

---

[1] Boiled dumplings filled with potatoes, cheese, or fruit.

Christian Aid Ministries is sending food parcels to Ukraine for us to distribute. Would you like to receive one each month?" He smiled gently.

"A box of food each month? For us?" Nadia's eyes were wide. "How do you keep it from spoiling if it comes all the way from America?"

"Well, most of the products are things that don't spoil quickly, like rice, beans, and other dried foods. You'll find the foods very nutritious, and they'll go a long way. So if you don't mind, we'll deliver a box here each month."

After singing a concluding grace song in Russian, the visitors prepared to leave. Nadia and the children followed them to their vehicle to say goodbye. It had been a pleasure to have them come.

A few weeks passed before Edward dropped by again.

"Here is your food parcel," he said, setting the large cardboard box on the wooden bench next to the lean-to door. "The Scripture says 'I delivered the poor that cried, and the fatherless, and him that had none to help him.'"[2] He smiled.

"Thank you so much!" Nadia exclaimed. "Larissa and Maxim, come see the gift God has given us."

"There are also forty U.S. dollars to help with your expenses," Edward said as Nadia and the children opened the box. "That should help with your electric or fuel bill, or wherever you need it most."

"This is more than I ever expected," Nadia said, her voice shaking. "Thank you."

The late spring breeze rustled the tree leaves and the sun peeked through the clouds for a moment. A few dandelion seeds drifted on the breeze.

As Edward left, Nadia and the children started taking things out of the box. "Mama," said Larissa, "this is sure nice of Edward to bring this."

To herself she couldn't help thinking, *Why can't it be my papa bringing us food? And what was he saying about God helping the fatherless?*

16

Mama's Story

1995

"I'm so hungry I could eat a whole loaf of bread," moaned Maxim. He leaned against Larissa. The darkness inside the bus hid them from the scrutiny of the other passengers.

"So am I," Larissa groaned. It had been a long day in the city as they wandered through the markets and the zoo. Even though they didn't have much money, every year Mama took them to the zoo to see the animals. It had been a wonderful day, but now they could think of nothing but their empty stomachs.

"Breakfast seems like days ago," whispered Larissa to her brother. "I could eat a whole grilled chicken and top it off with five ice cream bars."

"Time to get off the bus," Mama said as the bus slowed for the stop in Feofaniya Park. They had been too late to catch the bus to Lisnyky, so they had ridden the bus to this stop at the edge of Kiev.

Larissa spotted a few people she knew from previous visits to this bus station. Most of them lived close by and wouldn't need to walk far. *But we still have an hour's walk, and I'm hungry.*

At that moment, they saw Natalia, a lady they had earlier befriended at this bus station. She had just exited from the rear doors of the bus and was coming toward them.

"Hello, Nadia." Natalia heaved her bags closer. "It's kind of far for you to walk all the way home yet, isn't it? The least you can do is come to my house for tea before starting off."

Larissa looked at Maxim, licked her lips, and raised her eyebrows. Hot tea. That sounded good. Maybe she would give them some food too.

Natalia lived just a few minutes away on the outskirts of Khotiv. Her house wasn't fancy, but it was well-furnished and clean. A streetlight threw a faint light along the street and across the front of the house.

"So tell me more about your life, Nadia," said Natalia as they finished eating bread and fish. She opened a pack of chocolate wafers. "You've told me snatches before, but I'd like to hear more. Didn't you live in Siberia for a while?"

"Yes, I did." Nadia paused and leaned back in her chair. "When I was eighteen, I was working at a sewing factory here in Kiev. One day the director announced an opportunity for anyone who wanted to travel and at the same time help build the USSR. The project, the director told us, was in far eastern Siberia."

Siberia! Larissa leaned forward. She was now paying close attention. *Maybe Mama will talk about Papa.*

"I was living with three friends near the sewing factory. We talked about this and decided to go. We wanted to prove to the USSR how dedicated we were.

"There were fifty of us who applied to go. My friend Irina and I were delayed, so the rest of our team left a few days before us. They were sent to work on the railroad north of Lake Baikal, where the work was harder and the weather more frigid than where we went.

"Irina and I helped with the construction of the Ulan-Ude International Airport. We arrived in the city of Ulan-Ude in September of 1982. We lived in an apartment building reserved for the women who helped with the airport project. The weather was just beginning to change from fall to winter, and soon we were working in subzero weather.

"On New Year's Eve, we girls were invited by local Buryat girls to go out to the city center to have some fun. That evening I met Andre." Nadia paused.

"He was a year younger than I was and had dark, straight hair that fell over his ears. His dark eyes always seemed to be laughing. He loved to have fun." Nadia's eyes brightened for a moment.

"We began going out together each week as time permitted. Then Andre was called to the army and was scheduled to leave on May 20, 1983. We decided to quickly get married, and our wedding took place on May 19, the day before he left.

"Life was difficult with Andre leaving immediately to serve his two years of service. He was sent to an army camp a few hours northeast of Ulan-Ude. I stayed in Andre's room at his parents' house and commuted to work from there. I discovered soon after Andre left that I was expecting a baby.

"That was a tough winter. I continued to work at the airport until a week before Larissa was born. After she was born, I stayed at the hospital for another week before I was released to go home. The hospital was warm and they fed us well, although the constant crying of the babies sometimes bothered me.

"My in-laws had a drinking problem, and sometimes they shouted and fought. Once when I returned to the house, they locked me out. They told me to go but refused to let me have Larissa. My mother-in-law said she helped care for her, so she gets to keep her. Since Andre was serving duty, I went to the local army general and spilled my story. He sent authorities with me to get Larissa and our belongings and then helped me find another apartment.

"When Andre finally returned from the army, he too started drinking. Once when he was drunk he confessed that he had been unfaithful to me while he was in the army. He said he was sorry, so I forgave him. However, he continued to drink and smoke and was again unfaithful, so we divorced and I moved back here to Kiev." Nadia wiped a tear that had slipped down her cheek.

"That's too bad," said Natalia, reaching for another chocolate wafer.

"It has been hard to find a place to live and a job ever since," Nadia continued. "Pavel, a relative of my uncle Yakov, asked me to marry him, so we lived together for a while. Pavel is Maxim's father. But after I moved in with him, I discovered that he also had a problem with drinking. He would sometimes lock the two children and me out of the house when he was drunk, even in the winter. Poor man. He didn't realize what he was doing, but it was more than I could take, so Uncle Yakov helped me move to my mama's house. Since part of the house is legally mine, we blocked off one room for me and my children and built a lean-to to hold wood.

"When Larissa was in third grade, Andre sent a letter to us and asked if she could come visit him. I refused. Think about it—an eight- or nine-year-old traveling by herself for seven days on a train. I was upset."

Larissa listened in rapt attention. She had never heard her mother tell so much of her story. She hadn't even known her father had asked her to come visit him. The thought sent warm circles down her spine.

"This past winter I met the Americans. We have been attending their services at the Number 236 School. They rent the school's assembly hall on Sundays."

"Really?" Natalia poured herself and her guests more tea and added hot water. "What kind of service do they have?"

"It's similar to the Baptist service, but they call themselves Mennonites."

"Could I come see what it's like?" Natalia squinted her dark eyes.

"Of course," Nadia replied. She drained the rest of her tea and stood up. She really wasn't in the mood to elaborate more on the Mennonite church services.

"Sit down," commanded their hostess. "The night is still early. Why hurry off? You have never told me much about your childhood. I'd like to hear that too." She refilled Nadia's cup.

Nadia settled back into her chair and continued. "My uncle Yakov said my mama was not married but had been seeing my father Valera. He was a musician in the Orthodox church. Since Valera was living at Uncle Yakov's, he and my mother got to know each other. When I was born, Uncle Yakov and his wife wanted to adopt me, but Mama didn't want them to.

"My mama was a beautiful girl, but she had sporadic mental issues—and still does at times. For some reason, she didn't want Yakov to adopt me even though they were already caring for me. The offer just angered her.

"My father Valera also didn't want anything more to do with my mama or me. Uncle Yakov said he told my father that it was his duty to marry my mother, but he refused. This angered Uncle Yakov so much that he chased Valera out."

Larissa stared at her mother. She had never heard all these details before. She had been feeling sleepy but now was wide awake as she processed what she had heard. *Mama did not have a mother or a father who wanted her. At least I have Mama.*

"My mother tried to beat me to death when I was home from the orphanage one summer," Nadia went on. "Uncle Yakov had found an orphanage where I could live and be schooled. Then my mother came to the orphanage and took me home for the summer. She took me to the garden to help pick strawberries. I didn't know what strawberries were and stepped on some of them. She took her hoe and probably would have killed me, but the neighbors stopped her. Later when she and I were walking to Kiev to sell strawberries, she stopped beside an old dump. She caught me and beat me, but someone happened to be near enough to hear my screams and come to my rescue."

"God was watching over you," Natalia replied.

"It is time for us to leave," said Nadia, rising from her chair. She shook Maxim, who had fallen asleep on the sofa.

"It has been a great time together," Natalia said. "Thank you for telling your story."

"Yes," replied Nadia. "Thanks so much for inviting us in."

Orphanage Life

1995

"Mama, why do I have to stay here?" Larissa clung to Mama, her eyes wet with tears. "I want to go home."

"Do we have to go over all this again?" Nadia held Larissa close. "I told you that I lived and studied at this Pereiaslav orphanage when I was growing up. It's a good place to live and get an education."

"I don't care about a good school. I want to go home." Fearfully Larissa scanned the five-story brick building.

"The director agreed to take you, so you need to be brave. Share your candy, and you'll quickly make friends," Mama assured her. "Besides, you will have a nice place to sleep and three meals a day. I have to work hard just to provide for Maxim and me, but God will care for us."

Larissa watched Mama walk across the orphanage grounds to catch a bus at the intersection. Numbly she watched until the trees and bushes along the thoroughfare hid her from view. Larissa sighed, blinking to control her tears. She turned away. Life was not fair.

A stocky woman of medium height was approaching, along with a group of girls Larissa's age. The woman smiled at Larissa. "My name is Teresa," she said. "I am your caretaker." Her light brown hair was twisted into a low bun updo.

"You will like it here," Teresa predicted pleasantly, her blue eyes twinkling. "I will venture to say that by the time you have to leave, you will want to stay." The girls had hung back for a moment but now pushed closer.

"What is your name, girl?" It seemed they all spoke at once. Larissa wiped away the last tear from her cheek.

"Larissa."

"What did you bring along with you? Where are you from?" Questions came from all directions.

"The girls will show you around the orphanage grounds," Teresa said above the hubbub as she turned to leave.

Larissa relaxed as she realized the children were curious just like herself.

"I have something in my bags that I might share if you tell me your names," she said, warming to the girls surrounding her.

When the children began shouting out their names, Larissa frowned.

"One by one, please."

After Larissa had passed out a piece of candy to each of the girls and a few of the boys, they showed her around the orphanage grounds and the school building. Finally they took Larissa up to the girls' dorms. They showed her a large room with three beds.

"That is your bed and this is mine," said a girl who had introduced herself as Galya. The beds were across from each other.

"I'm Lana," said another girl. She tossed her flaxen hair and plopped onto her bed.

Larissa, center, in her room at the orphanage with friends. The girl with the white sweater is Galya.

There is so much space in these rooms, Larissa thought as she placed her bags beside her bed.

"You can put your clothes in here," said Lana. She hopped up to open the doors to a standing closet. "I sleep in this room too, so you will be sharing it with Galya and me." She tossed her hair back from her face. "It's too bad you came so late, or we would have taken you down to the river for a swim."

"Do you like to swim?" asked one of the girls crowding into the doorway.

"Of course I like to swim," Larissa replied. She smiled just thinking about it.

That night Larissa lay in her twin bed with conflicting emotions. As she snuggled under the thin blanket, a faint glow of starlight beamed through the window and touched her face. In one way, she wished she were still at home with Mama and Maxim. But in another way, she liked the thought of friends who were in similar circumstances to her own. At least they wouldn't mock her for not having a father like the M Street schoolchildren had.

A week passed with Larissa learning the schedule. The caretakers and teachers were clear about what they expected of her. She didn't care for the schoolwork or the chores, but she did enjoy the physical education and the friendships.

"You do well with exercising," remarked the physical education teacher. He watched as Larissa went through a set of chin-ups on the bars.

"I don't like to run track though," replied Larissa. She plopped beside Galya to rest.

"I wouldn't do any physical education if I didn't have to," Galya said with a grimace.

"I had physical education every day when I lived at home," Larissa smiled. "Mama made me work all the time, like it or not. She said we should never be lazy. That's probably why exercise is not difficult for me."

"I wish I had a mama," replied Galya. "My papa never told me about her."

Larissa didn't know how to respond. She didn't have a father, and Galya didn't have a mother. She wished she knew how to fix it. Just then her stomach growled.

"I'm hungry," Larissa said, changing the subject.

"Me too," Galya replied.

In spite of getting three meals a day, the children were sometimes hungry. The meals were usually soup with bread, and even though the soup was nutritious, it often did not feel like enough.

"Come with me," said Galya, grabbing Larissa's arm. She lowered her voice. "Let's go to the kitchen. Maybe we can snatch something or beg the cook for food."

The two girls slipped into the hallway leading to the kitchen. They could hear the cook's knife clicking against a cutting board. They tiptoed to the kitchen door and peered in.

The cook named Lyuba was cutting up potatoes for the evening meal. No one else was around.

"What shall we do?" Larissa whispered to Galya. She pulled back just as the cook turned toward the door.

"Let's ask her for something," Galya suggested. "She is nicer than most of the cooks."

The girls tiptoed into the kitchen.

"Oh!" Lyuba jumped. "Do you have to sneak up on me like that?"

"Lyuba, we are hungry," said Galya. "Can we have a piece of bread or an apple or . . ." Her voice trailed off.

"So you girls are hungry, are you? You can't wait until supper?" Lyuba's pudgy face broke into a wide grin. "Just like me when I was your age." She sliced two pieces of bread. "Take this and run."

"Thank you." The girls' eyes reflected their gratitude.

"Don't tell anyone, or we'll all be in trouble." The heavyset cook turned back to her job.

The two girls slipped the thick slices into their pockets. Now they needed to find a private place to eat. As they left the building, Teresa called to them.

It seemed to Larissa that the slice of bread in her pocket swelled as the caretaker approached. *Is she going to ask us where we were? I hope she doesn't ask us to empty our pockets.* Larissa stole a glance at Galya, who appeared quite unconcerned.

"Do you girls want to come to my house for tea this evening after your homework is finished?" Teresa asked. "A few others are coming too."

Larissa breathed a sigh of relief.

"Yes, of course," they answered together.

As Teresa turned away, Larissa broke into a jog. "I'll beat you around the track," she shouted over her shoulder to Galya. The two girls raced toward the track they normally avoided. At the far end and out of sight of the buildings, they stopped.

"Wow, I thought we were going to be interviewed," said Galya. "I almost laughed out loud when Teresa asked if we wanted to come to her house for tea." The girls finished their slices of bread as they talked.

"Do you have a papa?" Larissa pushed her hair back out of her face.

"Yes." Galya kicked at a stone. "But he lives in Russia, so I likely won't see him until school is out next spring."

"My papa lives in Russia too. In Siberia." Larissa glanced at Galya. "I wish I could see him."

"Let's talk about something else," said Galya, her face troubled.

Every day after lunch the children could choose a class such as acrobatics, dancing, sewing classes, or art lessons. Sometimes in the late afternoon, the caretakers and children went to the river to swim. Larissa couldn't have cared less about sewing, but she did enjoy the acrobatics and drawing, and she never missed an opportunity to swim.

Every ten days all the children had to shower and change their underclothes. Hot water was turned on in preparation for this special day. A large coal furnace heated the water for the showers.

After showering, the girls would sit in the open air, drying their hair and dreaming about the future.

One day while the weather was still warm, the children and a couple of caretakers spent the evening at the river. The children swam, splashed, dived, and shouted until they were exhausted. This was better than any shower. When the cool evening breezes began to stir, they huddled on the bank in the sunshine to dry off. Perched in a pine tree downriver, a kingfisher sounded its strident, mechanical rattle in response to the children's disturbing shouts.

"That was a nice dive, Kolya," Larissa complimented the friendly boy as he climbed out of the water and onto the bank. A large, flat rock jutting out from the bank served as a splendid diving board.

"Maybe someday you'll be able to swim as well as I can," Kolya teased.

Larissa made a face at him and ran to the rock. She dived into the water, disappearing below the surface with only a slight splash and barely a ripple. She came up grinning.

"Good job, Larissa. That was the best yet tonight." Galya linked arms with Larissa.

By now the sun had disappeared over the horizon and the sky was changing colors. It was time to head back. Slowly the children traced their way back to their dorms and waiting beds.

"I plan to move to America when I grow up," Larissa overheard one of the girls in the hallway say.

"You're dreaming out loud, Tatyana," Ira replied, laughing. The two teenage girls slept across the hallway from Larissa's room. "Maybe we will be able to visit Germany or Spain sometime, but not America. What have you been drinking?"

"I had some black tea for supper," Tatyana giggled. "If our grades are good enough we will be awarded a free trip to a country in Europe. But maybe someday I'll get to go to America too."

"Galya, is it true that we get a free trip to another country if our grades are good?" asked Larissa as she slipped into her nightclothes.

"Yes," cut in Lana, "but it's not just good grades, we also need good conduct."

"Poor me," Larissa groaned. "I have neither."

"If you could win favor with the orphanage director it might help," Galya suggested as she jumped into bed.

My grades are poor. And I got into trouble last week for taking apples from an orchard across town. Larissa's mind whirled. *The director does seem to like me though, so maybe that is a possibility.*

Larissa fell asleep planning her trip out of Ukraine. Little did she know how far her life's travels would take her.

A Sudden Death

1996

Nadia rode down the escalators and stood in line at the metro station. She was heading home after a trip to Kiev to buy seeds for spring planting. She could hear the train coming and the damp underground air whooshing toward her from the tunnel. As she stood in line, she felt uncomfortably conspicuous.

She was wearing one of the dresses Sarah Miller had given her. She was also wearing her veiling. The dress hadn't been so bad because she could wear a sweater or a coat over it, and few people would notice. But the white veiling was not so easily hidden.

As the doors of the city train opened, scores of people pushed and shoved as they disembarked. Then came the desperate rush for Nadia and the others to get on board before the doors closed and the train started for the next station.

"Maybe we should let the nun have our seat," Nadia overheard two young women say as they giggled, glancing in her direction. One of the women was dressed in a classy, knee-length skirt and a wine-colored coat. The other was also clothed in Paris fashion.

Nadia blushed and looked the other way. She hated all the sideways glances and laughter. She was just doing what the Word of God said a Christian woman should do, wasn't she? At least that's how Pastor Bruce had explained it.

The wind was cold and the skies dreary when Nadia got off the train to catch a bus for the rest of the way home. She stopped a moment to catch her breath. Just then the gray skies began to scatter sleet, and Nadia pulled her coat tighter. Her mind wandered as she waited.

She had started instruction class last May and really enjoyed the teaching and the social life. Nadia respected Bruce for his keen insight and ability to give solid answers to her questions. She thought about Bruce's response not long ago when she had been asking questions in class. "Nadia, you have many questions." Nadia thought she had seen a hint of a smile on Bruce's lips.

Her mind drifted to the food parcels. She had been so thankful for the food and money each month, but then several instruction class participants began to rib her about it. Even though it didn't happen every time she rode home with the villagers, often someone would say something about her parcel, and then someone else would mention the forty dollars she received. It had finally become too much to endure.

"I don't want you to put the forty dollars in the box," Nadia told Edward.

"Are you sure?" Edward asked.

"I am sure," Nadia responded reluctantly but firmly.

When Edward asked her again if she was sure about her decision, she was emphatic. "Please do not give me the forty dollars." Edward gave her a strange look, but Nadia refused to give him more details.

The next month when Peter dropped off the food parcel, sure enough, the money wasn't in the box. Nadia felt a twinge of regret, but she looked forward to telling the village women that she no longer received the money. She was also a little perturbed. Why didn't they just mind their own business? She couldn't help it that she didn't have a husband and a home of her own. She was doing the best she could.

Nadia was jolted back to the present as a bus pulled up to the curb. Soon everyone was pushing and shoving to get on board. She managed to find a seat just inside the back door. Soon the bus was crammed full, and there wasn't room for one more passenger. Just then an elderly woman with a large bag appeared in the aisle next to her. Her face was wrinkled with age and most of her teeth were missing. *I should let her have my seat,* thought Nadia.

"Over here, Grandmother," Nadia told her. "You can have my seat." She stood to let the elderly woman squeeze past and sit down. Slowly the bus crept through the outskirts of Kiev. Nadia stood sandwiched between other passengers and soon became drowsy with the sounds of the passengers' quiet murmuring and the sleet plinking against the windows.

By the time Nadia arrived in Lisnyky, it was late afternoon and the sleet had changed to snow. Walking carefully, she headed along the street toward her home. Out of the corner of her eye, she noticed a woman walking along on the other side of the street.

"Heretic!"

Just as Nadia turned to look, she saw the tall woman spit in her direction.

"Heretic!"

Nadia turned and hurried on. She hadn't gone more than a few steps when she felt a snowball hit her in the back. Soon another snowball exploded around her. Nadia felt hot as she hurried toward home. Her heart was pounding and her head hurt. Arriving at home, she locked the door behind her and fell to her knees beside the bed and wept. It was an hour before she arose with a sense of peace. God would sustain her. She needed to go get Maxim, whom she had left with Alla for the day.

The next day Nadia felt better as she sat in the Mennonite service, listening to the Word of God. Despite the hateful actions of some of her neighbors, listening to the sermon gave her new courage.

Nadia tried to follow along as Bruce taught the Sunday school lesson, but her mind kept drifting to the mocking and name-calling she had experienced. She thought of the second episode of the evening before.

After bringing Maxim home, she had gone to the village well to fetch water for their sponge baths. Another woman from the village had also come to the well. The woman had to wait as Nadia was drawing up her water, and Nadia heard her muttering something about "Shtundist." Nadia thought of calling her a name in return but decided that wasn't a good idea. She had simply grabbed her pails of water and hurried home.

Her mind flashed back to the present. Bruce had just said something that caught her attention. He was reading from the Bible. " 'If the world hate you, ye know that it hated me before it hated you. If ye were of the world, the world would love his own: but because ye are not of the world, but I have chosen you out of the world, therefore the world hateth you.' "[1]

"These are the words of Jesus," Bruce said. "If we face opposition, we can know that Jesus has also experienced what we are going through."

How does he know what I'm facing? Nadia contemplated. *Can he read people's minds?* No, God must have led Bruce to these words from the Bible just to meet her needs.

---

[1] John 15: 18, 19

That evening at home Nadia tried to find the passage Bruce had been reading in the Gospel of John, but couldn't. After a fruitless search, she finally turned to the Psalms again where she often read. Several verses caught her attention, and she read, "I will say unto God my rock, Why hast thou forgotten me? why go I mourning because of the oppression of the enemy? As with a sword in my bones, mine enemies reproach me; while they say daily unto me, Where is thy God? Why art thou cast down, O my soul? and why art thou disquieted within me? Hope thou in God."[2]

The following week as Nadia worked at the school, she met Shura. They were both in the kitchen getting hot water for their cleaning jobs.

"You're doing great now, aren't you?" Shura smiled. "At least you have enough food and clothing. But why did you reject the money they were giving you? It was a gift because you needed it." She looked puzzled.

Nadia paused before replying. "Some of the instruction class women kept talking about it, and I got tired of the drama. I have enough conflict with neighbors and relatives who call me a heretic and a Shtundist." Feeling overwhelmed, Nadia grabbed her bucket of water and left the kitchen.

When warmer weather arrived, Nadia took a stroll down the street to inspect her garden plot to see what needed to be done before planting. A small strip along the left side was her mother's plot and a larger plot—nearly half an acre—was hers. It technically belonged to her grandfather, but Uncle Yakov had said she could use it. The soil needed to be built up since it was a low-lying area.

Nadia took her time walking home. She jumped as a shadow flashed over her. She breathed a sigh of relief when she saw it was only a white

---

[2] Psalm 42:9-11

stork winging toward a large nest on the top of an electric pole beside the street. The nest had been there as long as she could remember. The return of the storks was a sure sign that spring was here.

The next week when Nadia returned to work in the garden plot, the weather was even warmer. She raked up the weeds and leftover stubble from the year before. She then burned the debris and scattered the ashes over the garden area. The sun rose, warming the earth and erasing the fog, leaving a partially overcast sky. Nadia's fire soon crackled, and smoke rose into the quiet breeze that drifted up the valley.

Working in the garden was a balm for Nadia's soul, and her spirits rose as the small plot of land was transformed. In her mind she sketched out the layout of the plant beds. Suddenly she heard someone calling her name.

"Nadia!"

She turned around to see Uncle Yakov coming up the street. He was bellowing and almost running.

"Nadia! You cannot use this land. You are a heretic!" He stopped for a moment to catch his breath and lean on a post next to the dirt street. "Go home, Nadia. I will not let you use this land anymore. I told you to discontinue your involvement with the American church, but you still go there." He dropped his garden tools on the ground beside him. His face was twisted with anger. Nadia stood frozen to the spot.

"Are you going to go, or do I need to chase you off?" He tried to yell, but his voice was weak. "GO! If I catch you here again, I will kill you."

Nadia's heart sank as she grabbed her rake and hurried out of the garden. Uncle Yakov shook his fist at her.

"You need to come back to the true church—the Orthodox church." He spoke with passion. "Forget those Shtundists."

The beautiful morning had suddenly turned into a nightmare. Uncle Yakov had been the one person in her life she could always depend on. It was hard to believe that now he too had turned against her.

When Nadia arrived home five minutes later, she dropped her tools in the lean-to, sat on a stack of wood, and tried to make sense of her thoughts. *Why, God? Why can't life be normal for me? What is the purpose of all this?* She dropped her head into her hands and wept.

She jumped as she heard someone opening the door. Maxim stood in the doorway.

"Hi, Mama. I'm home. Can I go play?"

"Hi, Maxim." Nadia smiled at her seven-year-old, then turned quickly to hide her swollen eyes. "Do you have homework?"

"Not much," he replied, tossing his head. He flopped his bag on the stack of wood.

"I suppose you can go out for a few minutes." Nadia gathered some wood chips to start the fire. She needed to make supper.

The next day Nadia worked hard at preparing a small plot behind the house where she could grow a few vegetables. She hummed a tune she had heard at the American services as she worked the soil. When she had a little spot ready, she planted some radishes since they liked the cool spring weather. She found an old piece of clear plastic to cover them and weighted down the edges with stones. She would need to be on the lookout so the chickens wouldn't scratch and tear the plastic.

When the month of May rolled around, the instruction class was interviewed for baptism, but Nadia didn't think she was ready yet.

"I still don't understand exactly what I am doing," she responded to their questions. "I need more time." So it was decided that she would continue another year in instruction class. The baptismal day was a special occasion for everyone, and Nadia was able to witness what it would be like to join the Mennonite church. She wanted what was right, but sometimes it was hard to do the right thing.

The next week a neighbor lady offered Nadia her extra cabbage plants. She had sowed the seeds into her starter beds and ended up with too many plants.

"You can have them," she said. "Just come over and get them out of my hotbeds."

Nadia was excited about the cabbage plants, but she wasn't sure when she could get them planted. Since Larissa was home from the orphanage for the weekend, Nadia wanted to be sure to wash her clothes. And she didn't want to work on Sunday.

Nadia was glad she had access to her grandfather's half-acre garden plot again. After Uncle Yakov had chased her away, she had talked to Alla and her husband about it. They had encouraged her to ask for legal rights at the land office in Lisnyky. She took their advice and had now been given permission to work the land regardless of what Uncle Yakov said.

That afternoon Pavel showed up to say hello. He stopped by occasionally to visit Maxim. Today his clothes were clean and his chin smooth.

"I'll stay and help plant the cabbages," he offered after Nadia told him what she planned to do.

"I need to hang these clothes out to dry yet," Nadia told him. "If you want to help carry water to plant the cabbages, you may."

"Not a problem." Pavel's eyes squinted as he grinned. He sat on a chunk of wood and waited. Pavel was a short man whose solid outlook on life had been skewed by drinking. Today, however, was an exception. He was sober.

When Nadia had all the clothes pinned on the line, she gathered her garden tools.

"Max-i-m," she called.

"What?" Maxim slid down from the sour cherry tree.

"Your papa's here." Nadia picked up her tools. "I need you and Larissa to help me plant the cabbage plants."

Everyone got busy. Pavel carried water from the creek that flowed along the street, Nadia and Larissa planted, and Maxim helped where he could. By evening, most of the cabbages were in the ground.

They were still hard at it when they saw a car coming down the street that led to their garden plot. The four stopped to watch.

"It looks like the police!" exclaimed Pavel. "I have to run!" He turned and ran up the terraces beside the plot and disappeared into the woods.

The car pulled up next to the garden. Two men and a woman crawled out. Nadia could see they were in uniforms.

"Good day. Are you Maria?"

"No," responded Nadia. "Maria is my mother."

"Do know Yakov Barbar?"

"Yes, he's my uncle. Why?"

"He was found dead in Kiev along the street next to the St. Volodymyr's Cathedral."

Nadia gasped.

"Pedestrians said he had just left the service and was walking along the street when he stumbled and fell. They suppose it was a heart attack."

"Did you tell his wife Marusia?" Nadia asked as she fought to remain stoic. Larissa and Maxim pushed close.

"We don't know how to find his wife. We found your mother's documents on him when we investigated his death. That's why we came to Lisnyky. Someone up the street told us where you live."

The police wrote down the address Nadia gave for Yakov and Marusia's home and climbed back into their car. When the lights from the vehicle faded into the distance and the evening was quiet once again, Pavel returned from the terraces.

"It was cold lying on the ground up there," he grinned. "I just didn't want to get caught since I haven't been working the last couple of months." Pavel suddenly noticed their somber looks. "What's wrong?"

"They said Uncle Yakov died of a heart attack this evening."

"No!" Pavel shook his head. "He wasn't that old."

"They wanted the address to find Marusia to tell her." Nadia wiped

A Sudden Death

her eyes and blew her nose.

The evening atmosphere had changed from cheerful to somber. By the time the last cabbage plant was in the ground, it was nearly dark. Night sounds echoed across the little valley and along the terraced hillside as they walked back to the house.

The next morning Nadia and the children slept late. It had been nearly midnight before they had collapsed into bed. Now it was Sunday morning and Nadia wanted to attend the Orthodox church for the celebration of the Holy Trinity. This was a special service, and Nadia knew there would be lots of food.

When Nadia and the children arrived at the church, the service was just ending. She stood in the entrance as the worshipers talked in groups and waited for the tables to be set up outside for the fellowship meal.

As Nadia looked around for someone to talk with, she spotted Marusia in the church talking with an elderly man. She was dressed in lively colors and a light scarf.

She must not know about Yakov's death, thought Nadia as she observed her aunt. *What should I do? I'm afraid if I tell her she'll make a scene and blame me. She'll say I'm upset because they don't like the American church and that I had something to do with Yakov's death.* Nadia's thoughts raced, and a plan formulated in her mind.

Stepping outside, she found the janitor. "Sir, did you hear that Yakov Barbar died last evening after he left the service?"

The janitor was shocked. "No, I didn't hear that." His face twisted with emotion. "I knew him well. I also know his wife Marusia and his sister Maria."

"Sir, could you help me out?" Nadia pleaded. "I am Maria's daughter. But could you go tell his wife what happened. I don't think she knows. She is not dressed appropriately for someone whose husband has just passed away. The police must not have found her yet to tell her what happened."

"Hmm." The janitor cleared his throat and stepped back.

"Please, sir. If I tell her, she will accuse me and create a big scene."

"Okay, I will tell her." He turned and looked in the direction Nadia was pointing. "Yes, I see her."

Nadia stepped back into the shadows of the entrance. Larissa and Maxim were outside watching the tables being loaded with food. Nadia could see the janitor approaching Marusia. He waited a moment until she finished talking to the elderly man, then stepped closer. She watched closely to see Marusia's reaction.

Marusia must have assumed Yakov was out helping someone last evening, as he often did. It was not unusual for Yakov to be gone overnight, either guarding the cathedral or visiting another town or village.

Nadia could see Marusia's expression change as she moaned and clutched at her throat. Nadia strained forward to catch what she was saying. At that moment Marusia happened to look Nadia's way and spied her.

"There she is!" Marusia cried. "I knew it. She's to blame."

Before the janitor could react, Marusia ran toward Nadia. She pounced on her and began beating her.

"It was because of you that he died! I know it was you!"

The janitor caught up to Marusia and pulled her away from Nadia. Marusia struggled to get away.

"I don't ever want to see you again!" Marusia shrieked. "Never! Don't you dare come to the funeral."

Onlookers began to crowd close to see the disturbance. Nadia grabbed Larissa and Maxim and hurried away.

Larissa's heart pounded as she watched Marusia shouting and crying. Quickly the three scurried away from the church and the commotion.

Spain

1996

*L*arissa scribbled on her scrap paper and frowned. She was now in grade six, but she still disliked mathematics. It seemed she could almost never get a good grade, and her deskmate Galya wasn't much better. The girl behind them, however, was a whiz at schoolwork. Sometimes Larissa stole a glance at this girl's work to get an answer. Most of her classmates did the same—as long as the teacher was looking the other way. Otherwise, they would be in trouble.

Mama hopes I get a good education, so I guess I should try my best. Larissa sighed and turned back to her work.

Since being at the orphanage, Larissa had visited home only a handful of times, usually on weekends. The first few times Mama came to ride home with her. But now that she knew which buses to ride and where to get on and off, Mama didn't come to get her. Last weekend she had been at home and had gone to church with Mama and Maxim.

After the services, Pastor Edward had presented them with some goodies, including several boxes of cereal. It was the second time they had received the brightly colored Froot Loops. Mama had said she could take a box back with her to the orphanage. As always, she was warmly greeted by her friends when she returned. *I enjoy being at home, but I enjoy being here too,* Larissa thought.

After math class, the teacher had some advice for the students. "You need to keep at your work," she said in a loud voice. "Some of you hand in unfinished homework, and that needs to improve."

"I am tired of school," Galya whispered, bending close to Larissa. "I wish it was summer vacation."

Just then Teresa walked in with the history teacher close behind her. As she spoke, something in her voice caught the children's attention.

"I just learned that anyone who wants to go on an award trip to another country has a chance to do so. Who all would like to go to Germany, Italy, or Spain?"

Larissa watched as almost all the hands went up. No one was thinking about mathematics now. A hum of voices rose as the students whispered to each other or shouted their preferred destination while the teachers wrote them down.

"We will see what we can do," Teresa replied. "I think everyone can go, but we will need to find homes and host parents for everyone."

After classtime, Larissa stood in the hallway gazing out the window. The hot water register under the window was an excellent place to keep warm. Sometimes Galya or some of her classmates would join her to watch the falling snow and to chat. From this second-story window they could watch an occasional student or the janitor walking along the shoveled paths across the orphanage grounds.

Sometimes Vasily, the director, would stop to say hello. His office was only a few paces up the hallway. The director appeared younger than he actually was since his dark hair had not yet been touched with gray.

"How are you doing, girls?" His black eyes and eyebrows made him look almost fierce.

"Good," Larissa and Galya responded respectfully.

"How's your schoolwork? Fun?" His eyes twinkled as the two girls shook their heads. "I understand," he continued. "I was young once too."

Larissa watched the director disappear into his office. Vasily was firm in his discipline but also kind and understanding with the orphanage children. She liked him. Not long after she had arrived at the orphanage, the director had called her into his office to talk with her. He had asked her about her family and her father. She could sense that he cared as she told him of not remembering her father. He had also given her a little bag of peaches.

A few days later Teresa announced that not all the children could go out of the country after all. Out of the nearly three hundred students, only a third would be allowed to travel. They would be the students with the best grades.

Larissa's heart sank. She should have known that she would not be awarded a trip anywhere. But perhaps if she prayed and asked God to help, it would happen. *Mama often prays about our needs, and God answers her. I will pray too. I will also write a letter to Mama to tell her about it.*

That evening Larissa wrote her letter to Mama.

> *Teresa said that only students with good grades will be allowed to travel abroad. Please pray that I can go. You can call me, and I can tell you more.*

The next day Larissa knocked on the door of the director's office.

She waited with pounding heart. She had decided to ask Vasily if he could help her get a trip to Italy with the other students.

"Come in." She heard Vasily's voice.

"So how can I help you?" Vasily asked after Larissa took the offered seat.

"I would like to go on a trip too," Larissa began. "I always dreamed of going to Italy, but now it looks like it won't happen after all."

"How are your grades?" Vasily asked quietly.

"Not the best." Larissa fidgeted. *I hope he doesn't ask about my conduct. Surely he knows my record though.* Larissa wiped the perspiration off her forehead.

"I will see what I can do for you." The director rose from behind his desk. "You are dismissed until I call for you at a later date." Larissa thought she could see a hint of a smile on his muscular face.

"I spoke with Vasily today about the award trip," Larissa told Lana and Galya that night. They lay in their beds after the lights were off. They could hear the murmur of girls' voices in neighboring rooms.

"What did he say?" asked Galya. "I wasn't chosen to go either. Actually, I don't really want to go."

"He said he would let me know what he could do about it," replied Larissa.

A week passed before Mama called. She had gotten the letter Larissa had sent. Larissa was in an art class when Teresa told her that she was wanted in the office on a phone call.

"Larissa, how are you doing? We miss you." The line crackled and Mama seemed distant, but Larissa could still hear her. "I got your letter about the trip abroad. Maxim and I are praying that you can travel with the others."

After talking to Mama, Larissa felt better. Even if she couldn't travel to another country this time, there might be other travel opportunities later.

It wasn't until the middle of April that Vasily called Larissa to his office. When Larissa stepped inside she immediately noticed how organized his desk was.

"The quota for those going to Italy is full," the director announced. "But I was able to get you a trip to Spain. I hope this works for you."

"Yes, of course." Larissa could hardly believe what she was hearing. An award trip to Spain would be just as good as Italy. It was a dream come true and an answer to prayer. *Maybe I don't have a papa to pay for the trip, but at least Vasily cared enough to make it possible.*

"Thank you! Thank you very much!" Larissa jumped up. She wanted to run and tell her roommates.

"One request from you," Vasily smiled. "Bring something from Spain for me as a token of appreciation for what I did for you."

"Oh, I will! Thank you again!" Larissa rushed out the door. Lana and Galya hugged her when she shared the news with them. They would not be traveling until the first part of July, giving the school officials time to complete the paperwork.

Larissa was glad to be at home after school was out. Mama soon received an official letter from the school giving details of the documents they needed for Larissa's trip.

"Alla gave me the address of a place that takes passport photos," said Mama. "We will go tomorrow morning."

After the passport photos were developed, Nadia sent them to the school, along with the other necessary documents. Since the orphanage was government funded, the government would pay for Larissa's passport.

The students who were traveling met at the orphanage on July 1 to receive travel instructions and to prepare for their trip two days later. On the morning of the trip, the students rose early and ate a good breakfast. Then, each shouldering a backpack with their clothing, they climbed onto the back of a dump truck for the trip to the airport.

The large diesel dump truck roared off with the children shouting in anticipation. Oksana, a caretaker, rode with the children as a Spanish/

Russian interpreter.

Tanya and Larissa sat together on their trip to the airport. Although Tanya was in grade five and a year younger than Larissa, they had become good friends at the orphanage.

"I can hardly wait to see Spain," said Tanya, leaning closer to Larissa.

"Were your parents okay with you going?" Larissa could see the light in Tanya's blue eyes as the wind whipped her blond hair around her neck.

"I don't have any parents." The light in her eyes darkened. "They both died when I was just a little girl. I don't remember them at all. I usually live with my grandmother during the summer."

Larissa felt troubled. *I don't remember my father because he lives thousands of miles away, and Tanya does not remember her father because he died.* Larissa wished she knew what to say, but the subject was too painful.

The sun was climbing out of its bed, and the sky glowed a faint pink. They would soon be at the airport. Above the tree line Larissa watched a jetliner lifting into the skies.

In the airport terminal, the children stayed close together while Oksana handled the passports and ticketing. It took nearly twenty minutes for all the names to be cleared and the boarding passes issued. Finally they were allowed to go through security and then to the gate, where they waited to board the plane.

Larissa and Tanya jumped to their feet with the other children at the boarding call. Once on the aircraft, the girls fastened their seat belts.

"I'm not sure about this," Larissa giggled nervously to Tanya. "I am scared." She grabbed Tanya's arm.

"We'll be okay," Tanya replied, looking brave. Just then the engines revved, and the large aircraft began to taxi toward the runway. As they thundered into the skies, some of the children clung to each other in fear, while others laughed with delight. But no one was laughing when the plane hit some turbulence and started bouncing up and down. A few of the children even needed to use the barf bags.

As they descended into Madrid, Spain, four hours later, Larissa sighed with relief.

"I don't know if I'll ever like flying," she said as the aircraft hit the runway.

"I love it," Tanya replied, her face flushed with excitement.

After deplaning, Oksana told the children to follow her through the airport and out to the waiting vehicles and bus. People stood along the sidewalk holding signs with children's names written on them. This allowed Oksana to hand over those children whose host parents were here to pick them up. The rest of the children, including Larissa and Tanya, boarded a large bus for an eight-hour ride south.

"I guess we will need to learn Spanish if we are going to get along here," Tanya remarked, pointing to the signs along the highway. The bus slowed as they passed through a town.

"I can say 'Hi' and 'Thank you' in Spanish," replied Larissa.

"That's a good start, but you've got a long way to go until you are fluent," Tanya teased.

As they traveled along, they saw lots of olive orchards. In the dry landscape, winds kicked up dust among the olive trees, giving the appearance of ghosts fading in and out. Farther south they began seeing more vineyards and even some citrus orchards.

It was dark when the bus rumbled into Lucena, a city in southern Spain, where the children would meet their host parents. The children lined up beside the bus with their belongings and waited to be called.

"Tanya, take care," whispered Larissa as she gave her friend a hug. They were both excited about meeting their Spanish host parents.

A burly, dark-skinned man accompanied by a beautiful woman and three boys stepped out as Larissa's name was announced. Oksana translated for the Pepe and Araceli Cabesa family as they greeted Larissa.

After a brief interchange and a big hug from Araceli, the family led

Larissa to a sport-utility vehicle. After a short drive they arrived at the Cabesa home and parked next to a four-story, white stucco house. Pepe explained that his mother lived on the first floor, his offices were on the second, their home was on the third, and the fourth was partially open-air. An elevator could be taken to the upper floors. It was obvious that the family was quite well to do.

Larissa was shown to her bedroom and was soon fast asleep. In the morning she awoke with a start. *Where am I?* Then it all came rushing back. She was in Spain.

She jumped out of bed and dressed. Before she pushed open the door that led into the living room, she stopped. *What shall I say? I don't know much Spanish, but I guess I can say "Good morning."* She tried to remember a few more words she had been taught earlier that week.

"Buenos dias," Larissa greeted Araceli, who was moving about the kitchen.

"Buenos dias," returned Araceli. She smiled and gave Larissa a hug and a kiss. She spoke a few more sentences in Spanish that Larissa didn't understand.

Araceli then rubbed her stomach while saying another Spanish word. *She's asking me if I'm hungry,* Larissa realized. Quickly she nodded her head. She certainly was hungry! She sat where her host mother motioned, and a plate was set down before her. The food looked different but smelled delicious.

I wonder where Pepe and the boys are? thought Larissa as she took a bite of pasta. Light streaming through the kitchen window revealed the sun to be high in the sky.

Adoption?

1996

"The cathedral is set on an oversized hill and has a great view," said Araceli. "It's a St. Mary's Catholic Church."

Larissa had been in Spain for just over three weeks. This evening the Cabesa family was going to the famous church on the hill.

The church could be seen from a distance, as it had been built upon a miniature mountain that seemed to have been pushed up out of the rolling terrain. Sunlight glistening from the spirals and windows of the ancient building drew attention from miles away. The road snaked around and around the small mountain until finally they arrived at the top. They pulled into a parking lot and got out to admire the cathedral.

Inside the church entrance, Araceli bought candles to place at the base of the statue of St. Mary holding Baby Jesus. Araceli showed

Larissa how to take the candles, ignite them on the candles already burning, and place them in the candleholder. Araceli also gave candles to her sons to light and place.

"Here, kiss the statue as I do," Araceli demonstrated. Eight-year-old Miguel paid his respect to St. Mary and Baby Jesus while Larissa watched.

His older brother, however, refused. "I don't want to kiss that thing." He turned away. Larissa also stood back and observed the demonstrations. *I can't kiss the statue,* she resolved. She feigned interest in the stained glass windows. *Mama told me that paying respect to icons and statues is wrong.*

After touring the church, the Cabesa family moved outside to take in the breathtaking view of the surrounding country. Since the sun had set, they could see the lights blinking on in the valleys and in the surrounding towns. After a walk around the hill and some conversation, they piled into their SUV for the trip home.

"It is beautiful here," Larissa murmured.

"Your Spanish is improving," said Miguel with a grin. "You are losing your accent and learning new words."

"Thank you," Larissa said. "I like learning your language."

"One thing that helps is your gift of gab," Miguel giggled.

The trip back to Lucena seemed to pass quickly with the lively bunch. *It would be fun to live with this family,* thought Larissa.

When Larissa got up the next morning, Araceli had breakfast ready for the family. Pasta was often on the menu.

"You are like a daughter to us," said Pepe and Araceli. They gave Larissa a morning hug and kiss. "What would you say if we would adopt you? We could provide a good home for you and a good education."

Larissa could hardly believe her ears. Adoption! It was almost too good to be true. *I would have a father and have money and . . .*

"You could write a letter to your mother and tell her of our suggestion." Araceli dished out spaghetti and eggs onto each plate, with plenty of olives on the side.

The cheerful morning dialogue centered on the possibility of adopting Larissa and the changes this would bring. Larissa ate heartily of the good food.

"Why don't I take you to the Catholic school in town where we send our boys?" Araceli continued. "I think you would enjoy touring it. There are a few summer classes in session."

They walked about ten minutes along the streets of Lucena until they reached the school. It appeared much more organized and up-to-date than the schools in Ukraine. Larissa noticed that the boys and girls playing on the grounds wore uniforms, and some of the women teachers wore a veiling. It would be a change from what she was used to, but she could adjust to it.

"I received a call from interpreter Oksana this morning," Araceli told Larissa as they walked home from the school. "They're planning a day at the ocean for all the orphanage children and their host families. It will be a way to reconnect with your friends during your stay here in Spain."

"Tanya! It's so good to see you!" Larissa hugged her friend. "Tell me how it's been going for you."

"I have good news." Tanya kicked through the sand on the beach with her arm linked through Larissa's. "My host parents are working on adopting me!"

"Really!" Larissa exclaimed. "I am so glad for you!" The ocean breezes flung their hair and tugged at their clothing. All the host families had brought their orphanage children to the ocean for the day. Some lived close by while others like Larissa and her host parents had driven for several hours.

"Yes, I am so excited. My host parents are not rich, but they do have enough money and are very kind to me." Tanya's eyes were moist.

"May I tell you my story too?" Larissa drew her initials in the sand with her toe as she spoke. The children around her splashed and shouted in the ocean waves.

"Tell me," Tanya encouraged. They continued walking along the beach.

"My host parents have asked to adopt me too!"

"Are you joking?"

"No, I'm not." They stopped a moment to look into each other's face. Dreams danced in their eyes.

"I have to go back to Ukraine at the end of our stay here to complete the process," Tanya said. "The next time I come back, which will likely be next winter or spring, I will stay here."

The girls rushed into the ocean together and swam out from shore. They treaded water, floated in the waves, and talked about the future.

During the afternoon, a lunch was set up on the beach for the children and the host families. As the sun sank over the Atlantic Ocean, the tired orphanage children joined their host families to gather their belongings and head for home.

I wonder what Mama will think when she gets my letter, Larissa thought as they motored along. Dust rolled up behind them as Pepe took a shortcut through a large olive orchard.

21

The New House

1997

The odor of wood smoke mixing with the damp, earthy smell of the morning fog drifted across the hillside. Sparrows twittered incessantly, hopping from branch to branch before fluttering to nearby trees. Two children climbed into the cherry tree to pick its fruit. The morning continued to brighten as the sun pierced through the blanket of fog. In the distance, a radio blared its music into the morning stillness.

"Stop eating so many cherries and fill your pail, Maxim," thirteen-year-old Larissa reprimanded as she reached for another clump of cherries.

"I only ate two," Maxim grinned as he stuffed another one into his mouth.

Almost a year had passed since Larissa's visit to Spain. It had been a summer she would never forget. But her mother had been very upset when she received Larissa's letter concerning adoption.

"If I would allow you to be adopted, I would have only Maxim. If Pavel would somehow get custody of Maxim, I would be alone. No, I will not allow any adoption."

Mama doesn't understand, Larissa reflected sullenly. *I could make a good living and then bring her and Maxim to Spain.* The orphanage had allowed her a four-week visit to Spain again during the winter months, which had only increased her desire to stay. *Maybe someday I will move to Spain.* She tossed a few more cherries into her nearly filled pail. *I can already speak Spanish fairly well.*

"I'm tired of picking cherries." Maxim sat on a branch with his small pail pinched between his legs.

"We need to hurry and fill the baskets, Maxim," Larissa replied, pushing aside a branch in her search for cherries. "The sooner we can get to the market, the sooner we can sell the cherries." *And the sooner I can buy some ice cream,* she thought to herself. She could already taste the cold sweetness.

Larissa slid down the tree and dumped her pail into the basket. Her thoughts kept returning to Spain. *I wonder how Tanya is doing.* At least her friend now had both a mother and a father.

"Would anyone want to go with me to see where Nadia and her children live?" Edward Miller asked the instruction class women. "I think they need a better place to live, but I want your opinion. Would you care to ride with me and see their living conditions?"

Nadia was not at the class that day. Although they missed her, it gave Edward an opportunity to share with the class his idea to build a house for Nadia and her children.

A number of the women expressed interest, so a few days later a group of instruction class women and an interpreter accompanied

Edward to Nadia's house.

Edward had told Nadia they were coming but had not told her why. The group pushed into the small room.

"You have an apple tree beside the house," one of the women murmured. "Are the apples good?"

"They're very sour," Nadia responded. "They're called Antonovka apples."

After visiting for a few minutes, the women slipped outside to investigate the fruit trees. "Here's a nice pear graft!" another lady exclaimed. "Look at the difference between the rootstock fruit and that of the grafted branch." The grafted branch was loaded with nice-sized pears.

As the vanload headed back toward Khotiv, the women talked about their visit. They had seen the inside of Nadia's house for the first time. The one room had two beds with a small space to walk between, a small table, and a smoky woodstove. The room had a damp beet smell from the borscht she had been cooking. The single window dripped with condensation. There was no shower and no kitchen—just one room, plus a little lean-to large enough to hold a stack of wood and a wash tub.

"Edward, it's such tight quarters," one of the women commented as they headed back. "And she doesn't even own it. It's awful. We need to help her."

All of them agreed that the house was barely livable, and Nadia really did need something better.

"I will discuss it further with my fellow pastors," responded Edward.

The next Friday Edward and several others traveled to Nadia's house with mission driver Meesha Kobets to present the idea.

"We want to build a house for you," Edward said. "Would you be okay with that?"

Nadia's eyes widened. "What? A new house? Are you serious?"

Tears of joy ran down her cheeks as Edward explained the plan.

"A house?" Larissa whispered to Maxim. "Did we hear right?" They hugged each other.

"Tell me, Nadia. You have a plot of land with a big garden, right?" Meesha asked. "Could we go see it?"

"It was my grandfather's land, but since he died and my mother and my uncle already had land and a house, the land officer in Lisnyky said I could inherit it."

They walked over to the half-acre plot and discussed where they should build the house. They decided to build it as far back from the street as possible.

"I have spoken with a builder who lives on M Street," Edward told Nadia. "He and his son built an attractive brick garage on his property and did a very good job. I think he would be a good builder."

"We will also help as much as we can," Edward went on. "But I do have plans to go back to America soon." His words caught not only Nadia's attention, but also Larissa's and Maxim's. They pushed close.

"What?" Nadia was aghast.

"But don't worry," Edward continued. "We will try to complete as much of your house as possible before I leave. I'll ask the builder to begin on Monday."

"Will you be coming back to Ukraine?" asked Nadia.

"I may come back to visit, but probably not to stay." Edward looked sober.

Nadia could hardly imagine Edward and Sarah leaving Ukraine. She had grown to love them. She tried to collect her thoughts.

"What about preparing food for the workers?" Nadia asked. "I only have a little kerosene stove to cook on besides the woodstove in my bedroom."

"I will try to come up with something," Edward replied. "I'll bring some food too."

The following Monday Edward brought a gas stove he had bought for Nadia.

"Oh," he said, "I forgot a propane tank." He shook his head. "You don't have one, do you?"

"No," Nadia replied. "Sorry."

"I'll run and buy one." Edward and Meesha were soon back and attached the tank to the stove.

"Wow!" Nadia clapped her hands when she saw the blue flame. It would be so much easier to cook now that she had a gas stove. The stove seemed almost out of place in such a small lean-to.

That week Larissa and Maxim frequently walked down to the garden plot with Nadia in hopes of seeing the backhoe there to start digging, but no one showed up. By Friday, they were bewildered. What was wrong? Edward had said the excavating would start on Monday.

After the service on Sunday morning, Nadia approached Edward as he talked to a visitor. They were standing outside the school building. Some of the people from Lisnyky were already climbing into the church van in preparation for leaving.

When Edward looked her way, Nadia caught his attention. "Have you heard when the excavator is coming? I was expecting him last week but nothing happened."

Edward's mouth dropped open. "No one showed up? The builder told me they would be there Monday or Tuesday. I'm sorry. I'll have to check into this."

The sun peeked through the clouds for a minute, throwing rays of sunlight onto the elderly pastor's shimmering white hair.

"Don't worry. He'll come," Edward assured Nadia. "I will be out tomorrow morning to get something going."

"Let's go visit Alla," said Mama that evening. "I want to tell her of our good fortune."

"Come in!" Alla called cheerily when they arrived.

"A new house?" Alla stopped stirring the soup and turned around. "Did you say someone is building a new house for you?"

"Yes, I did," Nadia beamed, hanging her sweater on the hook beside the door.

"Tell me about it," Alla ejaculated. She tested the soup that had cooled on a saucer.

Nadia started from the beginning and told her the whole story. "Our pastor Edward said he would come tomorrow and start digging the cellar by hand if he had to."

"Oh, Nadia," Alla laughed. "That's wonderful. Finally you and the children will have your own house away from your crazy mother. You will make all the villagers jealous. Remember how they laughed at your mother because she wore a felt boot on one foot and went barefooted with the other?"

"And they still make fun of me too," Nadia replied. "Just this afternoon someone threw a tomato at me when I was at the well." She peeked into the living room to check on Maxim, who was playing with Alla's two boys.

"Well, this will certainly make all the villagers in Lisnyky talk." Alla dished out soup into bowls. "I think your God is helping you."

Mmm, this soup is delicious. Larissa scooped up the last bit and handed her bowl back to Alla for more.

"Like my soup, do you?" Alla smiled. "You can have as much as you like, Larissa. I should adopt you for my own daughter. What do you think, Nadia?" Alla placed the filled bowl in front of Larissa.

Nadia didn't respond.

The next morning when Nadia, Larissa, and Maxim arrived at the garden plot, Edward was there with his shovel, digging. He

Edward working on Nadia's new house foundation.

straightened when he saw them coming.

"Good morning," Edward greeted them. "We talked to the excavator and he should be here today sometime. Maybe you can plan on making lunch."

"What time do you want to eat?" Nadia asked.

"Twelve o'clock will be fine."

The week flew by as the cellar and footers were dug. When the excavator finally showed up, the work went fast. The concrete for the footers was soon poured, and Edward found a crew that needed work from a collective farm in Khotiv to help lay the bricks.

As Edward and Sarah packed their suitcases to fly back to the United States, the first story of the new house was nearing completion.

Meesha Kobets was put in charge of completing the project and making contact with Edward in the United States when necessary. By November, the exterior of the house was completed except for the main door. Meesha's father laid up a brick stove in the wall between the kitchen and the bedroom to provide both heat for the

Nadia's new house nearing completion.

bedroom and a place to cook in the kitchen.

To provide easy access to water, a well was dug behind the house on the first terrace. Large cement rings were brought and lowered into the hole to keep the sides from caving in and contaminating the water.

Finally, in late November, they were able to move into the new house. Nadia took a heavy blanket and draped it over the entrance doorway, holding it in place with pieces of wood and cement blocks.

"I guess this will work until we get a door," Nadia said.

"I think we will be okay," replied Larissa. "I am just glad we have a new house to live in."

Larissa was back from the orphanage for the weekend. Nadia tried to stoke the fire and stir up some heat in the new brick stove against the frigid outdoor temperatures, but it continued to burn sluggishly.

"Maybe the chimney wasn't built right," said Larissa as she wrapped a blanket around herself and snuggled up to the new stove. "You should talk to someone about it. Maybe it can be fixed."

As the fire burned slowly, Larissa climbed into the bed next to Mama's. Tomorrow was Sunday and she needed rest.

The next morning Larissa, Maxim, and Mama stood next to the main road waiting for the mission van to take them to church. The wind was still, but the air was cold and crisp. Snow lay on the ground.

"Do you like your new house?" Pastor Arlan asked as he shifted the van into gear.

His Russian is broken, Larissa thought as she looked out the frosty glass window. *I guess they haven't been in Ukraine long enough to learn much Russian.* Pastor Arlan Kurtz and his wife Linda had recently come to fill the void left by Edward and Sarah's departure.

A young man in the passenger seat looked back at them and smiled. He too spoke in broken Russian, though his accent was more like Pastor Bruce's.

"My name is Rodney. I am from Canada. What is your name?" He smiled at Larissa.

"My name is Larissa." Larissa turned to breathe on the window. She made a hole in the frost. A few village women sitting behind her jabbered quietly. Getting a ride to church was much more interesting than walking.

Larissa could hear Arlan and Rodney speaking to each other in English. *I wish I could speak English,* she thought wistfully.

Keep Climbing

1999

As Larissa rode the bus toward the orphanage, she thought about Mama and Maxim back home in Lisnyky. It had been a year and a half since their house was built, but it still wasn't totally completed and had no indoor plumbing. They were thankful for what had been done, but someone needed to help them finish the interior work.

Money was also a problem. Mama had barely enough to buy food for the family and pay the electric and gas bills. At least they were still receiving the food parcel, which was something to be thankful for.

Larissa stepped off the bus and headed for the orphanage. Fifteen years old now, she carried herself with an air of maturity. She was shorter than many of her friends, but she was trim and tough and athletic.

"Hi, Larissa." Galya gave her a hug. "Welcome back. Did you bring anything good with you this time?" She smiled with anticipation.

"No Froot Loops today." Larissa flopped down on her bed. "Sorry."

"I can't eat your apology." Galya made a face.

"I can sing for you." Larissa dug in her backpack and pulled out a small songbook. "How was your weekend?"

"Like a normal Saturday and Sunday. Sleep. Do homework. Take a walk in the orchard. Eat some soup." Galya sighed. "I wish I could go home too."

Larissa listened to her friend as she flipped through the songbook and found a favorite song. She shoved a pillow behind her back and scooted up next to the wall beside her bed.

"Why don't I sing to cheer you up?" suggested Larissa.

Her clear soprano voice filled the little room and all became quiet in the dorm as the melodious sound floated through the building. Larissa sang while Galya and Lana dressed for the night and slipped into their beds. When Larissa finished her singing, a pounding sounded on the wall from the next room.

"Larissa, more."

When Larissa heard her friends, she smiled and turned the pages to find another song. She sang until her voice began to give out and then put the book back into her backpack. It was time for bed. As she prepared herself for the night, she again heard the knocking on the wall, but this time it was softer.

"Larissa. More. We love it."

I guess I can sing one by memory yet, Larissa thought as she flipped off the light switch. She quietly sang a couple verses by memory, and then all was quiet.

Larissa stood with the other orphanage children and listened to the announcements by the director. It was spring of 1999, her last year at the orphanage. After school closed for the summer, she would be going home to Lisnyky to live with Mama and Maxim again. She would then attend school in Lisnyky for the last two years of her schooling.

"We need to thoroughly clean everything before President Leonid Kuchma's wife arrives," announced Director Vasily. His black eyes flashed and his chin was lifted. "We want every room to be clean, the grounds spotless, and each student in place, working hard. We will have the showers open the day before she visits. We want you all to be clean and well dressed for this special occasion."

Everyone worked hard to clean the orphanage before the arrival of the important guest. This was a once-in-a-lifetime event.

"I think seeing the president's wife will be exciting, but it is not as exciting as summer vacation," Larissa remarked to Galya. "I am almost as excited about summer camp in Crimea as I was about going to Spain."

"I hope I can go too," Galya replied. Then she shook her head. "I don't know though. My father will have the last word on that."

"I could hardly believe my ears when Teresa announced that our summer vacation would be in Crimea," continued Larissa, setting the bucket of soapy water next to the window. She could see some of the boys raking the grounds while a few others were shaking out the rugs.

"Were you ever in Crimea?" asked Galya.

"No, but Mama was." Larissa ran her rag along the window trim. "It is much warmer there since it is at the southern end of Ukraine and mostly surrounded by water."

"You mean if we go we will likely be staying next to the Black Sea?" Galya raised her eyebrows.

"Yes, probably. We'll get to do lots of swimming." Larissa rinsed out her rag in the bucket of water.

"I can hardly wait either," put in Zorana, another of Larissa's classmates.

"By the way, when are you going to cut your hair?" asked Galya. "It's falling down around your shoulders. Mine needs to be cut too."

"I actually like my hair longer," replied Larissa. "I used to dream of having hair that touched the floor."

"It would get in the way, and it's not in style," countered Lana, who had been listening.

Mama would not be happy if I cut my hair, thought Larissa. She squeezed out the rag and continued washing their bedroom walls. *When I go to church with Mama, I wear a veiling, so I guess no one would know if my hair was a little shorter. But it seems Mama is really strict about whatever Pastor Bruce or Arlan teach.*

She wondered if her mother would ever be a member of the American church, or as they now called it, the Mennonite church. Her mother had gone through instruction class several times but still hadn't been baptized.

"I don't think I completely understand what I am doing," Larissa had overheard Mama telling Pastor Bruce. "I still have many questions."

The days leading up to the first lady's visit were exciting. The children cleaned, organized, and dreamed of someday being important too.

"Someday I may be the president of Ukraine," boasted one of the boys. He drew himself up tall with his black eyes flashing. "I will lead the country into great success."

"Not if I win the election," his friend retorted.

"I don't think either of you qualify," interjected Lana.

Finally the day arrived. The president's wife and her aides emerged from the vehicles and were welcomed by the director and his wife. First Lady Ludmila Kuchma warmly greeted everyone and then followed Director Vasily as he led her through the orphanage and school. At the end of her tour, she asked the students who were graduating from the orphanage school to gather in front of the building. She gave a short speech and then presented each student with a gift.

"Keep climbing upward," the president's wife encouraged as she finished her short talk. "Never let obstacles keep you from realizing your goals. Yes, life will happen and you will have moments of discouragement, but don't allow this to hinder you. Keep climbing."

As the last vehicle of her entourage disappeared from sight, the graduating class of '99 hugged each other.

"We can do it!" they shouted. Larissa hugged Galya, laughing. The sky was the limit. They would make progress in spite of their place in life. Neither she nor Galya had both parents, but that didn't have to hinder them from being successful. They would work hard. They would keep climbing.

Black Sea Summer

1999

Dusk was falling as the large bus descended the last slopes of the Crimean Mountains into the lowlands of southern Crimea and rolled into the seacoast town of Simeiz. Seagulls flew along the coast looking for food. On one section of rocky beach, a few gulls fought over the remains of a dead fish.

"We're here," the driver announced as he guided the bus through the large, open gates and up to the gray limestone buildings. Surrounding the headquarters were several playgrounds and open areas. Along the fences that enclosed the grounds were trees and shrubbery.

"During the school year this is a kindergarten school, but during the summer it is used as a camp," explained the lady guide. "I will introduce you to the camp caretaker. Please bring your luggage with you."

The excited youth grabbed their belongings and descended the steps into the remaining light. They were greeted by the fishy, tangy smell of seawater. Evergreen trees graced the street leading up to the beach, their branches waving gently in the evening breeze.

"I am so glad to be off that bus," Larissa remarked as she swung her backpack onto her shoulder. "I hope we get some food soon."

"You mean you want to eat?" laughed Kolya teasingly. "Maybe you should diet."

Larissa made a face at him.

"The only kind of diet for me is to eat everything," retorted Galya. "I'm as hungry as a wolf."

After the children were shown their rooms, they were led to a dining hall across the street. The meatballs, cooked buckwheat, and fresh bread seemed tastier than usual. Trays of vegetables and fruit followed the main course.

"Now, after such a delicious meal, I'm ready for some sleep," Zorana said. "I think I'll sleep like a log."

"Me too." Larissa flopped onto her cot as her classmates also prepared for the night. "Don't wake me up until noon."

The next morning, loud knocking awakened the children. Kristina, the caretaker, was beating on the doors and calling them for breakfast.

"After breakfast I will take you out to the Black Sea for a swim," she called. "Be ready to follow me to the cafeteria in ten minutes."

Larissa rubbed her eyes as she walked to the window. She shoved it open and leaned on the windowsill. The sun had not yet risen over the treetops. A lone rosebush beneath the window sparkled with dewdrops. She savored the freshness of the morning.

After breakfast was over, the children played along the beach. The older boys and girls walked out onto the pier and dived off into the sea. Just to the left and within sight of the pier, a large rock called the Virgin Rock jutted out of the water. A fishing boat bobbed in the distance.

"We should climb the Virgin Rock to jump," Larissa declared. She tossed her head, sending a spray of water. "I dare you, Kolya, to climb up and jump from the first cliff."

"I will if you follow," he retorted.

A few of the braver youth proceeded to climb the treacherous rock. Once at the top, Larissa waited until she worked up the courage to jump. It felt like a long time before she hit the water. Returning to the surface, she shook her head to clear her ears, then swam with the waves to shore.

Wow, that was exhilarating! But I think it was enough excitement for one day. Larissa kicked through the sand and joined the other girls who were sitting and soaking up the sun.

The summer passed with the orphanage children swimming in the sea, eating extra good meals, and visiting a botanical garden. Larissa wished she could stay forever.

One day Larissa stood and gazed at the mountain towering to the west. *I am going to climb that mountain before we leave this summer,* she thought. She was sure she could do it in one day. All she needed was someone to go with her.

"I want to climb that mountain," said Larissa. A few of her classmates turned to look where she pointed. "I plan to climb to the top before we leave here this summer."

"You can if you want to, but not us," retorted the other ninth graders.

Finally one day Larissa convinced one of the younger girls to go with her. It would be a good hike to the top of Cat Mountain, as it was called.

When the two girls finally reached the summit of Cat Mountain, the view over the town of Simeiz and the Black Sea was breathtaking.

"I wish I could fly," laughed Larissa as she jumped and whirled in the wind.

By the time the two girls retraced the descent, they had both worked up a tremendous appetite.

I'm glad it's nearly suppertime, thought Larissa. *I'm ravenous. But at least I got to climb the mountain!*

Finally the day arrived for them to leave for home. As they were preparing their things, caretaker Kristina suddenly stood in front of them. "Listen," she said. "Someone messed up. I am not sure whose responsibility it was, but no one bought bus tickets for you. We can't leave until we have the tickets. In the meantime, we need to find another place for you to stay since the kindergarten children will be here next week."

"How could anyone forget about a whole camp full of children and youth?" complained Lana. "It's ridiculous!"

"Oh, well. At least our vacation will be longer," said Larissa with a smile. "I'm not really looking forward to a new school anyway."

Kristina found a bus to transport the children to an empty facility two hours northeast of Simeiz. This camp was dilapidated, and the cook made terrible meals. Larissa soon decided she was ready to leave after all.

One day as Larissa was playing hopscotch with a few other girls, she heard someone scream. The girls stopped to listen. Soon Oksana came running up. She was almost beside herself. "Girls," she exclaimed, "one of the boys has drowned!"

"No! Who?" the girls gasped.

"Kolya."

The girls were stunned. Kolya had been a friendly, outgoing boy who was well liked by everyone.

That evening the boys explained how it had happened. "It was terrible," one of them said, his face contorted with fear and grief. "We found a bottle of vodka and sneaked back to a small lake to have a drink. Afterwards, Kolya went out into the water for a swim. He never made it back."

It was late the next afternoon before the body was brought from the morgue for the orphanage children to view. Larissa could see tears in Kristina's eyes as she announced that the children would be able to pay their last respects before Kolya's body was taken back to the orphanage. The children slowly came forward to the simple wooden coffin in which Kolya lay. They were terrified at the sight of death. Larissa's heart was smitten. *Where is he now?* she wondered.

The children gathered around Kolya's body one last time before it was taken back to the orphanage. It was awful. Larissa turned away, her thoughts in turmoil. *What happens after people die? Would I be ready to die?*

New Desires

2000

The simple church room was packed full. Those who came in late sat in a small, open room to the right. The white brick building was not well insulated, but with the heating system chugging steadily along and so many people inside, the rooms stayed comfortable.

Master's International Ministries (MIM) had bought the thirty-six-foot-square, three-story building to use for church services and as a mission center. It was located in southern Kiev in an area called Teremky, within walking distance of the M Street school they had utilized earlier. The building's first floor was used as a church auditorium. The second floor had three rooms—an office for MIM, a walk-in clinic, and a sewing room. A two-bedroom apartment was on the third floor.

Master's International Ministries in Kiev.

The property included an old house out back that could be remodeled and a large garden where a good-sized warehouse had been built the previous autumn for storing humanitarian aid, as well as chainsaws, tillers, and other equipment. A two-car garage was included at the end of the building for vehicle and small-equipment maintenance.

This morning Larissa had arrived early to make sure she got a seat in the small room to the right of the auditorium. Her heart pounded as she pondered how she would say what she wanted to say. She had been thinking of this for the past few months, and this morning was the morning. She bowed slightly and prayed for courage.

The service progressed as normal with a few songs led by Pastor Bruce's son Michael. *I like when he leads the singing,* thought Larissa. *Everyone sings better.*

The window behind her whistled as the angry January wind tried to pry open the large single pane to get inside.

Since it was cooler near the back wall, Larissa pulled her sweater close. The Spirit spoke to her conscience. "What about all the times you knowingly disobeyed Mama? Remember when you cheated on your test in school?" Memories flooded back of the times she had stolen cabbage from the collective farm or pilfered food at the market. *But I was hungry,* she tried to justify herself. "But taking something that does not belong to you is wrong," the inner voice told her. Larissa sighed. She knew she was a sinner. She had heard the Gospel preached and knew she needed to repent. The process had already begun in her heart.

Larissa jerked back to reality when she heard Pastor Bruce comment on the message and then ask if anyone would like to come forward to repent. She hesitated.

The church room was full, and a few women were murmuring to each other. Larissa got to her feet.

"I would like to repent."

Bruce turned to her with a smile. "You may come forward."

"Do you realize that you are a sinner and in need of a Savior?"

"Yes," Larissa nodded. "I have sinned, and I want to give my heart to Jesus and follow Him and obey Him."

"Do you want to pray?"

"Yes."

"You may kneel to pray, and then I will also pray."

On the way home, Larissa's heart overflowed with thankfulness. She had made a public commitment to follow Jesus. It seemed every bird and every tree was clearer and more beautiful than ever before.

It feels so good to be clean and to have my sins forgiven, Larissa rejoiced as she walked. The words of a song came to her mind and she started singing.

> "So I'll cherish the old rugged cross,
> Till my trophies at last I lay down;
> I will cling to the old rugged cross,
> And exchange it someday for a crown."

New Desires

The next day in school, it seemed the other youth were extra vulgar and rude. But maybe it was her imagination. Perhaps the students had always talked about these topics in this way. *Maybe I'm the one who has changed.* She frowned at her classmates' immoral talk. But she knew she had talked like that too.

Larissa's mind drifted to the previous day. After her commitment, Brother Arlan had stood to give a word of encouragement. "In 2 Corinthians 5:17 it says, 'Therefore if any man be in Christ, he is a new creature: old things are passed away; behold, all things are become new.' You are now a new creature in Christ. Old things are passed away, and now you are made new."

Life looked different now that she was living for Jesus. She had been enjoying youth Bible study since she returned to Lisnyky and could hardly wait to begin attending instruction class.

"Larissa, what are you daydreaming about?" whispered Alina, the girl beside her at school. "Get to work or you will have lots of homework."

Larissa smiled to herself. Yes, she had better get to work for more than one reason. First of all, she wanted to show she was different now that she was a believer. But she also didn't want homework. Even though schoolwork wasn't more fun today than last week, at least she had a purpose in life and wanted to do her best.

After Larissa's return from Crimea, she had started tenth grade in Lisnyky. She wasn't impressed with the school or the teachers, but it had been her only option. It felt good to live at home, although life with her mother carried its challenges. Pavel had stolen Maxim away, so Mama had been alone until Larissa arrived home again. Although she was glad to be at home again, she often missed her friends at the orphanage.

"Let's go to the nightclub tonight and dance." Alina leaned close as she whispered to Larissa. "Maybe we will get to dance with Sergey."

Larissa studied her paper. She tried to hide her feelings as she worked on her grammar sheet. *I don't want to go to the nightclub.* Thoughts raced in her head. *What should I say?*

"Mama needs help tonight," she whispered. "I can't go."

When the last class was dismissed, Larissa grabbed her bag and stuffed her unfinished work inside. As she walked down the street, she noticed that even the sun seemed to be cheerful.

"Hello, Mama," Larissa greeted her mother. "I'm hungry. Is there anything to eat?"

"Not much, but what we have, we can eat." Mama handed her a large bowl of buckwheat soup and a piece of bread. "I need to find a job to make some money so we can buy meat and cheese. Bruce told me yesterday that he would let me know when a new shipment of books arrives."

"What do the books have to do with us?" Larissa asked.

"He said they need a Master's International Ministries address stamp in each book. Each book needs to be stamped and then put back in the boxes for distribution. He said it's something I could do. Maybe you could help too."

"That would be interesting." Larissa sipped on a spoonful of soup. The kitchen area was cool, but the soup was hot.

The next day at school Alina approached Larissa.

"We had a smashing good time last night at the dance." Alina tossed her head. "You should have been there. Sergey was there, and I got to dance with him."

"I'm not interested," Larissa replied. She went on into the classroom and plopped her books on her desk.

The Struggle

2001

Larissa approached the Lisnyky School with trepidation. She stood outside the fence for a moment. *I don't want to go in there. I didn't bring any food so I should not eat at the party either.* Larissa was wearing her pink dress but not her veiling. She had let her hair fall about her shoulders. It was still too much for her to wear her white veiling to the village school.

"Maybe after I am out of school I will wear the headship veiling," she told Mama. "The villagers and some of my classmates already mock us for attending the Mennonite church. I don't need more trouble."

The evening was cool and the sun had disappeared. A few neighbors loitered outside.

"You are one of the graduation students, aren't you?" asked a neighbor.

"Yes," replied Larissa nervously.

"You need to get inside with the rest of your classmates," the woman scolded. "Your name may be called soon."

Yes, Larissa knew that, but she felt so out of place. *I would not be here if it wasn't for the diploma.* Slowly she turned toward the entrance and stepped inside.

Larissa stood in the back of the auditorium and watched the celebration. As each student's name was called, there was a round of applause as he or she walked forward to be presented with a diploma.

"I like your dress," commented Alina after Larissa walked to the front to receive her diploma and then returned to her spot in the back of the auditorium.

"Thank you. It's my favorite."

After each eleventh grader was recognized for his or her hard work and achievement, the students and families moved to the tables loaded with food. As the laughter and dancing began and the music increased, Larissa slipped out the back door. It was time for her to go home. The others would party through the night hours and then go out to a distant hill to watch the sunrise as a symbol of a new phase in life. Some of the students would go on to university or college and learn a career. Others would go home and get a local job.

As Larissa walked home, her feelings were mixed. On the one hand, she missed her village friends; on the other, she wanted to please God. She resolved to make it her choice to please God. Mama had also encouraged her to find a job for a year before starting college, but this also brought fear.

Where could she work? What if she didn't know how to follow instructions? Her mind continued to race through the options and possibilities.

The instruction class was ending, and soon the applicants would be interviewed in preparation for baptism. Larissa was excited. It had been several weeks since the graduation party.

"Could we meet with you Tuesday evening of this week?" asked Pastor Bruce. He looked sober as he spoke with her. The interpreter shifted nervously. For two days Larissa wondered why the ministers wanted to meet with her. She knew it was almost time for her to be baptized, but she had a sinking feeling that this interview was about something more than that.

It is likely about my going without a veiling at the graduation, she mused. *Most likely someone from church saw me.* She tried to remember who she had seen that evening. *I was wearing my cape dress though*, she consoled herself.

Tuesday evening finally arrived. "I'm going on a walk," said Mama. "I will leave you to your meeting."

Larissa watched out the big kitchen window. As she waited, butterflies increased in her stomach. When the mission van pulled up, Larissa hurried toward the door. In her haste, her dress caught on the corner of the woodstove. *Oh, no.*

The two pastors and an interpreter sat in a circle of chairs. Pastor Lloyd cleared his throat. His light brown hair was parted neatly and his blue eyes were sober. Lloyd and his wife Betty and their three youngest children had been in Ukraine now for about eight months.

"We really appreciate your life and your enthusiasm about instruction class. We do not doubt your relationship with God. There is a concern though, and I will let Bruce express himself."

Larissa's mind raced.

"Someone notified us that you do not always wear the headship veiling. You were seen in public without it." Bruce paused.

Larissa felt hot as she looked at the kitchen floor. Then anger crept into her heart.

"Is this true, or not?" continued Bruce.

Larissa looked up. She could see tears in Lloyd's eyes. He pulled

The Struggle

out a handkerchief and wiped his nose and eyes.

"Yes, it is true that I went into the village once recently without my veiling." Larissa cleared her throat. She looked down.

"We were hoping you could be baptized with the others, but we are thinking it might be better to wait until next year." This time it was Bruce's turn to look down. "We are sorry about this."

"Is there anything else you would like to say?" Bruce asked quietly.

"I am sorry," said Larissa. She felt hot. She had known better than to go out in public without her veiling but had ignored her conscience.

After Bruce led in prayer and the pastors had left, Larissa climbed the terraces behind the house. "God, why did this have to happen? Was it really so wrong not to wear my veiling? Others who are church members do worse things and are not caught." Her heart ached.

A thrush nightingale flew to a nearby birch tree and began to warble a song. Its song soon changed to a scolding melody. Larissa turned to observe the gray-brown bird. Normally she enjoyed its ever-changing song, but today it was irritating. She searched for a stone to throw at it.

In the distance Larissa could see Mama walking down their short valley toward home. What would she say when she found out?

That night Larissa could not sleep. She tossed and turned with troubled thoughts. What would the others in her class think about her? Finally she fell into a restless sleep.

As Larissa worked in the garden the next day she continued to think about the meeting the day before. *If I can't be baptized, maybe I should just quit going to this church.* Then Larissa recalled the tears she had seen in Pastor Lloyd's eyes. It must have hurt the pastors to tell her she had to wait. No, she would continue to attend.

On Sunday Larissa joined a few of the other youth girls after the service. She was still hurting over the turn of events but wanted to be included in the group. She was extra quiet however.

"Did you hear that the youth will be taking a trip to the Carpathian

Mountains?" asked Lena. She and her sister Sveta were becoming Larissa's good friends at church. "I am sure Sveta will be going," Lena continued, "but I don't know about me. I may be too young."

"I am going for sure," declared Harmony, Pastor Lloyd's daughter.

Larissa smiled at Harmony's fierce look.

"You won't go if they say you can't," Sveta informed her airily.

"It would be nice if we could all go," interjected Bethany Sommers with a quiet smile. Bethany, the daughter of Christian Aid Ministries' field director Edwin Sommers, was quickly becoming another of Larissa's friends.

A week later the youth were bouncing along the rough roads toward Chernivtsi, Ukraine, the first stop on their planned trip.

The hike through the gorgeous Carpathian Mountains proved to be a balm for Larissa's soul. It was a time of spiritual growth and of developing better relationships with the youth group.

The guide was a man three times their age, but he knew his way well through the mountains and was tougher than any of the youth boys. Although he carried a large pack, he still had to wait on the youth following him. One incline was so steep that they had to help each other up through the boulders and trees.

Larissa and a friend, Twila Yoder, in the Carpathian Mountains.

This mountain hike was similar to the Christian experiences the youth were encountering. There were many steep places, but the guide was thoughtful and knew when to stop and how to help them. He always chose the right path. *Just like*

The Struggle

our heavenly Father, Larissa mused.

St. John's wort, forget-me-nots, buttercups, wild carnations, and many other wildflowers grew profusely. There were pine forests, a grove of beech trees, and oak trees scattered here and there. At one campsite, wild hogs snuffled around the tents during the night in search of goodies.

The fresh mountain air was easy to breathe, and the strenuous hiking was a great stress reliever for Larissa. She was very thankful to have come along.

Friendships

2002

The MIM warehouse was filled with the sounds of youthful chatter, clacking staplers, and pouring seeds. Seed Team 2002 was hard at work. Local youth were helping package the seeds into individual packets and then into family bags with a variety of seeds and a Gospel tract. Their goal was twenty thousand family bags to pass out at seed meetings in villages across Ukraine.

Even though it was cold and snowy outside, the inside of the warehouse was warm. Around the tables, groups of young people worked diligently.

"I'm ready for a break," said John Mast as he filled another container with beet seeds.

Me too, thought Larissa. She hadn't eaten breakfast and her stomach was growling. She enjoyed her time with the youth and was glad to help with a worthwhile project like this. It would make a difference for thousands of families.

"Where do the seeds come from?" Larissa asked as she filled another packet.

"Christian Aid Ministries buys some of them in America and some in Europe, and then sends them to us," responded Bethany. "My dad works for Christian Aid Ministries, so that's how I know."

"They look like quality seeds." Larissa quickly filled the next packet and passed it on. She felt secure among the American youth, although she wished she knew the English language better.

She filled another packet with seeds and continued to talk almost nonstop.

"I think you should be quiet now," Harmony's brother Harold told her with a grin. He too was helping pack the seeds.

"I like to talk," retorted Larissa. Harmony and Lena nodded knowingly at each other and laughed.

"Don't we know that!" Lena replied. She grinned at Larissa as she stapled another packet and grabbed the next one.

The youth told stories, teased each other, or simply chatted as they packaged the garden seeds. There was never a dull moment.

At the end of two weeks the last seed packet had been stapled, the family packs assembled, and a number of songs memorized. Now it was time to pass out the seeds.

Larissa attended several of the seed meetings in the villages around Kiev. A few of the men or youth boys would share messages, then the youth would sing some songs they had practiced. Afterwards the packets of seeds would be passed out. They also handed out Bibles and Bible storybooks. Larissa enjoyed watching the villagers leaving the building with a Bible in one hand and a bag of garden seeds in the other.

The spring months passed with Larissa again attending instruction class. She enjoyed it, but it wasn't as new and interesting as it had been the previous year. Still, it was refreshing to learn more of God's Word and to learn to know the new class members.

From time to time the American families would return to the States for a furlough. *I wonder what America is like,* thought Larissa. She had many friends in America now. She missed Edward and Sarah. She imagined America filled with the beauty of palm trees, spraying waterfalls, and lots of breathtaking plant and animal life. A bird she wanted to see sometime was the cardinal. She had seen photos of these bright red birds of America. Someday she would go. Somehow.

Although Maxim still lived with his father Pavel part of the time, right now he was living at home. One day Larissa spoke to him about her idea. Perhaps they could visit America together.

"If you get to go first, then you have to help me come," said Larissa. "If I am able to go, I will help you come."

"You're just dreaming," Maxim replied. He wrinkled his nose. "It will never happen."

"Would you like to come over to our house and help us snap green beans?" asked Harmony, breezing up to Larissa one day.

Larissa looked up from the fabric she was cutting. She was in the sewing room on the second floor at the MIM mission.

"What are green beans?" she asked, wiping the sweat from her forehead. The windows to the sewing room were open, and a warm breeze touched her face.

"Well, come on over and find out."

After the sewing classes were over, Larissa hurried out of the room. She nearly bumped into Diane, who was backing out of the clinic

Friendships

room with an armful of meds.

"Sorry," murmured Larissa as she stepped around the nurse.

"That's okay," Diane smiled. "I should have watched where I was going. How was your day?"

"Okay. I was sewing a dress today."

"That's nice."

Larissa walked with Diane out to the street, where the nurse bade her goodbye. It wouldn't take long to walk to Pastor Lloyd's house just around the block.

"Hi, Larissa," Harmony welcomed her. The warm, cozy kitchen had an appetizing smell of chocolate.

"I am baking some bars," said Harmony. She pointed to the little oven. "While they bake, let me show you something I bought at the market."

Larissa enjoyed Harmony's bubbling conversation as she led the way to her room and showed Larissa what she had bought. *I wish I had a sister,* Larissa thought. When they returned to the kitchen, the acrid smell of something burning greeted them.

"Oh, no!" Harmony gasped. She grabbed two hot pads and jerked open the oven door. Quickly she yanked out the bars and flopped them onto the stovetop. "I'll need to let them cool a few minutes to see if they are edible."

Larissa noticed piles of skinny, green vegetables on the table in the dining room. She peeked in and saw Lloyd's wife Betty.

"Hi, Larissa," Betty greeted her. "Did you come to help?"

"Yes, are these the green beans?" Larissa picked up one and ran her finger along its green slenderness.

"Yes," Betty nodded. "Is it something new for you?"

"They are even good to eat raw," interjected Harmony. She grabbed a bean and stuck it in her mouth.

"We never grew green beans," Larissa replied. "So it is new for me." She took the bowl Harmony handed to her. "Are they actually good to eat?"

"Of course," Betty laughed. "They're very tasty. If you stay for supper, we'll make some."

Larissa watched Betty break the beans into smaller pieces and followed her example. Her bowl soon filled with the snapped green beans.

I hope they have something more to eat than this, thought Larissa. *I'll eat anything they serve, but I'm not sure about these beans.*

Her mind went back to the frog legs she had once eaten at a youth function. She and some of the other girls had shuddered with horror at the thought of eating them.

The young man frying them had just smiled and said, "For every creature of God is good, and nothing to be refused, if it be received with thanksgiving."

The strange thing was that once they had tasted the frog legs, everyone liked them. Most of them had even gotten a second helping! *Maybe the green beans will be the same.*

At the supper table, Larissa took a spoonful of green beans to be polite. They had a different taste, but Larissa could honestly say they were good. Betty had sprinkled them with salt and pepper and cooked them with finely chopped onions.

Everything is super, Larissa thought as she reached for another piece of bread and lathered it with strawberry jam. *Betty sure knows how to make delicious food. I would come back for more of this.*

27

Sewing College

2002-2003

Rain pitter-pattered against the windows. Heavy clouds scurried across the sky, dropping their moisture. As Larissa leaned against the kitchen table, a mouse scurried along the wall and into the storage room.

"I don't want you to be a cook," said Mama. "Look at Alla. She works in the Lisnyky school kitchen and it's hard work. She has to carry heavy boxes of vegetables, kettles full of food, and buckets of drink."

"But I want to be a cook." Larissa was not worried about the mountains of vegetables she would work with. It sounded like fun to her. She could almost smell the sweet aroma of freshly baked bread. If only she could go to college to learn how to be a professional chef.

"You would also need to buy food to take along to college during your training," Nadia continued. "I don't have money for that, and neither do you. We hardly have enough to live on."

This was true. Larissa watched the rain pounding the garden plants. *If only I had a father. Then he would have a job, and money wouldn't be an issue.*

"You often look pale," Nadia continued. "I am afraid with such hard work you might pass out sometime." Nadia's face was creased. "My answer is no. If you really think you have to study something, I'd rather see you go to sewing college."

Larissa stood with Sveta outside the mission. They were waiting for the evening Bible study.

"Do you think I could attend sewing college with you and Lena?" asked Larissa. "You've been going a year now and could tell me the steps needed to register."

"Sure, I could do that," Sveta agreed. "I can introduce you to the director."

Larissa's mind raced as she considered all the problems this might bring. *How will I pay for public transportation? What will I eat for lunch? Will I be able to sew well enough to please the teachers?*

"Let's go find a seat," said Sveta, interrupting Larissa's thoughts. She led the way.

Larissa and Sveta found seats near the front of the auditorium. As she waited for the service to begin, Larissa prayed quietly. *Dear God, in Jesus' name, help me to trust in you when I am afraid.*

As Pastor David Miller rose to open the service, Larissa was still lost in thought.

"Greetings to you in Jesus' name. Let's stand for prayer to begin our service."

Larissa jumped as people around her began to rise. She had better pay attention.

It was August before Larissa was finally enrolled in the sewing college in Kiev. There were twenty-three other students in the class.

Larissa rose early on the morning of the first day of classes. She dressed quickly, ate a piece of bread with butter, and headed out the door. Since there were no buses in Lisnyky this early in the morning, she had to run for Khotiv. She started off briskly, hoping someone would stop and offer her a ride. A large truck roared past.

The sun was just peeking up as Larissa jogged into Khotiv and stood in line at the bus stop. Mama had given her a little money to pay for transportation. *I have enough for this week, but then what?* Worry pushed up into her heart once again. *Please help me, God. In Jesus' name.*

When Larissa finally arrived at the last station near the college, she hopped out and ran the rest of the way. She wanted to be on time. She slowed to walk up the large steps to the college entrance. Before entering, she paused to catch her breath.

Along the street, vendors struggled with their carts, and pedestrians pushed their way around them. The bus Larissa had ridden was pulling away from the curb, leaving behind a cloud of smoke. A green taxi-van slowed with a squealing of tires as a young boy darted across the busy intersection.

After entering the tall brick building, Larissa walked quickly to the restroom to check her hair and veiling. She was glad Lena would be in her class. That way she wouldn't be the only girl who dressed differently.

Yelena, the teacher, was an older woman who hardly ever smiled. Today she would be teaching the class how to sew men's clothing.

"This is interesting," said Lena during a break. "I think it's exciting."

"Yes," replied Larissa, "I like it too."

Over lunch Larissa went to the restroom and then outside for some fresh air. She lingered long enough to allow her fellow students time to eat their lunches before returning to sit with the others. *I don't want them to see me without lunch,* she thought. She joined the conversation and hoped no one would notice that she wasn't eating.

Yelena soon started teaching in two shifts since the class was so large. She preferred small, manageable groups. This way everyone could use a machine.

When Larissa was on the last shift, getting home was always a problem. The last Lisnyky bus would have departed the Kiev station, so the only option was to take another bus to Khotiv and walk the remaining hour to Lisnyky.

As she walked home through the darkness, she was usually tired but happy. Since her recent baptism, she had a stronger sense of peace and joy. It had been another milestone in her walk with God as her Father.

One evening as Larissa and Lena were preparing to start the first leg of their trip home together, they missed the bus to Khotiv. With darkness rapidly settling over the city of Kiev, the two girls looked at each other in despair.

"Maybe we can stay overnight at Bethany's house," Larissa finally suggested. "Edwin's family is friendly enough. I could call my mom and let her know."

"Why not?" laughed Lena. "Okay with me. We can at least try." The girls turned back the street that led to Edwin's house.

"Are you sure we should?" asked Lena as she raised her hand to knock. She gave a few light raps. The door swung open. Bethany stood at the entrance with a quizzical but friendly look. They briefly explained their dilemma to her.

"Sure, you can stay overnight. Come in." Bethany waved them in. The house was warm and inviting.

It was late before they settled down, but soon they were fast asleep.

Early in the morning, the sound of a train whistle awoke the two girls with a start. *Vreeeeeeeeeee.* Thinking she had to get out of the way of the thundering locomotive, Lena started screaming and rolled out of bed and down onto Larissa, who was in a lower bed.

After both screaming for a bit, Larissa finally came to her senses and started laughing. "Oh, we are not on a train track!" she said, her voice shaky. Wide awake now, the three girls laughed until their sides hurt.

"I am glad no one is hurt," chuckled Bethany.

"I'm glad it was Lena that landed on me and not a train," Larissa laughed. She winced as she wrapped a blanket around her shoulders.

Alvin and Leona Kramer and their adopted daughter Ashley arrived in the spring to serve with MIM. Their house was within sight of the mission, and Larissa soon learned to know the new pastor and his family.

"Come over to our house," Ashley pleaded one day. "We will eat some popcorn, and Mom can make tea. Maybe you can even stay overnight."

Although grateful for the invitation, Larissa little realized how much she would come to appreciate it. That fall when Larissa missed her bus to Khotiv or had afternoon and evening classes at college, she began staying at Alvin's house occasionally. Their home was cheery and warm, and an extra bed next to Ashley's always welcomed her.

"I really appreciate that you love my daughter and make an effort to talk to her, Larissa," said Leona Kramer the first evening she arrived. "Some youth avoid her. You know, when someone looks or acts a little differently, some people just don't know how to take it. I'm thankful that you accept her and have taken her under your wing. Ashley needs friends like you."[1] She smiled as she pulled the oven door open and peered in. "I think the bread is done," she murmured. Her tall figure moved easily.

Larissa took off her shoes in the entrance and dropped her backpack to follow Ashley into the dining room. Alvin sat in his chair along the wall, drumming his fingers on the arm of the chair. He was a slender man with a scrubby beard and short, curly hair. His rugged features made him appear stern, but he actually had gentle ways and a love of humor.

"Howdy," he drawled. "Where have you been?"

"Oh," giggled Ashley. "Out and about, Daddy."

"Behaving yourselves?" Alvin's blue eyes twinkled.

"Of course," Ashley giggled.

The next morning Leona prepared a delicious breakfast for Larissa before she left to catch the bus. She also packed a big bag of food for Larissa's lunch. Tears came to Larissa's eyes as Leona handed her the large bag of food. "Thanks so much!" Larissa said, giving her a grateful hug.

After leaving Alvin's house, Larissa took a bus to the college. *I am so thankful for Alvin and Leona's thoughtfulness*, she mused as she watched the traffic slide by the bus window.

When Larissa arrived at the classroom, it was still locked and a few other students were waiting. Teacher Yelena had not yet arrived to unlock the room.

"I hope she's in a good mood today," Larissa's friend Zoya remarked as she tucked her short hair behind her ears and hitched up her pants. "If not, I'll make up for it," she joked.

"You better not be too lighthearted." Lena pushed a strand of hair

---

[1] Ashley was killed in a traffic accident on March 26, 2010. She was a friend of the John Esh family and was a passenger when they were struck head-on by a semi truck.

back from her forehead.

Yelena soon arrived and unlocked the classroom. As usual, her face remained indifferent as she greeted them.

Later that morning Larissa wrote down the measurements that Yelena gave to the class. As her teacher sketched the shape of the outfit on the chalkboard, Larissa drew it in her copybook in preparation for the actual sewing lesson.

The next day, eight sewing machines hummed as eight students bent over their machines. The remaining students were given other assignments until the sewing machines were not in use.

It was important to sew exactly as Yelena instructed. If the sewing was off even a fraction of an inch, Yelena would get upset. "Take it apart!" she would yell. "Now!"

She would make them do it over until it was almost perfect.

Larissa at sewing college.

By the second year of her studies, Zoya had become a good friend of Larissa's. They often sat together over lunch break. Sometimes Larissa had nothing to pack for her lunch. One day Zoya probed to find out why.

"Why didn't you bring any lunch?" she asked. "Aren't you hungry?"

"Yes, I am sometimes hungry," Larissa replied. But she tried to avoid her friend's questions and didn't explain why she had no lunch. With no father to support the home and Mama without a regular job, there just wasn't much money.

"Do you have a boyfriend?" Zoya asked Larissa. "Or doesn't your church allow that?"

"Of course our church allows it," cut in Lena, who had sat down beside the two. "We want to get married sometime."

"I don't have a boyfriend yet," said Larissa. "But when I do, it must be the first one that asks me. I asked God to allow no young man to ask me that I am not supposed to marry. The one who asks me first is the one God wants me to marry. Of course, he must be a believer."

"What?!" Zoya's eyebrows shot up. "What if he's ugly? Or mean?"

"I prayed, so I believe God will bring me the right one first."

"Well, that's not my way," Zoya replied.

"It's not mine either," Lena agreed.

As Larissa sketched the next sewing project in her copybook that afternoon, she thought about the lunchtime conversation. She did want to marry, but she did not want to marry just anyone—she wanted a good husband. *God, please be sure he is a good man.*

The second year of college proved better than the first. Since Alvin's home was always open to her, Larissa stayed there quite frequently. This also resulted in having a packed lunch more often.

As Larissa's experience in sewing grew, she started picking up small sewing jobs to get a little income. This made it possible for her to buy some clothes and pay for transportation.

"Could you sew me a dress?" asked Leona one day. "I will pay you for it."

Since she now had some money, Larissa was interested when Becky, daughter of David and Ruth Miller, invited her to their yard sale. "We are going back to the United States for a while," Becky said, "so we're having a yard sale. You should come!" David and his family had served with the MIM mission for a number of years.

"What's a yard sale?" Larissa asked.

"Come and see," Becky replied with a smile.

When Larissa hurried into the mission compound the day of the yard sale, she was surprised to see tables set up outside in the yard.

Clothing, books, and other items lay on the tables for anyone to touch or observe. *So this is a yard sale?* Larissa looked through everything carefully. Other church girls and mothers were also there.

Larissa's heart did a flip when she saw the coat. It was just her size—black with a fur-lined hood. It would make an excellent winter coat. She checked to see how much cash she had. It wasn't enough. *Maybe they will let me pay the rest when I get more money.*

"Could I give you what I have now and pay the rest later?" Larissa asked, her heart pounding.

"Yes, I think that would be okay," Ruth replied.

Larissa was thrilled with her purchase. Now she would have a cozy fall and winter coat. It had pockets on the outside and even one on the inside with a zipper. That was where she would keep her hard-earned money.

The coat was a godsend. That winter when Larissa stood in the snow and the sleet to wait for her bus, she was warm—except for her feet. Her sneakers just did not keep out the moisture and frigid weather. *I wish I could save enough money to buy a pair of boots,* she thought.

One evening Larissa arrived home late, nearly eleven o'clock, with her feet soaking wet and cold.

"Oh, my feet are almost frozen!" she exclaimed when Mama greeted her at the door.

"Come to the kitchen, and I will heat some water." Mama quickly heated a kettle of water and poured it into a basin. While Mama sliced bread and heated some soup, Larissa soaked her feet in the hot water. As her feet and legs warmed, she nearly fell asleep.

"I'm so glad you can sometimes stay with the Kramers when it is late," said Mama. "Alvin and Leona are such good people." She sat on a chair opposite Larissa. "How was your class today?"

"Good. Zoya asked me today if I can come to her house next week one night." Larissa ate the last of her soup. "I would enjoy that."

"Come," said Mama. "Let me wrap blankets around you so you stay warm and sleep well." Feeling warm and loved, Larissa snuggled down in bed and drifted off to sleep.

Cross-Cultural Relationship

2004

"I have a secret to tell you," Larissa told her two friends. Lena and Nina leaned forward. Nina was a young woman attending church whom Larissa had learned to trust and appreciate.

The white Sprinter van bounced its way out the long cobblestone road to the main highway. A vanload from Kiev had been to the village of Berezyanka for an afternoon service.

Berezyanka was a small village out in the middle of nowhere. Because of family connections, one of the villagers had joined the Mennonite church in Kiev. As a result, Lloyd and Betty Troyer and their three youngest children had moved out to the village to begin a new church outreach.

The two-hour drive was a good time to fellowship as it was normally uneventful except for the roughness of the infamous cobblestone road.

As the van's headlights pierced the darkness, a barefooted boy could be seen following a cow along the road. The scantily clad boy stopped and stared as the van passed. A new vehicle was seldom seen in this area.

"Well, are you going to tell us?" Nina asked.

"Pastor Lloyd asked if I would consider writing to his son."

"What?!" the two girls exclaimed together.

"Which one?" asked Lena.

"He said his name is Harold. He lives in America but was in Ukraine a few years ago."

"Do you remember him?" Nina wondered.

"His sister Harmony showed me a photo," Larissa replied. "I do remember filling seed packets with him. But I'd almost forgotten how he looked."

"You're lucky," Lena told her with a twinge of jealousy.

Larissa was quiet for a moment as she thought about her future. She remembered her orphanage friends laughingly predicting that she would marry a foreigner.

Larissa talked with her mother and prayed for wisdom. After nearly a month of praying and seeking God's will, Larissa agreed to begin writing Harold.

"I will let him know," Lloyd said. "He will write to you first."

Larissa was excited at the turn of events. She greatly appreciated Pastor Lloyd and his wife Betty.

How will this work out? she mused. *I can barely write a letter in English. I'll just have to do the best I can.*

Larissa found it hard to control her emotions. What would it be like to have a man in her life? A protector. A provider. Her heart quickened and her mind raced as she thought of her father far away in Siberia. Yes, he was her father, but he had not protected her nor provided for her.

"You need to stop daydreaming and get to work," Lena and Zoya teased during class at college.

Whenever Larissa was at home for the night, she checked the mailbox. When would the letter arrive? What would it say?

Then, one night, there it was—a letter from America! She took the envelope and ran up the terraces behind the house. It was a late summer day, and the tall grasses crackled as she sat down among them, her light blue dress spread around her. She opened the envelope, and out fell a photo and a few sheets of stationery. Eagerly she pored over the letter, reading it and then rereading it. It was actually happening. A man was seeking her friendship!

That fall Larissa wrote a few letters to Harold and received a few more in return. Harold wrote that he was teaching at a local Mennonite school. During their winter break, he was planning to fly to Ukraine to visit her. Her heart fluttered. She wanted to see him, but at the same time she felt terrified. *What will I say? What if he asks to come to our house? It is not even finished. What if he wants a meal?* Her thoughts whirled.

On Christmas Day, Lloyd's family and a few youth headed for the Boryspil International Airport. Harmony bubbled to Larissa as usual, but Larissa was strangely quiet. Her thoughts were on meeting Harold. What could she talk about?

Larissa recognized Harold as he exited the airport doors. As she remembered, he was tall and slender. He pushed a cart with his luggage. Her heart did a flip when he looked at her. After greeting his parents and siblings, he turned in her direction.

"Hi, Larissa. It's nice to see you." He smiled and stuck out his hand.

His handshake was really firm, Larissa thought. *But his face looks gentle.*

Soon the van was heading back to the mission. As they drove along the snowy streets, the youth sang some of the songs they had memorized.

At the mission, they stopped to drop off the Kiev youth before heading south to the village of Berezyanka where Lloyd and Betty lived.

It was nearly nine o'clock when the Sprinter pulled up to Lloyd's home. After unloading Harold's luggage and the groceries Betty had bought in Kiev, they settled down for hot tea and a snack.

Larissa sat next to Harold to talk. They looked through a photo album that had been lying on the coffee table. There were photos of the multipurpose building that had been built next to Lloyd's house for services. *He has a quiet nature,* Larissa observed. Gradually she relaxed as they talked.

"It's been a long day." Harold rubbed his eyes. "I have a gift I brought for you that I want to give you yet. We can talk more tomorrow."

As Harold left the room, Larissa took the empty mugs to the kitchen.

Harold returned soon with a little gift bag. Larissa took it.

"Thank you," she said, smiling up at him.

"Good night," said Harold. "I'll see you tomorrow."

"Good night."

Larissa hurried to Harmony's room where she would be staying for the night and closed the door. She untied the gift to find a small box. Opening the box, she saw a small English Bible with a black cover that snapped shut. She removed it gently and fingered its newness. A tear slipped down her cheek. How had he known that she wanted an English Bible? When she opened it, she found his handwriting on the inside. She wasn't sure how long she sat there, just looking at it. When she heard someone turning the door handle, she knew Harmony was coming to bed, so she quickly put the Bible back in its box.

The week flew by rapidly. Larissa and Harold took walks through the village and talked to the local children. They helped wash dishes and carry wood. *I didn't think he would wash dishes,* Larissa thought. *He does about everything.*

On Thursday, December 30, Lloyd's family took her and Harold to a pizzeria for his birthday. Larissa sat at the table and observed the restaurant. It was the first time she had been in a pizzeria. She savored the Coke and watched it fizz as they waited for the meal.

The pizza was delicious, but the black olives were not to her taste. Harmony agreed to take them, but then put up her hand. "Wait," she said, "Harold likes olives. Why don't you give them to him?" With a big grin Harmony passed the olives on to her brother.

He seems to enjoy almost any kind of food too. Larissa's heart warmed at the blessing of learning to know a young man who loved God. After never having a father who prayed with her or loved her, it was so good to feel cared for.

It was Friday morning when the Troyers and Larissa headed for Kiev to take Harold back to the airport for his flight home. It had been a wonderful week of learning to know each other.

"We need to stop at the Teremky market for a few minutes before we go to the Kiev mission," Larissa heard Betty remind Lloyd. As they entered Kiev, the traffic slowed.

Dear God, prayed Larissa silently as the van moved into the city. *Please have Harold give me a single white rose before he leaves as a confirmation that he is the man you sent for me.*

Snow flurries were falling when the van pulled up to the market. Larissa's heart took a flip when she saw Harold climbing out of the van too. As she went with Harmony to a few vendors, her mind was in a whirl. People pushed their way around the shops and booths. A small dog hopped along on three legs. A few sparrows pecked at sunflower seeds in the snow along the path leading through the market. High-rise apartments loomed behind the marketplace like sentries. Finally Harmony was finished.

I wish Harold wouldn't have to leave, thought Larissa as she climbed back into the van. Harold was already there. He smiled as he handed her a flower. Larissa gasped. She took it and sat next to him. It was a single white rose. Her heart leaped. *God, I can't believe how you answered my prayer. Thank you, God.* She raised the rose and inhaled the delightful fragrance.

Larissa wished the trip to the airport would last longer, but all too soon they arrived. They talked as they waited at the check-in counter.

"Will you call me when you get home?" Larissa asked, looking up into Harold's face. "I will wait for your call."

"I will call as soon as I get back," he promised.

Engaged

2004-2005

"Where have you been?" Leona was squeezing lemons for lemonade. "You're wet. You must have walked quite a distance."

"I walked from the Teremky market." Larissa placed her boots on the register and wiped them with a paper towel.

"Where did you get your rose?"

Larissa blushed. "Harold gave it to me before he left."

"Well, that was nice of him." Leona filled the pitcher with water and stirred the contents. "Did you enjoy your time together?"

"Yes, I did."

The next two weeks were midterm vacation, so Larissa spent a lot of time at the mission sewing room with some of the other youth girls.

She sewed a nightgown and several dresses, as well as a few other items people requested.

Larissa looked forward to the phone calls, letters, and cards she received from Harold. She enjoyed talking more than writing since she could speak English better than write it. *Thank you, God, for the opportunity to learn the English language better.* It was another answered prayer.

One of the frustrations with the phone calls was the poor service. Sometimes she could barely hear what Harold was saying and would struggle through the call. She was glad, though, that calling was an option.

Larissa's heart was light and free. It was so good to have a man in her life. She loved to hear his voice. As she walked along in the darkness of the street, she could see a street lamp throwing light across the mission grounds. She was almost back to Alvin's house from her walk.

She enjoyed Harold's letters and faxes but was embarrassed that she couldn't send many letters back to him. A stamp simply cost too much for her to write very often. She could buy two loaves of bread for the price of one stamp.

Every time a letter arrived, Larissa had mixed feelings. Her heart pounded with anticipation, but she felt guilty that she didn't write back more often. *I can't even call him much because of the cost. Perhaps I should get a job somewhere so I have more money to buy stamps and pay for phone minutes.*

It was the first part of February. The students were sewing on their projects, the room full of humming machines. As Larissa busily sewed, her mind hummed along with the machine as she mulled over her need. She needed money, but how could she get it?

That weekend Larissa decided to ask her mother if she could get a job working with her. It would at least be a start. Her mother had recently found a new job at a seed packaging factory in Kiev.

"Mama, could I quit college and work with you?" Larissa sliced another piece of Ukrainian rye bread and slathered it with butter.

"Since Harold and I are dating, I would like to have more money to buy the things I need."

"Hmm." Nadia paused for a moment. She took the teakettle off the stove and poured the steaming water into her mug. She dipped in the tea bag a few times.

"I could ask the director if he has work for you." Nadia sipped her tea. "This may be a good idea. We really do need money to pay for the gas and electric and to buy clothes and gifts. And if there is a wedding, we will certainly need money."

The next day when Nadia approached the director, he responded positively. "We can always use good workers here. She can start any time."

Larissa felt a tinge of regret at quitting her sewing classes but began working immediately at Interflora, a seed and bulb business. *Finally Mama and I both have a job,* she thought with a sense of satisfaction. Now they would have money to pay the gas and electric bills, purchase shoes, get some meat and cheese ... maybe even some ice cream. Her mouth watered.

The third floor of the building the company used was crowded with tables and boxes of seeds, bulbs, and roots. Larissa was dressed warmly since there was little heat in the building. She sat at a table with three other women who were counting out pumpkin seeds, stuffing them into little packets, and sealing them. Larissa took a small sponge and wiped the open flap. Then she closed it, holding it until the flap sealed.

"What is your name?" a tall, dark-haired girl asked.

"Larissa. And yours?"

"Olenka. I don't work here often, thankfully. Just when I run out of money." She brushed back her shoulder-length hair. "How long have you worked here?"

"I just started this week."

"Why do you wear such a long dress and that white veiling?" Olenka wrinkled her nose. "It draws too much attention."

Engaged

"The church I attend practices this because the Bible says a woman should wear a veiling and be modest." Larissa hurried to place her box of sealed seed packets at the spot the supervisor had shown her.

As Larissa worked alongside the other women and girls, Olenka would sometimes ask embarrassing questions. When Olenka learned that Larissa was dating an American boy, she asked whether he had been with her overnight.

"Of course not," said Larissa. "We have a hands-off practice until we are married."

"What!" Olenka raised her eyebrows and stepped back. "How do you know if you want to marry him?"

"Marriage should be based on love and commitment," replied Larissa. "We marry only in the Lord and not based on sinful desires."

When the Interflora secretary handed Larissa her wages for the week, it felt like a milestone. *My first real wages,* she thought. Carefully she placed the money inside her coat in the special pocket and closed the zipper.

It was a frigid March day when Larissa received a special card from Harold—the kind she had only dreamed about.

> You are someone special,
> Someone who will forever
> have a home in my heart.
> I'm so glad we are together.
> I don't know how else to express it,
> except to say—
> I love you!

In Harold's handwriting were the words:

> *Dear Larissa, do you think we could get married this summer? Please call or write as you think best. May you find God's will.*

Larissa read and reread the card. She wished he had written more. Could it be true? She opened the card again. Her heart was warm and her mind lost in thought. "Thank you, God," she breathed.

Soon the snowdrops were once again pushing up through the thawing drifts of winter. Milder winds began to blow, and rivulets of water trickled along the ground in an attempt to find lower levels across the landscape.

That week, after a time of prayer, Larissa called Harold to talk. She decided she could afford this special phone call.

"I liked the sweet words you wrote in that special card," Larissa said as she shared her heart with Harold. The phone connection seemed to be much clearer this time. "Yes, I will marry you."

The two young people discussed how they would tell their parents and announce their engagement. They were both excited.

It was a few days before Larissa shared the news with her mother. They were relaxing in the kitchen next to the registers.

"Harold asked me to marry him, and after praying about it I have agreed." Larissa studied her mother, who continued to gaze at the seed catalog in her hands.

"We wanted to share this with our parents before we announce our engagement," Larissa went on.

Finally Mama looked up. Her eyes seemed extra bright. "Did you say you're getting married? Really?"

Mother and daughter embraced for a long moment.

"He will make you a good husband," Nadia told her, pushing back. "You will be blessed."

The engagement was soon announced in church, and plans began for a June wedding.

Crushed

2005

"Larissa," said Nadia one evening, "are you sure you are ready to get married?"

"Why not, Mama?" Larissa stopped and looked at her mother in surprise. The gas had been turned down for the day and the room was cool.

"I think you are too young," Nadia replied. "Besides, I will be alone at home when Maxim is away with his father."

"We can't change our plans now." Larissa looked puzzled. *Why does Mama talk like this? She wished me God's blessings. Why is she changing her mind?*

"I don't understand, Mama." Larissa sat down next to the table.

"You would understand if you were me." There was an edge to Nadia's voice. "Mama didn't want me. Andre was not faithful to me.

And now you want to leave me. Don't you care about your mama?"

"Of course I care about you," insisted Larissa. Her head hurt. Why was Mama talking like this? The wedding date was already set.

The next week seemed like a long one. Larissa could feel the tension when she was with her mother. They tried to be congenial, but some days the lack of peace was almost more than Larissa could stand.

Some days her mother seemed to change her mind and talked favorably about the marriage.

"I suppose it will be good for you to have a husband," she said. "Then I would have some grandchildren. That would be a good thing for me. Maybe it's okay for you to go ahead."

Larissa's heavy heart and the way she felt must have been transmitted over the phone when she spoke with Harold.

"Are you doing okay?" Harold asked her. Larissa tried to avoid the question by asking about his teaching and other work. She could sense that he knew something was wrong.

As the days passed, Nadia continued to bring up the idea of canceling the marriage.

"I just don't think you should marry Harold right now," she argued. Larissa could see that her mother was becoming more upset with time. "I still need you at home."

"But you gave me your blessing," Larissa pleaded. She was nearly in tears. She watched as her mother prepared for the spring gardening.

"Yes, but I should have given it more thought first." Nadia continued to poke seeds into the potting soil.

A few days later Larissa spent the night at Alvin's house. She enjoyed escaping from the tension at home.

"You look tired and sad about something," remarked Leona. "Would a cup of sweet tea help?"

"Can we talk?" Larissa leaned against the counter. Leona was slicing bread for supper.

"Sure. What's wrong?"

"It's Mama. She's changed her mind about Harold and me getting married." Larissa's voice trembled. "I don't know what to do."

"I think your mother doesn't know what to think." Leona gathered Larissa in her arms and held her tight until the sobs subsided.

"I want to please my mother," Larissa went on. "But she changes her mind every few days." Larissa reached for a tissue on the shelf. "Last Wednesday evening one of the sisters in church asked me why I don't care about my mother. She asked why I am leaving her. Mama was probably telling her what she has been telling me. It's not fair. I do care for Mama, but Harold and I are engaged."

"I think it will work out," said Leona. "You must respect your mother, but eventually you can marry Harold. You just might have to wait a bit longer."

Larissa felt better after talking with Leona about her trouble. *But what should I tell Harold? He will be hurt if I tell him Mama says we must wait.*

Another week passed before Harold called. Larissa didn't answer the phone. She felt horrible, but she simply could not talk to him. Not now. The phone rang again, and it was his number. Larissa ran to her bedroom, shut the door, and fell on her bed. She wept huge sobs until she couldn't cry any longer.

"Hi, Larissa," Harold's mother greeted her. "How have you been?"

"Not too good." Larissa looked away. She and Mama were attending the outreach church in Khotiv, and Pastor Lloyd and Betty were also present. Now the service was over, and people were leaving the church building.

"What's the matter?" Betty asked.

"Some days Mama is okay with Harold and me getting married, but the next day she is against it." Larissa sighed. "Did Harold ask about me?"

"He said he tried to call you, but either it didn't connect or you didn't hear the call."

"I am sorry about that. Mama thinks we should wait. Maybe you can tell Harold." Larissa could feel tears welling up in her eyes. Troubled in thought, she turned and walked toward the mission van.

Harold could hear the traffic going by the house. It was a snowy evening with temperatures hovering near freezing. He was living in his parents' house while they were serving in Ukraine. The house sat right beside State Route 655, the main road running through the Big Valley of central Pennsylvania.

That evening as he cleaned the kitchen, he noticed the wallpaper coming loose above the stove. He would need to find some wallpaper glue and fix it, or maybe he could just use some Scotch tape. He smoothed the wallpaper tighter. As he did, another paper behind it slid out a fraction.

Oh. What's this? He pulled the large paper from behind the wallpaper and stared at it. It was someone's pencil artwork.

His heart stopped. It was a drawing of a heart cracked in half with a large dagger stuck in the crack. His sensitive nature took over, and his heart sank. Was this a premonition of something between him and Larissa? Surely not. But it had seemed Larissa wasn't in the mood to talk when he called the last time.

Harold laid the artwork on top of the fridge and finished his cleaning. He prayed as he worked. He would call and ask Mom if she knew of anything happening with Larissa that could be affecting their courtship. As he lay down to sleep that night, he felt as if a weight was upon his chest. He turned to find a comfortable position, but sleep evaded him.

"Hello, Mom." Harold could hear his voice echo faintly as he spoke. "How are you all doing?" He was making a phone call to his parents in Berezyanka.

"Oh, I think we are doing okay. Dad and Henry are out on visitation, and Harmony is over helping an elderly neighbor lady. How are you?"

"Okay. We are getting ready for our year-end program, which will be here before we know it."

"Do you have your songs and parts all picked out?"

"Pretty much," Harold responded. "I need to choose one more song yet."

"How's Cameron doing—that boy with the learning disabilities?"

"Much better than last year."

Harold could wait no longer to ask his question. He would have to change the subject.

"How's Larissa?" He hesitated. "I still haven't been able to get through to her."

"I was finally able to talk to her at church this last Sunday. Dad was asked to preach in Khotiv, so I saw her there."

"Good." Harold breathed a sigh of relief. "Is she okay?"

"Yes, she's okay." His mother paused. "But the way it sounds, Nadia is not sure about Larissa getting married. I think she needs more time to get used to the idea."

Harold's heart felt like a knife had pierced it. He could not believe what was happening. Even though he had suspected that something might be wrong, he couldn't believe that there might be no wedding.

After the phone call, he knelt and prayed. "Dear God, you know what is happening. Can you please correct whatever is wrong? I trust in you and trust my future into your hands. Please, dear God, help me accept your will concerning Larissa and me and our plans."

As the days passed, there were no more phone calls to or from Ukraine between him and Larissa. He sent a card saying he was praying for her so she would know he hadn't forgotten her.

One evening after school, Harold gathered up his books and headed for home. As he motored along, he pondered his recent change of plans. He thought of the words of a song: "God's way is best; I will not murmur although the end I may not see." He wanted to believe this, but found himself struggling. *It's sure not easy to be thankful for what is happening, but maybe God has something greater in mind.*

Along Route 655, or the Big Valley Pike as the locals sometimes called it, Amish farmers were bouncing along behind horses as they plowed the unbroken soil. A few brave ones were already planting corn in hopes of beating the late spring rains.

As Harold traveled northeast along the main road, Jack's Mountain rose to his right and Stone Mountain to the left, like sentinels guarding the many farms and homes across the rolling landscape between them. The valley at its widest point was about four miles across.

During that week, Harold fasted and prayed about his travel plans and his future with Larissa. *If there is a future,* he mused soberly. *Surely it will work out.*

The next Sunday morning, Harold drank in the sermon. It seemed to be a message from God especially for him. The theme was about trusting in God's sovereignty, and Harold's mind wandered briefly to his courtship that seemed to be on hold. God knew this was going to happen, and maybe He was allowing it for a reason. He would have to trust that God was in control.

After the service, Harold spoke briefly with a few of the youth boys, then moved back the aisle. He shook hands with a few of the older men. He had been a member of the Pleasant View Amish-Mennonite church for a few years now.

"Are you happy?" asked Sam Peachey, whom they called "Driver Sam."

"I have much to be thankful for," Harold responded with a smile as his mind immediately went to Larissa. "But I suppose I am not always happy."

"Well, you should be," chuckled Sam. "You look healthy, and you've got a roof over your head—and you even have a girlfriend."

"Yes, you are right. I am blessed." Harold was ready to move on. He paused to shake hands with Kore Yoder.

"God bless you," Kore greeted him. "How's school going? What grades do you teach?" He smiled. "You probably told me before, but my forgetter is getting better with age."

After answering the older man's questions, he turned to move on.

"Stop by sometime this week," Kore said.

"I'll try," Harold nodded.

Leaving the church house, Harold drove over to his cousin Calvin Yoder's home where he enjoyed southern hospitality, chicken and rice, and sweet tea. He enjoyed the down-to-earth atmosphere, the many small and not-so-small cousins playing at his feet, and a relaxing Lord's Day afternoon. Through the open window he could hear a goat bleating and a few clucking chickens.

The week passed quickly with final quizzes and tests, program practices in the school basement, and a number of extra-curricular activities.

On Thursday evening after the youth singing at the nursing home, Harold decided to stop and see Kore Yoder. The old man shook his hand heartily and told him to find a seat.

"Did you buy your ticket yet?" asked Kore.

"I have been looking for a ticket, but I haven't bought one yet." Harold studied the older man. Kore's thin frame was getting weaker as he grew older. He could still walk well, but he took his time getting around.

"I figured you would be flying over as soon as school is out," Kore replied with a smile. He sank back into his recliner. "The reason I asked is because I want to buy it for you."

"I wasn't expecting that." Harold shifted nervously.

"I have been wanting to do something for you and your girlfriend, so this is what I have decided to do. You buy a ticket and bring me the receipt."

Harold's heart swelled with gratitude. It was a blessing to be part of a loving fellowship. He knew he wasn't worthy of the gift, but the best thing to do was graciously accept it.

After the end-of-the-year program and picnic at school, Harold packed his luggage. His cousin Miriam agreed to take him to the airport in State College to catch his flight.

"Have a good trip," Miriam smiled. Her dark eyes glistened. "I'll be praying for you that things will work out."

Harold had grown to appreciate Miriam's kind and compassionate responses to life. She had been a helper in his classroom the past year, and they had learned to know each other better.

Harold closed his eyes as the small commuter jet whistled down the runway and winged its way into the sky. He wasn't thinking much about the flight. His mind was on a special girl over in Ukraine—one who seemed to be escaping him. His thoughts eventually turned to prayer, and a calming peace surrounded him as he dozed off.

Larissa returned to the sewing college in May. With her marriage postponed, she decided she might as well finish her year and get better grades for her diploma. She was glad, however, for the money she had saved during the three months she had worked at the seed and bulb business.

The small city bus rumbled along, stopping to pick up passengers and drop others off along its normal route. The bus vibrated as it traveled down the cobblestone road, but the occupants of the bouncing vehicle thought nothing of it. This was Kiev. Some roads were paved, but many were still cobblestone. Stone buildings a thousand years old dotted the city as a testament to its ancient history.

Larissa, on her way home from a day at the sewing classes, sat in the back of the bus and watched the city slide by. Her thoughts drifted to Harold, who had written that he would be flying to Ukraine as soon as school was out. She looked forward to their meeting with mixed feelings.

Since she had returned to college, she was again frequently spending the night at Alvin's house. One evening when they both happened to be in the living room, Alvin spoke to her about Harold. "I heard that you and Harold have stopped dating. Is that so?" Alvin wrinkled his nose and tapped his fingers on the arm of his chair.

"Well, yes . . . Or no. I don't know," stammered Larissa. "Mama said she thinks I should wait. So I decided to stop for now."

"I want to give you some advice. Look, who do you want to marry? One of the other boys around here? Who would you ever find as good as what you have?" Alvin glared at her. "Harold is a decent young man. What more do you want? Do you hear me?"

"You're probably right," replied Larissa, blushing.

"You need to keep on dating him and marry him," Alvin continued. "Where did you come up with this idea anyway?"

"It's because of my mother. One day she says she doesn't want me to marry him, but then a few days later she says it might be okay."

Larissa sighed. "I don't know what to think about it. She says I don't care about her and that I just want to leave her."

As Larissa pondered Alvin's words that night in bed, she made a decision. Out of respect for her mother, there would be no wedding this summer, but she would continue to date Harold. Alvin was probably right. After all, she had gotten a number of confirmations that if she wanted to get married, Harold was the one to be her husband. Her heart lightened and the future looked a little brighter.

Bible Camp

2005

The July weather along the Dnieper River outside of Kiev was sultry, with just enough breeze to disturb the mosquitoes that hovered along the water's edge. The water in the Dnieper River flowed from the turf swamps of the Valdai Hills in western Russia. The river then wound its way south through Russia, Belarus, and Ukraine until it reached the capital city of Kiev. From there it flowed on south until it emptied into the Black Sea near Crimea.

South of Kiev, the MIM mission had set up a Bible camp along the river. Larissa had been asked to help with the children at the camp and was in charge of the physical education class for the girls. Today they planned to go swimming. A few large tents for the children and several small tents for the caretakers were scattered among the trees back from the river's edge. A few puffs of smoke curled out of a pile of ashes and log ends as the last wisps of the morning fog disappeared in the piercing rays of the sun.

Throughout the camp, groups of children sat in circles, listening to their teachers. If the teacher was English, a Ukrainian interpreter helped bridge the language barrier. After listening to a Bible story, each child was given a paper with questions to be answered.

At lunchtime, an excellent meal always awaited the hungry children and teachers. Sometimes there was borscht, and often there were meatballs and seasoned potatoes and cooked buckwheat. Large kettles of compote, a cooked fruit drink, had been prepared, as well as hot tea and coffee.

Larissa smiled with anticipation as she gathered up the children's swimming clothes and some towels. The morning classes were over, lunch had been eaten, and now it was time for some recreation.

"Let's go to the river," she called to the girls in her care.

"Yay!" The lively youngsters grabbed their towels and ran for the water. It didn't take long for the girls to splash into the river for their daily swim and bath.

Larissa hung her towel on a branch close to the water's edge and then splashed into the water. She swam out with a few older girls to a deeper area. Soon some of the other youth girls who were helping with camp came to join them.

"Don't come out too far," Larissa warned the younger girls. "Stay close to the shore."

Larissa slapped at a mosquito that had pricked her shoulder and dived underwater to escape a few more that were hovering about her head. When she came up, she shook the water out of her eyes and looked around. It was a beautiful day to be at the river. In the distance she could see a few fishing boats crawling along in the deeper areas.

After their hour of bathing in the water, it would be the boys' turn for their daily swim. Larissa helped the younger girls dry and dress to return to camp.

Larissa's heart went out to the girls in her supervision since she knew that some of them, like herself, didn't have a father. Others had drunkard fathers, with mothers who could barely provide for them. Perhaps her love and kindness to the youngsters would give them hope. Her mind drifted to Harold, who was also in camp.

He had flown over after his school let out, and they had been together a number of times since he had arrived. They had enjoyed touring the Botanical Gardens in Kiev, shopping in the city, and taking walks around Teremky near the mission. Now that he was also helping at the camp, they saw each other more frequently.

Larissa noticed that Harold enjoyed helping with the children, and they respected him. *No wonder he enjoys teaching school. I am sure he will love our children too if we marry. He does seem quieter than he was earlier. I hope he's okay.*

That night as Larissa and her friend Nina lay in the large girls' tent, they talked quietly. Most of the younger girls were sleeping, and through the crack in the door drapes Larissa could see the stars. Tree frogs croaked their summer songs, and somewhere a long-eared owl hooted.

"So how do you get along with Harold?" murmured Nina. "He's so quiet, and you are more outgoing and fun-loving."

Larissa was quiet, pondering her friend's comment. Yes, Harold did seem quiet, but maybe it was because of the change of plans in their lives.

"He has always been kind and respectful to me," Larissa replied. "It seems like he always has good advice. I guess I could say I trust him."

"But he's tall and you are short."

"That doesn't matter a bit!" Larissa retorted.

The next day during a break in activities, Larissa and Harold took a walk down to the river. Suddenly Harold turned to face her.

"Larissa, would you like to fly back to America with me and visit the States? If I applied for a visa for you now, you could fly back at the same time Dads and I do." A ray of sunlight burst through the treetops, illuminating his face. Larissa stared. The picture was so serene and pure. He did love her and cared how she felt.

Larissa sighed. "I don't know. I'll have to talk to Mama." They continued walking along the sandy shore of the river.

After the week of Bible camp was over, Larissa found herself at home again. It was Saturday, and Mama wanted her to help with cleaning and weekend preparation.

"Harold asked if I would want to fly back with his family to America this summer." Larissa wrung out the last article of clothing for her mother, who was hanging them on the line tied between two trees.

"Where are you going to get the money for your ticket?" her mother replied. "We don't have money to buy one."

"I know." Larissa turned to catch sight of Maxim trudging up the dirt path toward them. "Here comes Maxim."

Maxim gave his mother a kiss and then entered the house.

"What if Harold would offer to pay for the visa and ticket?" Larissa continued.

"Did he offer?" Nadia asked as she hung another dress on the line.

"No, but I suppose he knows I don't have the money."

"But you wouldn't want to be obligated to him," Nadia said.

I don't care about being obligated to him if I can fly to America, Larissa thought. *Besides, we are dating, so it wouldn't matter to visit his country even if we don't marry.* Still thinking, she carefully swept the dirt walkway leading to the house. *At least Mama didn't say no.*

32

The Visa

2005

The third week of Bible camp was for the youth of the Mennonite churches, other Christian youth from around the country, and some local unchurched youth. It was a time when young people could feel free to ask the hard questions of life. It was also a time when youth could make friends with other youth and listen to their testimonies and struggles.

"My name is Lecia." The tall girl had an awkward but friendly smile. "What is yours?"

"Larissa."

"It looks like you got overbaked," Lecia said with a grin. "I am glad you crawled out of the oven before you burned up." The girls laughed.

"My mother and I were in Crimea last week for a vacation beside the Black Sea," Larissa explained. "There was lots of sun there." She picked up her songbook. "Do you like to sing?"

"Like a bird," came the answer from her new friend.

"Why don't we sing then?" suggested Larissa as she pulled out her songbook. Lecia dug around in her backpack for her books and Nina moved closer. The girls sang for a while, and then talked quietly until it was time for bed.

As Larissa lay wrapped in her blanket, her mind drifted to her relationship with Harold. *He seems like a good man. I think I want to marry him. I will go to America if he offers to help me get there. I will tell him.*

The next day at lunch Harold and Larissa moved through the lunch line together. The sun was high in the sky, so they sat under the trees to avoid the heat. The sandy soil was dry and they kicked up dust as they found a place to relax. A few youth sat on folding chairs, and others found chunks of wood to sit on.

"So what did you decide about going to America with me?" Harold asked. His voice was quiet. "I need to fill out the paperwork for a visa for you if you want to go along."

Just then a breeze kicked up, and a napkin fluttered away. A few of the youth boys were laughing heartily about a story one of them was telling. A bullfrog croaked from his perch near the river.

"Yes, I'll go along. Let me know when." Larissa smiled at Harold as she got up. They stepped in line with the others to get dessert, which consisted of honey cake, slices of apples, and hot tea.

"I think I will grab a cup of coffee yet." Harold stepped into the food tent. He poured some hot water and pitched in a spoonful of Nescafé instant coffee.

After lunch was over, Larissa met Betty, who had come to camp along with Pastor Lloyd. Betty gave her a big hug.

"How are you doing?" Betty smiled.

"Okay." Larissa returned her smile.

"Can we talk a few minutes?" Betty motioned to the large white Sprinter.

"Of course."

"Has Harold talked to you about going to America to visit?" Betty cleared her throat. A fly buzzed around them and landed on the dash. Its feet made marks in the dust as it landed.

Larissa glanced outside and could see the youth moving toward the afternoon class taught by one of the MIM board members. Harold was moving to find a spot among the youth boys.

"Yes, we just talked about it today, and I told Harold I'd go along."

"Good!" Betty replied. "I'm so glad. I think it will be good for both of you. You will be able to see what America is like and see Harold's home. You can travel with our family to visit other friends and relatives across America. I think you will enjoy it."

Larissa's heart beat faster at the thought. Was it really becoming a reality?

Larissa felt light and free as she pushed into the girls' tent to grab her Bible and study papers before hurrying to the assembly tent. She hoped Harold would be able to get a visa for her. Her mind kept drifting from her lesson to Harold and the trip to America.

"Where are your affections? Do you love the world's system, or do you love God?" Brother Andy Miller's voice cut through her consciousness. *Is he talking to me?* Larissa tried harder to keep her mind on the lesson.

Larissa enjoyed the conversations around the campfire, the messages by the pastors, and the daily Bible teaching they received. She especially enjoyed Jake Yoder's expressive preaching. He made the message come alive.

Two days later, Larissa and Harold found themselves traveling to the American Embassy. Driver Meesha was taking them in the large white Sprinter van at a fast clip. He careened around vehicles and punched the brakes frequently for pedestrians. Larissa hung onto her seat and tried to talk as they flew along the streets.

"The way he is driving, a person would think this was an important trip," said Harold with a grimace. "An emergency trip."

"Maybe it is." Larissa braced herself on the seat in front of her.

There were a few people ahead of them when they arrived at the embassy. A street sweeper was cleaning the paved area around the brick building. She paused to stare at Harold and Larissa for a moment before continuing her assignment. After waiting for a few minutes, the door opened and a guard waved them into the building. They passed through security and then spoke with the guard about their purpose in coming. Harold showed them his passport and documents, explaining what he needed. The guard waved them in.

"Go down the hallway to the end. Then turn left and you'll see a waiting line. Seat yourself until you are called." The guard pointed down the hall. Larissa could see the end.

Nearly thirty minutes passed as they awaited their turn. The building was immaculate. There was no dirt or dust, and the air smelled fresh.

"I am sure glad you are doing this," Larissa murmured, leaning closer. "Paperwork is not my thing. I would rather work in the garden."

"I don't mind it. Actually, I sort of enjoy it." Harold smiled.

The week after Bible camp, Larissa worked at home with her mother. There was plenty to do during the long summer days. Both she and Harold anxiously awaited news from the American Embassy.

At the Wednesday evening Bible study, Lena slid in beside Larissa. The service was just beginning, with Alvin Kramer beckoning everyone to stand for prayer.

Lena turned toward her as soon as the service came to a close. "Are you going to America?" she asked. They were heading outside to the waiting Sprinter—their ride back to their villages.

"If the embassy gives me a visa," Larissa replied, hugging her friend.

"We are waiting for their approval."

"I wish I could go." Lena made a face.

"Your turn may come," Larissa assured her. "You never know." They hurried outside with the others. Some of the elderly were already in the waiting van while others stood around the mission center talking.

"Where is Harold?" Sveta asked as she pushed close.

"He is in Berezyanka with his family for a few days," Larissa said. She turned to see who had nudged her. Galina was staring at her with admiration.

Galina was an elderly sister in the church whom they sometimes referred to as the "goat lady." She was a retired teacher who raised goats on her little farm. Short and wrinkled with a broad smile extending from ear to ear, she always seemed happy.

"God bless you, Larissa. I am so happy for you. I hear you may be going to America. Will you be staying there?" Galina's eyes were bright in spite of her age.

"I don't think so," Larissa responded. "I am going with Harold's family to visit America. He wants me to see his homeland."

"That is a good idea." Galina gave her a big hug and a kiss. "God be with you as you go. May He keep you safe on that big bird you'll be riding over the waters."

The next day Larissa received a call from Harold. She was so glad to hear from him.

"We need to appear at the embassy for an interview," Harold explained. "The officer wants to interview you before giving his answer about your going to America or not."

"When is the interview?"

"Next Tuesday. Will that work for you?"

Of course it'll work, thought Larissa. *I will make it work.* Her heart quickened as Harold explained the procedure.

"On Monday evening, I will plan on coming to Kiev," he said. "Meet me at the mission Tuesday morning, and we'll go out by public transportation to the embassy."

As Larissa and Harold sat and waited for Larissa's call for the interview, they were both thinking the same thing.

"What if they don't let me go?" Larissa voiced her thoughts as she looked into Harold's quiet blue eyes. "Then what?"

"Why don't we pray."

As the two prayed for God to reveal His plan and to work it out for His glory, peace stole over both of them, replacing worry with calmness.

"Zaikova Larissa Andreevna." The call had come for the interview. Larissa walked back the hallway to the enclosed compartment. There was no door, just an opening between two walls. The officer leaned across the counter toward her.

"Why do you want to travel to America?" Larissa answered his questions and then signed a paper he pushed toward her.

"You will be issued a visa, and your passport should be delivered to the address you provided in a couple of weeks. Any questions?"

"No." Larissa shook her head. Her mind was in a whirl. She was going to America!

"He said I can go!" Larissa told Harold excitedly. Her eyes shone with excitement.

"Great!" said Harold, getting to his feet. "God answered our prayer."

As the two young people rode the metro train and buses back to the mission, they discussed their future. What should they take along on the trip? It was exciting to think of purchasing airline tickets, packing suitcases, and telling their friends the good news. They were flying to America together!

After a few weeks, Larissa started checking the mailbox every time she passed.

"Those mailbox hinges are looking shiny from all the activity," remarked Maxim with a grin as he wolfed down his breakfast of buckwheat and fried eggs.

"At least it won't rust shut," Larissa grinned. She sliced a piece of Ukrainian bread.

"Maybe you should check at the post office," said Mama. "They would have noticed a special package from the American Embassy."

Larissa was glad her mother and her brother were looking forward to the visa almost as much as she was. They were excited that one of them would be going to America.

Then the letter came. It was an official letter saying that more time was needed and the information for the visa had been sent to Washington, D.C., to verify a discrepancy in the spelling of her name. Larissa immediately called Harold.

"I think everything will be okay," Harold responded. "Does the letter say when the passport and visa will be returned?"

"The date is around the same as our departure date. That's on Tuesday only two weeks away." Larissa could hardly hear Harold since the connection was not the best.

"We will pray and ask God to work it out," Harold encouraged her.

Larissa continued to watch for the passport and notified the postmaster of the important mail. Surely it would come in time.

In preparation for the trip, Larissa packed a light brown backpack she would use for a carry-on. She had bought the backpack with her hard-earned sewing money.

Harold had told her she could take a purse or backpack on the aircraft and a larger suitcase as check-in baggage. What would she take? She didn't have enough to fill a large suitcase, much less the two suitcases that the airlines allowed for international traveling.

Finally it was the last Sunday before she and Lloyd's family were to leave for America, and the passport still had not arrived. Nadia was not feeling well and decided to stay at home, but Larissa wanted to attend the morning worship services. She was a few minutes late since she had to wait on the bus. She sang as she walked back the street toward the mission. Rounding the turn, she saw the three-story mission building looming before her. She could hear someone inside preaching. Quietly she took a seat in the alcove to the right of the main auditorium.

Brother Peter Vasilyevich was teaching a Sunday school lesson. He spoke about trusting God for all our needs. "The Scriptures say that God will supply all our needs," Peter instructed. "In Isaiah 40:11, it says, 'He shall feed his flock like a shepherd: he shall gather the lambs with his arm, and carry them in his bosom, and shall gently lead those that are with young.'"

Larissa's imagination ran wild for a moment. How peaceful it would be for Jesus to gather her in His arms. *He would be able to answer all my questions. He could work a miracle and make the visa come immediately. But I guess I can pray to Him.*

After the service was over, Larissa greeted Naomi Zehr, a clinic nurse from Canada, who was also sitting in the alcove.

"Are you excited about your visit to America?" asked Naomi.

"I am, but I am also a bit worried about my passport, which hasn't come yet," Larissa admitted. "Our flight is on Tuesday, so we only have tomorrow for the passport and visa to arrive in time for me to go."

"I will be praying for you." Naomi's smile was gentle and caring. "I will pray that your passport comes tomorrow."

The church folk moved about and fellowshipped as the two girls talked. Soon the call came for those riding the Sprinter van to get on board.

"Would you like to come to our house for lunch?" asked Leona.

"Yes," interjected Ashley, who had pushed close. "You need to come over one last time before you fly off to the States." Her face wrinkled into a small smile.

Larissa enjoyed the meal with the Kramers. She relaxed in the warm hospitality and friendship.

That evening Larissa looked over her few essentials she had laid out for the trip. She prepared for bed, then knelt to pray.

"Dear God, I want to live in a way that pleases you," she prayed. She concluded her prayer with, "Please send the passport tomorrow so I can go along to America if it's not against your will. In Jesus' name, Amen."

She would go to the post office tomorrow and check with the postmaster, but now she must get some rest. She and Maxim had taken a walk in the evening to their cousin's house in Lisnyky. She was tired from a long day and ready for some sleep.

Monday morning dawned clear and beautiful, with sunshine streaming into Larissa's room. The large windows on the south and east sides of her room afforded a wide view of their little valley. It was the day before her flight to America. Her dream flight. If only the passport would come. Then her prayer would become a reality.

That morning Larissa helped Mama tidy the house, water the garden, and wash a few clothes. She drew water from the well behind the house. She boiled some water, made a cup of black tea with plenty of sugar, and tried to think about something other than the passport. A mouse scurried along the wall.

When the afternoon sunrays heated the little valley, Larissa climbed to her bedroom and looked through her luggage once again to see if she had missed anything. As she perused her belongings she heard voices below her. She peered out her bedroom window and saw the mail lady talking with her mother, who had been relaxing in the shade of their house.

Larissa dropped the shoes she had been holding and ran down the stairs. She had one burning question: Had the passport come? She burst out of the house just in time to see the mail lady hand a package to Mama.

Both women turned to see Larissa hurrying toward them. Mama handed the package to Larissa.

"I think this is what we have been looking for," she said.

Larissa scanned the package. Yes, there was the official stamp. She tore the package open and out dropped her international passport. Flipping through it, she found the single-page visa. It was a single-entry fiancée visa—her pass to America! It had come in time. Her dream was coming true.

There was just one little problem: Larissa still did not like flying. Although she wanted to visit America, she didn't relish the idea of being in an aircraft. *I'll make it,* she finally decided. *I wonder what America will be like.* She indulged in a pleasant recollection of her trip to Spain nearly ten years earlier. Pushing aside her worries about flying, she carefully packed her backpack.

33

A New World

2005

The flight from Kiev to Munich, Germany, lasted only a couple hours. After landing and deplaning, Harold and Larissa said goodbye to the rest of the Troyer family, who were taking a different route back to the States. Since there was nearly a three-hour layover, the two young people took their time, strolling along with their carry-ons and enjoying each other's presence.

"Why don't we stop and get a drink." Harold pointed to a small café. "Would you like some tea or coffee?" They drew up closer to read the chalkboard menu. Airport pedestrians moved past them. Some were walking leisurely, while others ran to catch their next flight.

"I would like something cool," Larissa replied as she scanned the menu. "How about a milkshake or smoothie?"

"Sounds good. Do you also want a muffin or maybe a Schnitzel sandwich?" Harold grinned.

"No." Larissa shook her head. "It's too expensive. Besides, I am not that hungry since they served us a light breakfast on our flight from Kiev."

It is so relaxing to be with Harold. Maybe that's why the flight was not as bad as I anticipated. Larissa finished her milkshake and sat back. *He seems to be at ease and unworried. Why is he so calm? Does he ever worry?* She kept her thoughts to herself as they discussed their upcoming flight and their plans once they reached America. *Perhaps he is calm and unworried because he is older,* she decided. *He is twenty-eight years old. Maybe that makes him more confident.*

"We should find our gate so we know where it is and check for any changes or delays." Harold picked up their carry-ons. "I'll carry yours for now."

The next flight was a much longer one since it crossed the Atlantic Ocean. Larissa and Harold chatted for a while, then tried to sleep. Since they were going in the same direction as the sun, it was hard to rest. Finally they dozed off.

After several hours, the lights came on again for the meal service. Groggily Larissa awoke from her sleep. Somewhere a baby's crying could be heard above the hum of the engines and the murmur of waking passengers.

"How long do we have yet?" Larissa unstrapped her seatbelt and stood up. "I need to stretch a bit."

"I don't know for sure, but I suspect we have two or three hours yet." Harold slid out of his seat and stood in the aisle. The flight attendants with their food carts were slowly moving toward them.

After a good meal and some walking about the cabin, Larissa felt better. *I am ready to get off this plane though,* she thought. She breathed a silent prayer. It was so good to know that God was directing her life.

He was caring for her and leading her each step of the way.

She thought of the monthly food parcel they received from Christian Aid Ministries, the house that Edward Miller had built for them, and Alvin and Leona's care of her while she was in sewing college. God had never failed to provide for her and her mother. She could also see that even though God had never changed the situation with her earthly father, He had now sent Harold into her life. *Why, God? Why are you doing this for me? I am not worthy, and yet you keep answering my prayers and providing.*

When the giant aircraft touched down at Dulles International Airport in Washington, D.C., Larissa could feel her heart pounding. She was here. In America. Excitedly she peered out the window. She could see the airport terminal, the runways, and a distant tree line.

After taxiing for a few minutes, the aircraft came to a lurching halt and the seat belt sign was shut off with a quiet *dong*, signaling a stampede to disembark. Passengers grabbed their carry-on luggage from the overhead bins and stood in the aisles waiting for the cabin door to open. Harold and Larissa collected their carry-ons and followed the other passengers off the plane.

People were walking and talking on all sides of them as they moved toward the baggage claim. They moved down a long ramp with other passengers to pick up their luggage. Everyone seemed happy, and people were respectful of each other's space. A tall man walking beside them caught Larissa's eye.

"Hi," he said. His ponytail swung with an audacious flop.

Larissa moved closer to Harold. It almost seemed as if these people had been drinking vodka.

"Why is everyone so happy?" she whispered to Harold.

"What do you mean?"

"The people."

"I don't understand." Harold looked bewildered as he looked around.

They were now beside the baggage carousel waiting for their suitcases.

"Everyone smiles at me."

Harold relaxed as he finally understood. He chuckled.

"That's just the way it is in America. Most people are friendly even if they don't know you. It's not unusual for folks to smile and wave even if they are not family or neighbors."

They soon recovered the suitcases and headed for immigration. The luggage needed to be checked through customs, and the passports stamped at entry. Then they needed to place the suitcases on a belt to be sent to the next plane taking them the last leg to Pennsylvania.

The flight to State College, Pennsylvania, lasted only about an hour. As Larissa descended the steps that had been pushed up to the aircraft's door for deplaning, she could see a small cluster of buildings.

"This is just a small airport," remarked Harold, seeming to read her thoughts.

When they entered the airport terminal, a man and a girl moved toward them. They were smiling.

"Well, howdy." The man was dressed in plain clothes and wore a black hat. "How are you, Harold?" He shook his hand, then turned to Larissa.

"My name is Calvin, and this is my daughter Miriam." Miriam smiled and gave Larissa a hug. She was also dark-haired, but it was her eyes that Larissa noticed. They were eyes that appeared kind and understanding. Larissa liked her immediately.

"Let's go find your luggage," said Calvin.

Where are the palm trees? wondered Larissa as they motored along the outskirts of State College. Most of the trees and foliage were much like the ones she knew in Ukraine. She had imagined palm trees growing profusely, immaculate lawns around every house, and large, expensive homes on every corner. She did see some upper-class houses, but many were not even brick. Maybe America was not what she had thought it was.

Larissa was impressed with the roads, however. They were like smooth glass. *I have not felt one pothole or bump yet,* she thought. *And the traffic is moving along so decently and lawfully. I think it would be fun to drive in America. Maybe someday I will.*

"This valley with mountains on either side is beautiful," Larissa remarked as she observed the rolling landscape with farms spread across the wide valley. On both sides of the road were fields of corn and beans broken only by an occasional fencerow. They passed a farm where a team of horses was pulling a hay baler and a wagon. An Amish family was putting up hay. Most of the places they passed were well-kept and organized.

"This is what we call the Big Valley," Harold replied. "Ahead of us is the village of Belleville."

This is about the size of Lisnyky, Larissa thought as they drove through the little village. After driving through town they pulled into a lane off the main road they had been traveling.

"Here is the house Mom and Dad bought last year and where I am living." Harold pointed to a two-story house with vinyl siding.

"Your parents should be here soon." Calvin looked at the vehicle clock. "Sam Peachey, who most of us call Driver Sam, went to pick them up at the Harrisburg airport."

A few weeks later Larissa traveled with Harold's family to the Midwestern states to visit friends. As the van sailed along the interstates, Larissa gazed across the landscape in amazement. She clung to the seat as they crossed bridges high above rivers that cut through the Pennsylvanian mountains. The farther west they traveled, the flatter the terrain became. As they passed through the states of Indiana and

Illinois, the land was like an even plain with fields of corn as far as she could see. Most of the farms were well kept and clean. Finally, on the second day of travel, they arrived at the Jake Yoder farm in Kalona, Iowa. It was exciting to see where her friends in America lived.

"Well, come in," Jake's wife Esther greeted them. She gave Larissa a big hug. "It is so good to see you. All the way from Ukraine."

"Yes, it's good to see you, Larissa." Jake's hand swallowed hers. The menfolk moved to the living room while Larissa followed the women to the kitchen.

"It's so good to see you all," bubbled Esther. "You probably are just taking it easy while you are in the States, Betty. You work so hard in Ukraine."

Larissa felt at ease. It was interesting to watch Americans talk and listen to what they talked about. Their conversations seemed gentle and mellow compared to her own people. Perhaps it was just a difference in culture. Larissa joined Harmony and her sister Hope, who had pulled out a few chairs in the dining area.

"Edward and Sarah will also be coming for supper," informed Esther. "We thought it would be nice if they could be here too."

When Larissa greeted Edward, his eyes filled with tears. It was like old times.

"Edward has been affected by a stroke," explained Sarah to Larissa. "That's why he can't talk as well as he used to."

After a hearty Iowa meal, Jake and Esther showed Larissa and Harold around the hog farm, with the rest of the Troyer group in tow.

"Look at how clean the pens are!" exclaimed Larissa. A mother pig was lying on a perfectly clean grate over a trench. Any droppings falling through the grate would be carried out.

"We normally have a whole barnful." Jake waved his hands at the rows of empty pens. "But we just shipped out, so we are waiting on the next shipment."

Larissa took note of the spotless barns, the immaculate lawn, and the weed-free flowerbeds. Everything seemed so organized and clean.

The next morning after a delicious breakfast of eggs and bacon, Jake suggested they go see where Edward and Sarah live before they leave. "They don't live too far from here, and Esther and I can take you."

Later as they sat in their living room, Larissa could see a tear sliding down Edward's cheek as he gazed at her. Her stomach hurt as she saw his emotion. Edward simply sat and watched them talk. His hair was extra white. It had been only eight years since he had left Ukraine, but his debilitating stroke had aged him considerably.

I hope I don't spill this coffee on their heads. Larissa carried the coffee cup with both hands. She and Harold were drink servers for the bridal table. It was Harold's brother Hector's special day. Larissa's hands shook as she neared the table. She breathed a sigh of relief when the cup was safely on the steady surface.

They look so happy, thought Larissa. *Maybe it will soon be my turn.* She hoped Harold would bring up the subject of marriage again sometime, but maybe it was better to wait until the summer was past and they were both sure.

"Would you like to go to Lewistown with me?" Betty asked when she called Larissa one morning. "I need to get some groceries, and I thought I would drop by the job where Lloyd and Harold are working. If you want to go along, I can stop by and pick you up."

Since their return to Belleville, Harold was working with his father on a Keystone Builders masonry crew, and Larissa was staying with the Calvin Yoder family. She kept herself occupied by doing some sewing and helping the Yoder family.

Larissa was ready to go when Betty arrived. It was another late-summer day with temperatures in the upper eighties. A few clouds scuttled across the sky, and the sun shone brightly. She was so glad Betty had asked her to go along. It would be interesting to see Harold at his job.

"I also want to stop at the Aldi store," said Betty. She flipped on the blinker as they approached the intersection. After another left-hand turn, they pulled into the parking lot.

My, this is an amazing store, Larissa thought. *It is so clean, fresh-smelling, and organized.*

"Should we get a few cold drinks for the men?" asked Betty. "Here are some bottled strawberry smoothies."

At the checkout line, Larissa stared in amazement at the speed of the cashier. As fast as she swiped the items across the barcode reader, it beeped. In what seemed like seconds, she gave them their total. After checking out and loading up the groceries, they headed out.

At the jobsite Larissa was glad when Harold saw them and came to the van. He greeted her warmly.

"How are you doing?" He was dressed in work clothes, making him look a little different than usual.

"I'm okay," she smiled shyly. "We brought you all some smoothies."

"Good. Would you like for me to show you around?"

"Sure. What are those green metal things standing along the house?" asked Larissa.

"That is scaffolding that can be cranked up as needed as we lay the rows of bricks." He turned the crank a couple turns to illustrate. There was a metallic, clicking sound.

It's amazing how these people do things, Larissa thought. She watched an older man push a wheelbarrow full of mortar along the scaffolding.

He stopped every so often and shoveled some mortar onto a large square board. Between these boards were stacks of bricks to which another worker was adding more bricks. Larissa took Harold's empty smoothie bottle and moved back as he stepped up to the wall and grabbed a tool and dipped into the pile of mortar on the board. He spread the mortar on the brick wall. He grabbed another dip of mortar and spread it too. Then another and another until a long section was covered. He moved back quickly, grabbed a brick, and laid it on the wall. Then he grabbed another brick. And another. *Wow*, thought Larissa. *What next? This is incredible. No wonder people in America have money. They really work. No one is loafing around.*

As Larissa walked back to the van she heard someone holler behind her. She turned to see what was going on. Then she heard it again.

"MUD!"

Why is someone hollering about mud? She watched curiously as the older man with the wheelbarrow pushed it up to the fellow who had been calling for mud. He filled the mud board with mortar.

She stared in amazement at the sight. *No one has to wait for anything. It all goes on without stopping.*

34

An Understanding Heart

2005

"I'll be over to pick you up around seven o'clock," Harold had said when Larissa called him about the evening activity. They would be going along with the youth to the Valley View Nursing Home to sing.

Larissa stepped to the window when she heard Calvin's daughter announce that someone had arrived. Sure enough, Harold's black car was coming to a stop in the drive. The small black Saturn with a hint of brown metallic color had won her heart immediately. She could hardly believe it was Harold's car. Maybe someday it would be her car too.

Her heart pounded a little faster. She had come to America to see where Harold lived and what his country was like, and now she was learning to love not only him but also his culture. She hadn't been sure if she wanted to marry him when she had left Ukraine. *At least it's a free ticket to America if nothing else,* she had thought with a twinge of guilt. But now she was becoming more certain that he was the man for her.

Harold and Larissa in Belleville.

She had never quite understood Americans, even the ones in Ukraine, but she knew without a doubt that she loved them. Her mind relived her relationship with the Kramers. Alvin and Leona had shown their love for her not only by their words but also by their deeds. She remembered all the meals and rides they had given her, and she vividly remembered Alvin's gruff advice to keep dating Harold. She would never forget these dear people and their kindness to her.

Larissa watched Harold's tall form step out of the car, his light brown hair teased by the wind. Then he disappeared from sight as he climbed the steps to the door below.

She quickly patted down a few loose hairs and smoothed her veiling into place. Tonight she was wearing her dark green dress. She quickly donned her white sneakers with pale blue stripes.

"Hi, Harold." He seemed as calm as ever, his blue eyes smiling as he leaned against the doorway.

"Ready?"

The drive to the nursing home didn't take long since it was just across Belleville. Other youth were already there, chatting as they waited for everyone to arrive. After a few minutes, they all headed inside.

After the youth numbered off, they split into two groups, going into different wings of the nursing home. *This nursing home is so clean.* Larissa glanced into the rooms as they walked by. *And it even smells good.* She couldn't tell what the smell was but assumed it was some kind of air freshener.

After singing at the home, the youth met at a farm just outside Belleville to play a few games of volleyball. *This is fun,* thought Larissa. *I guess youth are the same everywhere. We all enjoy a relaxing game and good fellowship.*

Soon it was time to head for home, and the youth dispersed for the evening, calling out their goodbyes. Harold and Larissa headed back to Calvin's house. It wouldn't be appropriate to get back too late. By the time they pulled into the Yoder drive, the sun had disappeared over the horizon, leaving only a dusky light.

"Could we talk for a minute?" Larissa turned to Harold.

"Sure, I'm not in a hurry." Harold waited.

Larissa was quiet for a moment. Then she told him of a recent happening that was causing an inner struggle. "I know I'm probably overreacting, but it is affecting me."

Harold listened quietly with only an occasional nod of understanding and a few comments. He handed her his unused handkerchief to wipe her tears and blow her nose. He then suggested they pray, after which Larissa was quiet.

After listening to Harold's advice and praying with him, Larissa felt better. She was glad she had shared her problem with him. He seemed to understand exactly what she had been facing. Yes, she would marry him. He would provide well for her, both physically and emotionally.

Outside the car it was dark, but inside, Larissa's heart was filled with light and joy. She wished she could hug him and tell him how much she loved him. But they had been taught that courtship was to be hands-off, and she knew that was the better way. Anyway, she was sure Harold would not approve if she made any move to touch him.

They hadn't yet, and she was sure he would never violate that trust.

No, she must not even dwell on the thought. Harold was faithful to her, and she would also be faithful to him. She cringed as she thought of her own father who had not been faithful to her mother. Sometimes those thoughts caused anger in her heart against a man she had never known. She knew, however, that she must forgive if she wanted to be forgiven.

"Good night, Larissa." Harold's voice was gentle and quiet. "I will be praying for you." Larissa watched until the taillights disappeared down the street.

As Larissa prepared for the night, she hummed to herself. She felt light, as if she could fly. "Thank you, God."

The next morning Larissa jumped out of bed, threw back the curtains, and raised the window to let in the fresh air. This was the normal morning procedure for her. She loved to see the sun and feel the fresh morning breeze. It helped clear her mind and awaken her heart.

It was Friday, and she was trying to finish a new dress she had begun to sew the day before. She wanted to wear the dress when she and Harold went shopping tomorrow.

It was a beautiful Saturday in early September, and the two young people had been shopping in Lewistown. They had bought sandwiches and drinks and were now pulling up to the Juniata River that wound its way through town.

Larissa gazed out the window at the river next to the street. "Down there is a shady spot." She pointed to a park bench under a group of maple trees.

As they ate their lunch, they discussed their future. Larissa hoped Harold would bring up the subject of a wedding. If he didn't, she thought, maybe she would have to.

A bright red bird flashed along the path and among the trees.

"What kind of bird is that?" gasped Larissa.

"That's a cardinal." Harold donned his glasses that had been lying beside him to get a better look.

"It is beautiful. Oh, I love it!" Larissa continued to watch the bird as it flitted from the tree to a bush next to the river. "It's the prettiest bird I've ever seen."

"They have a beautiful warble too." Harold laid his glasses on the bench beside him and turned his attention back to Larissa. She met his gaze.

"Larissa, we need to talk about our future. How do you feel about things by now? Would you still agree to get married?" The river flowed silently by while large, puffy white clouds floated lazily overhead.

"Yes, I do want to marry you. If I had known everything I know now, I would have married you this summer in Ukraine as we had planned. I would have pressured Mama until she agreed."

Harold was quiet, but his blue eyes showed his excitement at her revelation. "Why don't we plan our wedding now while we're both over here?"

"Should we get married here or in Ukraine?" Harold asked next. They watched two squirrels chase each other around a willow tree next to the river.

"If we get married here, Mama and Maxim would miss it unless we could get visas for them. Would that be possible?"

"Hmm. Probably not." Harold leaned back on the park bench. "You do have a fiancée visa, which means if we get married here you become a permanent resident. If we go back and have a wedding there, I will need to apply for an immigration visa. But why don't we talk to our parents about it?"

"I am glad we are invited to your friend Jesse Troyer's wedding,"

Larissa said, changing the subject.

"Me too. And the main reason is because you and Dads won't be leaving as soon." Harold chuckled as he removed the lid from his drink and pitched the ice. "This way I get to see you longer."

Larissa sighed contentedly. More than one dream had come true today.

35

Married Twice

2006

Dearest Harold,

"I am the Good Shepherd, and know my sheep, and am known of mine" (John 10:14).

Dear, thank you so much for all your letters and faxes. I am so happy for them.

Today is Monday night, February 23. It's Alvin's birthday, and I was so busy. I was helping make the supper for the seed team and clean the house.

Today I cut out my wedding dress and your shirt. When you come, I will measure you for your suit coat . . .

I feel like I want to go to bed for a whole week and not get up. Good night. ~Larissa

I think this fax is long enough with my poor English, thought Larissa as she placed the paper into the machine. By now she knew how to send faxes and didn't need Leona to help her. Besides, she was uncomfortable with anyone besides Harold reading them.

She dialed the number, making sure the paper was aligned as it fed through the machine.

That week Larissa worked on her wedding dress and Harold's matching shirt. While sewing, her mind drifted to the fun the other young people on the seed team were having. Since the seeds wouldn't arrive for another week, they had decided to visit the church at Chernivtsi and the CAM orphanage in Romania.

Thursday morning, as Larissa was busy taking apart a seam to correct a mistake on her dress, she heard Alvin bang into the kitchen. He was usually more careful coming into the house, but today he sounded in a hurry. Larissa could hear the excitement in his voice as he talked.

"Mama, I just got a call from the seed team. Johnny Esh was killed in a snowmobile accident!"

"What happened?" Leona dropped the fresh bread onto the counter and turned to stare at her husband.

"I didn't get many details yet. The youth went out for a ride this morning." Alvin poured himself a cup of sweet tea and dropped into his chair.

"They did say one of the girls was riding with him."

"That's awful!" Ashley cried. She and Larissa had come into the dining room to listen. Larissa couldn't speak. How could this have happened?

Alvin tapped his fingers on the arm of the chair. The Kramer household was sober.

As the day passed, more details filtered in. After consulting with Bishop David Peachey, who was in Berezyanka, Alvin and Meesha Kobets drove down to Chernivtsi to meet with the youth to make plans for the body.

That Sunday as Larissa listened to David Peachey preach, she was impressed by the sermon. Everyone was.

That evening Larissa sent her weekly fax to Harold.

> Dear Harold,
>
> Greetings from Ukraine, from me!
>
> This morning we had a good service. David Peachey preached about who will go to heaven and who will go to hell. In other words, we need to be ready when Jesus comes. I think it really touched the people's hearts. Vita (Nina's sister) confessed, and most of the people cried, and of course, we all feel sorry for Johnny's family. Do you remember that he was the server at our table at Jesse's wedding? I talked to him at Alvin's house on Monday evening and he asked me if I remembered him. I also played volleyball together with the seed team a couple of times. I think Johnny was a good boy. All this has made me think about my future—about my life . . .
>
> I talked to your mom and she said that when I write to you to tell you to bring a bag of 50 tea light candles along for the wedding tables. Also could you bring my shawl I left in Harmony's bedroom?
>
> I finished your wedding shirt and my wedding dress. What about the suit coat material for your suit? Shall we buy the material here?
>
> ...Goodbye. Love, Larissa

The weeks slowly drifted by for Larissa as she spent some of her time at Alvin's and some of her time at home with her mother. She made a few trips to the city to look for shoes and other essentials for the wedding.

On Saturday, February 11, Larissa found herself bouncing along in the van with Lloyd and Betty to meet Harold at the airport. Harold's sister Hope was also along.

Larissa's heart fluttered as she saw Harold emerge from the terminal, pushing a cart loaded with luggage.

"Hi, Harold! Welcome back to Ukraine!" Larissa greeted him. "Here, let me take your briefcase." She took it from his hand. "You look tired."

"Hi, Larissa! It's so good to see you." Harold's heart warmed with her presence. "But yes, I am tired. It was a long trip."

They loaded up the luggage and headed back to Kiev under an overcast sky. By the time they arrived at the mission, a fine snow was falling.

"We will be having supper at Alvin's," Larissa said as they rounded the turn to the mission complex. "Are you hungry?"

"Yes, I am." Harold rubbed his eyes. "Though I did eat well on the flights."

When supper was over, Harold and Larissa washed dishes while the others visited. *I love when he helps me like this,* Larissa thought. Carefully she washed the last dish, rinsed it, and handed it to Harold to dry. She thought back to her childhood. *What a blessing it would have been to have had a father like Harold.* As she realized anew her great loss, her eyes stung with tears.

"I want you to try on your wedding shirt so I can see how it fits," said Larissa, regaining control of herself as she dried her hands. "Could you do that for me?"

"Sure." Harold hung the damp tea towel on the rack.

After checking to see if the shirt fitted Harold properly, Larissa handed Alvin's suitcoat to him.

"Try this," she said. "If it fits, maybe I can use it as a pattern."

"Good," said Larissa with a sigh of relief after Harold tried it on. "It's almost perfect."

Harold spent the weekend in Berezyanka with his parents but returned Monday morning by bus. Larissa met him at Alvin's house in the morning to discuss their wedding plans and their wedding trip. Since they wanted to begin the process of obtaining a marriage license, Harold needed to fill out paperwork confirming that he had not been formerly married. Meesha Kobets agreed to take them to the American Embassy to fill out the paperwork.

"Is that all?" asked Meesha when they came back out. He grinned. "Anything else?"

"We need to go to the Minister of Foreign Affairs to get the consul's signature approved." Harold handed Meesha the address. When they arrived, the office was closed.

"That was quick," Meesha commented when they came back to the vehicle. "Were they closed?"

"Yes," replied Larissa. "They are only open till twelve o'clock."

The streets were covered with snow and slush, but that didn't keep people at home. Pedestrians dressed in long winter coats and boots moved along the wide cobblestone sidewalks. An older grandma pulled her bag of wares along on her little two-wheeled buggy. As a light wind kicked up, a sidewalk vendor selling hot sausages pulled his cap further over his ears and put up his hood. By now the snow was falling steadily.

After Meesha dropped Harold and Larissa off at the mission, they walked back to Alvin's house in the swirling snow. *Harold is probably hungry, and I don't know what to make,* Larissa worried. *I don't know how to cook. Especially not American foods. Maybe Leona will have some leftovers from lunch.*

"Are you hungry?" asked Larissa as they hung up their wraps.

"If there is something to eat, yes, I will eat." Harold placed his shoes beside the hot register.

After looking through the fridge and finding a few items, Larissa served hotdogs, green beans, and bread. She felt better after seeing Harold eat and apparently enjoy the food.

Larissa spent the afternoon sewing, while Harold worked at the MIM office.

The following day Larissa and Harold again visited the Minister of Foreign Affairs and this time the office was open and the consul's signature was authorized.

The next stop was to get Harold's passport translated by an official translator. The secretary made copies of Harold's passport, and they headed back to the Sprinter van where the faithful driver Meesha was waiting.

"Where to now?" asked Meesha with an almost imperceptible grin. His shock of dark brown hair was covered with a fur hat. He could patiently wait on Americans in the vehicle for great lengths of time but would then drive like Jehu for the next destination.

"Next stop is Megalon," responded Harold. Megalon was a large three-story shopping mall with an up-to-date grocery store and a modern restaurant. It was almost out of place in the poverty-stricken country of Ukraine.

"Shall I wait on you?" Meesha asked when they arrived at Megalon.

"No," said Harold. "We can walk back to the mission, can't we?" Harold looked at Larissa.

"Sure, we can walk," Larissa agreed. "It's only fifteen minutes away."

"What do we need here?" asked Larissa.

"Come with me," said Harold. He led the way through Megalon to the restaurant. "How about my buying lunch for you today?" Larissa could see Harold's blue eyes twinkling.

"Are you sure?" Larissa's heart leaped. She had been to a restaurant only a few times in her whole life.

"Something special for a special person." Harold escorted her to the food line.

After lunch and some shopping, the two young people struck out for Alvin's place. It was exciting to walk through the falling snow through the market, around the high-rise apartments, and along the back streets toward the mission. Soon it would be their wedding day—March 4.

"Where have you been?" Alvin asked when they arrived. His voice was extra deep and gruff, but his eyes were smiling.

"Out and about," Larissa smiled.

"Did you get something to eat for lunch?" asked Leona. "Or do you want me to make something for you now?"

"Harold took me to Megalon for lunch," Larissa replied with a big smile. "For something special."

That evening after supper at Alvin's house, Harold suggested that they read and study Ephesians chapter five together. The topics ranged from submitting to one another to child training.

"A home built upon Jesus Christ is important for a solid home and a good home life," Harold said as they concluded their study. After praying together, Harold bade Larissa good night.

"Do you have keys to get into the house?" Larissa asked as Harold stepped out into the snowy night. Harold would be sleeping at the CAM guest house not far up the street.

Harold double-checked his pocket. "I do. Thanks for reminding me, and good night."

Larissa watched as her beloved was swallowed up by the drifting snow and the darkness.

The next morning after breakfast Alvin and Leona headed to Nadia's house to work on Larissa's bedroom, which still needed to be finished. Meesha took Larissa and Harold to the city for more paperwork. Larissa also found a little Christian bookstore a friend had recommended that sold Ukrainian wedding invitations.

The next few days were filled with sewing wedding clothes and getting all the paperwork done.

That weekend Larissa and Harold, along with Nadia and Maxim, traveled to Berezyanka to be with Harold's family for the weekend. They had a grand time planning the wedding with Harold's parents and siblings. It was late by the time the final plans had been made.

Mama has settled down and seems to enjoy the idea of our marriage, Larissa thought with relief. She had not spoken against the idea once since Larissa had returned from America. Actually, she seemed supportive of all the plans, though she voiced concern about her inability to help pay for the wedding arrangements.

"Don't worry," said Betty. "Some of our friends donated money to help with the cost of the wedding. God has supplied."

On Saturday Harold and Larissa helped paint some of the inside walls of the multi-purpose building in Berezyanka that was used for Sunday services and would be used for the wedding and reception. *I love working with Harold,* thought Larissa as they painted. Her thoughts continued. *But what will I cook after we are married? All I know how to make is soup or fried eggs. I don't want to disappoint him.*

The next Tuesday Meesha once again picked up the couple at the Kiev mission to finalize paperwork for their marriage license. After two and a half hours the paperwork was completed, and they were told to come back on March 1 to receive their license.

The following day Harold and Larissa met with David and Rhoda Peachey for premarital counseling. They enjoyed David's jolly humor and wise counsel.

Later that day they contacted Tez Tours who asked them to come to their office in Kiev to finalize their planned honeymoon to Egypt.

As they passed through a metro station, Larissa wanted to stop and buy some flowers.

"Here," she said, thrusting a bunch of yellow daffodils into Harold's hands. "I couldn't resist buying these for you."

"How did you know they are my favorite?" Harold grinned.

Larissa just smiled.

On Wednesday, March 1, Alvin and Leona took Larissa and Harold to the government office to obtain the marriage license. There was a large room with beautiful Slavic decorations and a platform with a special table. On the raised table lay the official book where Harold and Larissa needed to sign their names. They also signed the license. The government official rattled off a poem about marriage and asked them to kiss.

Larissa blushed and was glad Harold did not understand what the official said. Alvin and Leona took a few photos of the ceremony. According to the Ukrainian government, Harold and Larissa were now legally married. The certificate read, "Harold and Larissa Troyer, married March 1, 2006."

Harold and Larissa's civil marriage.

Now for our Christian wedding on Saturday, thought Larissa as they drove the snowy roads back to Nadia's house. Alvin and Leona spoke with Nadia and Larissa briefly while Harold pulled up two buckets of water from the well behind the house.

Larissa stayed at home with her mother, and Harold rode back to the mission with Alvin and Leona. He would be staying at the CAM guest house for another day.

The morning of March 4 dawned with a beautiful sunrise. As Larissa and her mother rode with Alvin and Leona from Kiev to the village of Berezyanka where the wedding was to be held, she tried to enjoy the morning beauty in spite of the butterflies in her stomach.

When they pulled up to the mission house in Berezyanka, the cooks were already busy preparing the Ukrainian meatballs and salads. Potatoes were being peeled for the various dishes to be made. Laughter and conversations filled the room.

On cue, the large bus from Kiev arrived with the guests from the city. Alla and her daughter had come from Lisnyky and wanted to spend some time visiting with Larissa and Harold before the wedding. *There is so much to do, and I need to get dressed yet.* Larissa's mind whirled. *I hope Harold likes the wedding dress.*

When Larissa was finally dressed and ready, she peeked out of the bedroom. Harold was patiently waiting. But where were the flowers? *Surely he has flowers for me.*

"Harmony, do you think Harold forgot to buy flowers for me?" Larissa turned to Harmony and Nina who had helped her dress. "Surely not?"

"Let me ask him," said Harmony, going out to talk to her older brother who was quietly waiting.

"Oh, I sort of forgot, but I really have no way of getting a nice bouquet way out here in no-man's-land." Harold paused. "What shall I do?"

"We'll help," consoled Harmony. "Quick, someone. Get some of the roses we are using for the tables, and I'll make a bouquet. They won't have long stems, but at least it will be a bouquet."

Soon Harmony handed her older brother the small bouquet of white roses with baby's breath. It would have to do.

Larissa's heart sank when she saw the small spray of flowers. *Oh well, he doesn't understand our culture, so I can forgive him.* She gave

Harold a sweet smile and accepted the offered bouquet. *He looks so innocent and ... handsome.* Larissa gazed into his eyes. Her heart fluttered for a moment. *I have to keep myself together.*

The wedding service started a few minutes after ten o'clock with a song by the youth as Harold and Larissa walked in. All of Harold's siblings were at the wedding, as well as Larissa's mother and brother. Even though Larissa had sent a wedding invitation to Siberia to invite her father, there had been no reply.

After two congregational songs, Alvin shared an opening message and David Peachey performed the ceremony.

"Brother Harold, will you in the presence of God and these witnesses take Larissa, the sister by your side, to be your wedded wife? Will you love ...?"

After the vows were said and a blessing was given, Harold's father Lloyd preached a message. The building was filled to capacity. When the message was over, the youth sang another song as Harold and Larissa walked out of the auditorium and then outside. Since it was frigid outdoors, they ran to the house.

"We are finally married! Can you believe it!" Harold grinned as he picked her up and started up the stairs. Larissa shut her eyes and felt herself being borne aloft—literally. *He is carrying me up the stairs. He is a strong man!*

"We need to get back as soon as the tables are set up," murmured Larissa a few minutes later. They went to the window and could see the folks milling around in the cold while the folding tables, benches, and chairs were set in the place where the guests had been sitting for the service. In record time, the guests were flowing back inside to the warmth of the building.

Harold and Larissa found their seats at the bridal table. Matt Coblentz as best man and Harmony Troyer as maid of honor sat next to them. Jason Zook and Nina Krevchoon were next in line at the bridal table.

The reception lasted most of the afternoon with a variety of Ukrainian dishes served. Compote, hot tea, and coffee were also available. During the reception, many poems were quoted and songs were sung by different groups of people. The guests gave gifts and many also offered comments. Even the MIM director, Delmar Erb, spoke words of encouragement by telling an interesting and humorous story. Some of the Berezyanka village women sang a secular marriage song for the newlywed couple. The village boys watched the American/Ukrainian wedding with amazement and ate food, dessert, and candy until they ached.

It was late before the reception was concluded with a dismissal prayer. Slowly the guests found their way back to the large bus that was warming up for the trip back to Kiev.

Harold and Larissa spent time with guests who wanted to talk and helped load the wedding gifts into Alvin's car trunk. Larissa helped Harold gather his personal belongings to take with them to her mother's house in Kiev where they would be staying.

This has been a beautiful day, thought Larissa. *In more ways than one. Now we are twice married.*

At 3:45 the next morning the alarm rang. It was time to get up and prepare for the trip to the airport. Larissa and Harold quickly dressed and grabbed their bags, checking to make sure they had their passports and money.

Jason Zook pulled up to Nadia's place a few minutes early to give them a ride. They arrived at the airport at five o'clock. After thanking Jason for his kindness, they hurried to find the service counter for check-in.

The lady at the counter checked their passports, issued boarding passes, and pointed them to the stairs.

"That way," she said with a yawn.

Larissa and Harold slept most of the four-hour flight to Hurghada, Egypt. They awakened at the announcement of their imminent descent into the seaside city. A flowing expanse of sand stretched as far as they could see to their right—the Sahara Desert. Next to the desert was a blue-green sea stretching out to their left. It was the Red Sea, although it didn't appear very red. The winds were warm and dry, and a giant thermometer next to the airport terminal confirmed the temperature to be seventy degrees. Not a cloud was in sight.

The next few days were spent swimming in the Red Sea and enjoying the warm sunshine and good food. The honeymoon package included a morning and evening meal, which was plenty for the two of them. After a big breakfast, they spent time reading the Bible, singing, and praying together.

On the fourth day they were awakened at 1:15 a.m. for their tour of Cairo and Alexandria, Egypt. They stopped by the hotel restaurant to pick up their packed breakfast and then headed to the waiting bus.

The bus traveled with an armed caravan since there was danger of ambush from rebels. At one checkpoint the passengers had to show their passports to officials who boarded the bus. The extra-large windows allowed a grand view of Egypt as they traveled north.

It was almost noon before they drove into Cairo, crossed the Nile River, and then continued a few miles southwest to the pyramids of Giza. After buying tickets at the office, a tour guide walked them across the complex and explained how the pyramids were built.

"The largest pyramid is called the Great Pyramid and is one of the Seven Wonders of the Ancient World," he said proudly. "It is by far the oldest of these wonders and the only one still in existence."

The group walked around the pyramids. At one of the smaller ones they were allowed to descend into the manmade tombs to see the interior. Steps were hewn into the solid rock. At the bottom was a coffin-sized hole hewn into the solid rock into which the mummy had been laid.

"I am working up an appetite with all this walking," said Harold as his stomach growled. Larissa stood close as they gazed at yet another wonder of the ancient world.

"The Great Sphinx of Giza was cut from limestone bedrock into the form of a gigantic lion with a human head. It measures 240 feet from paw to tail, is 66 feet high, and is 62 feet wide at its haunches." The guide pointed to the head. "The face is most commonly thought to be the face of Pharaoh Khafre."

"This is what I call history," commented Harold on the second day of their tour. "The history of the United States only dates back a few hundred years, but these archaeological findings and sites are over a thousand years old. Some of these historical buildings are over two thousand years old, with the oldest pyramids being over four thousand years old. It's incredible."

Larissa yawned. "I would rather go wading in the Mediterranean Sea."

Late that night the tour bus rumbled into Hurghada and unloaded its stiff, tired occupants. The Aqua Blue Hotel looked inviting after the two-day trip.

"I am ready for some solid sleep," sighed Larissa, grabbing her purse. Harold shouldered their duffel bags and followed the group into their hotel.

"These blankets are again tucked under the mattress," Larissa grinned. "Here goes our nightly ritual." She yanked the tucked blankets out from under the foot end of the mattress and let them hang. Every day while Larissa and Harold were out, the cleaning boy would come to sweep up the fine desert sand that collected daily. He would also make their bed and tuck the sheets and blankets firmly under the foot end of the mattress. Every night Larissa and Harold would yank the blankets and sheets back out from under the mattress and have a good laugh.

"He tucks it in, and we yank it out," chuckled Harold.

One day during the second week they boarded a boat for a tour of several islands in the Red Sea. Larissa and Harold had the privilege of seeing a pod of dolphins near their boat. The dolphins seemed to ignore the boat full of people as they continuously dived and resurfaced to breathe.

"All my life I have dreamed of seeing dolphins," Larissa beamed at Harold. "That was the best part of today."

"The best part of my day was seeing you," Harold teased. Larissa punched him with her elbow.

Immigration

2006

$\mathcal{L}$arissa cracked the egg and dropped it into the frying pan. *What if he doesn't like how I make it?* They were now living in Larissa's room at her mother's house.

When breakfast was ready, Larissa and Harold sat down together in the simple, unfinished kitchen. Harold had brought in water the night before and filled the containers and pails for their morning sponge baths, cooking, and cleaning. An electric teapot heated the water for their morning tea.

After a breakfast of eggs sprinkled with fried pieces of bacon and green onions, a piece of Ukrainian bread on the side, and a cup of hot tea, the couple read the Bible and prayed together.

"You better run if you don't want to miss the bus to the mission,"

Larissa said. She helped Harold get his backpack filled with his papers and a snack she had made. "Have a good day." She kissed him goodbye.

"Thanks for the breakfast, dear. It was excellent."

Larissa stood at the large kitchen window, watching as her husband trudged toward the main road to catch the bus. It was almost embarrassing to have this wonderful American living in these poor conditions. Harold never complained about living in an unfinished house with no running water, although he did talk about installing a pump and water lines sometime. She suspected it wasn't so much for himself as it was for her mother. Since Maxim was now living with his father again, there was a little more privacy for her and Harold.

On the terraces behind the house they had planted a miniature garden with radishes and green onions. Larissa had covered the seeds with plastic weighted down with boards to protect the seedlings from the nighttime temperatures. Now that the weather had turned warmer, she had discarded the plastic.

As usual, Larissa spent some time praying for herself and the day ahead of her. She also prayed for Harold, who was now likely getting off the bus and walking back to the mission office. She remembered his words about her breakfast. "It was excellent," he had said. *I hope he was honest,* she mused. *Now what shall I make for supper?*

Larissa often thought fondly of their time together in Egypt. They had simply relaxed and spent time together learning to know each other and talking about their plans for the future. Harold had enjoyed listening to her sing the many songs she had learned over the years. She loved to hear him pray.

As Larissa reflected over her life, she realized that she had been guided and protected by an unseen force. *God has always been with me, even when I didn't realize it.* She pondered how God had brought it all together. Harold had recently told her about a vision he had a few years ago of getting married in Ukraine and living with his in-laws. When he saw her upstairs bedroom he recognized it as the same room he had seen in his vision.

Her classmates had told her she would not marry a Ukrainian but a foreigner. This too had happened. She had prayed that God would show her who to marry by it being the first boy who asked her. That prayer had also been answered. Larissa felt her eyes fill with tears as she washed the breakfast dishes and set them to dry. *God, why do you love me? I am not worthy.*

It was July 4. Larissa was emigrating to America with her husband. They would fly to the John F. Kennedy International Airport in New York City where they would meet Jake Beiler. Jake had a four-passenger Cessna and would be flying them to Belleville, Pennsylvania.

As Harold and Larissa passed through customs in JFK Airport, Larissa was admitted into the United States of America and had her

Larissa beside Jake Beiler's plane.

passport scanned. Now her permanent residency status would begin.

After finding their luggage, they met Jake, who showed them the way out of the building to his small airplane. They shoved the suitcases and boxes into the rear compartment and one of the back seats and then buckled the seat belts in preparation for takeoff.

As the light aircraft taxied out the runway to line up with the passenger airliners, Harold and Larissa cringed. A huge 747 passenger jet loomed behind them while a large jet ahead of them blew hot gases at the little aircraft behind it. Finally the small airplane was given clearance for takeoff, and after it bounced into the air, Larissa relaxed a little. She leaned back and tried to sleep under the droning of the small plane. Darkness fell, and far below they could see lights twinkling. After flying for an hour, Harold and Larissa began to see exploding lights below them.

"Fireworks," Harold called to Larissa and pointed down. They could see the miniature explosions far below them. They were too high to see any beauty in them, but it reminded them of America's Independence Day, which they had forgotten in all the excitement.

When they landed at the Mifflin County Airport and taxied up to the sprinkling of buildings, Harold's parents were there to meet them. A few of his siblings and cousins were also there to welcome them.

The remainder of the week was spent preparing for the reception on Friday evening for those in America who had not been able to attend the wedding in Ukraine. The reception would be held at the Locust Grove Mennonite Church in Belleville. Harold and Larissa were overwhelmed at the support of family, friends, and church members. Hundreds of people showed up to enjoy the food and fellowship. Bruce Jantzi led a group of people in some Russian songs. Relatives from far-off places came, as well as old-time friends, making it a splendid evening.

Lloyds had been preparing to return to Ukraine, but they had stayed long enough to help with the reception. When they returned to Ukraine, Harold and Larissa rented their house. Harold went to work for Keystone Builders, and Larissa became a homemaker.

"Why do you keep looking at your watch?" Larissa asked as they prepared for the Sunday morning service. "We will be on time."

"I guess it's just in me to be punctual." Harold slipped on his black shoes. "In America, we know the value of time."

"It would be more relaxing if we didn't have to be pushed by time schedules," Larissa replied, donning a light sweater.

"Yes, but don't you remember how frustrating it was in Ukraine when people made no effort to keep schedules and were constantly late?" Harold paused thoughtfully. "Don't you like the way our culture works? I mean, when you go somewhere to an office or a meeting, you know it will be at the time it was planned."

"Yes, you're right," agreed Larissa. "But I still wish you would throw your watch away." She smiled and took his offered hand as they left the house.

In August, Harold consented to teach at the Pleasant View School at their home church, so he decided to also attend Faith Builders Teachers Week. Since Harold and Larissa had already planned a trip to Niagara Falls and Ontario, the school board consented for the term to start a week later.

Going through customs and crossing the Niagara River Gorge on the Rainbow Bridge into Canada went without incident. Harold followed the signs to the Niagara Horseshoe Falls. They found a parking space, grabbed the camera, and headed to the lookout over the falls.

"This is absolutely gorgeous," breathed Larissa. "I can't believe I'm here." They watched the water thundering over the falls and felt the ground tremble under their feet from the force. They raised their voices to be heard over the roar of the falls.

"Those distant falls are on the American side." Harold pointed across the gorge to where they had come from. A gentle rain began to fall.

"Why don't we go inside the Visitor Center and find something to eat," suggested Harold.

After finding a small café and getting a bite to eat, they asked directions to the ferry under the falls. They were directed to a booth where they bought tickets to ride the *Maid of the Mist* and were given ponchos since the spray from the gigantic falls would settle over the boat. As the ferryboat motored along the cascading water, the gentle rain and the spray from the falls soaked their heads and feet.

"The water drops nearly 170 feet." The attendant on the boat had to raise his voice to be heard. "Every second approximately 750,000 gallons of water pour over these falls."

"My shoes and socks are wet," Larissa spoke into Harold's ear. They held the rail to keep their balance on the bobbing boat as they absorbed the power and beauty of the Niagara.

After enjoying a few hours at the falls, they realized they needed to move on since Bruce Jantzis were expecting them for supper. The Jantzi family was now living in Ontario since they had left Ukraine a few years before. Bruce's son Gabriel had just undergone brain surgery, which was another reason for Harold and Larissa's visit.

"Come in. Come in," welcomed Ruthann. "Do we have some tired travelers?"

Larissa gave Ruthann a hug. She could hardly believe she was visiting the Jantzi home in Canada. *It would never have crossed my mind ten years ago,* she thought.

"You may bring your luggage in if you like," Ruthann called over her shoulder. "You'll be staying here."

Bruce met them as they lugged their bags inside. He seemed happy, but also sober.

"Welcome," he smiled. "Larissa, you are a long way from home. I mean Ukraine."

"My home is in America now," Larissa smiled. "But I understand what you mean."

"Make yourself at home," Bruce instructed. "Gabriel came home yesterday, but he is still weak. He can handle some company, but it should be kept at a minimum."

Harold and Larissa greeted Gabriel, who was on the recliner in the dining room. They visited quietly for a few minutes, and he responded cautiously and slowly. He seemed paler than Larissa remembered him, evidence of the trauma he had gone through.

Larissa enjoyed the lively conversation around the table. She noticed that after the meal Bruce and the boys helped clear the table and washed their own plates. *How would it have been to have a father like Bruce in my home when I was growing up?* Her heart again flamed briefly with resentment against the father she had never known.

The next morning they ate eggs and pancakes for breakfast, after which Bruce read from a devotional booklet. Following the meal, they knelt for prayer before preparing to leave for the Sunday morning services.

That autumn in Belleville the leaves took on their fiery hues as the weather cooled, but Larissa did not always enjoy it. On their trip back from Canada she had been extremely nauseated, so they stopped and bought a pregnancy test. It showed positive. On one hand, Larissa was filled with joy and anticipation, but on the other hand, she felt some apprehension. *I don't know anything about this,* she thought. *My mother never taught me since her mother never taught her. How can I learn?*

37

Godly Seed

2006-2007

Her pillow wet with tears, Larissa lay nauseated and miserable on the couch in their living room. She wished Harold would come home. The clock showed nearly 2:30; he would be dismissing his students from the classroom.

It was the middle of October. School was in full swing, taking lots of Harold's time and energy. He often came home exhausted, and Larissa would give him a head and neck massage to relieve the stress.

But now, sick with her pregnancy, Larissa was finding it increasingly hard to cope. Her mouth watered as her mind traveled to her native homeland and its culture and foods. Oh for some salty fish with buckwheat and rye bread! She wanted it now! She seemed to almost suffocate with the weight of her emotions. As the pressure released, she cried again quietly. *I must tell Harold. I just have to find some of my native foods.*

An hour passed before Larissa heard the entrance door bang as Harold entered the kitchen. She could hear him placing his lunch box on the counter and setting his book bag on the table. Footsteps approached the living room.

"Dear, how are you?" Harold knelt on the carpet next to the couch. "Are you not feeling well again?" His kind words opened the floodgates of tears again.

"I feel so sick." Larissa tried to stem the tide but failed. "I tried to make something to eat for lunch but nearly fainted from nausea."

"I'm sorry. Shall I pray for you?" After prayer, they both felt better.

As Larissa walked along the back streets, she observed the brilliant maple trees and chattering squirrels. Occasionally a rabbit bounded across the street and into the shrubs next to the houses.

While Harold was in school, she enjoyed many walks in the fresh, outdoor air—if the local farmers weren't spreading manure on their fields. That ruined it, as the horrible smell made her feel even more nauseous.

On one of her walks, she met neighbors who were from Kazakhstan, a country bordering Russia. When the lady found out Larissa was from Ukraine, she invited her into her house.

"Come on in," she said, opening the door wide. "My name is Olga. Sit down for some tea." Olga was a tall, trim woman with dark brown hair. She welcomed Larissa with a beaming smile.

Larissa was overjoyed at having found neighbors who could speak Russian. Olga set out kolbasa, cheese, rye bread, and some other Russian specialties on the table.

God heard our prayer, Larissa thought as she savored a bite of the cabbage rolls Olga dished onto her plate.

"Where do you get the ingredients for these foods?" asked Larissa, reaching for another salty, fermented pickle. "These taste just like the pickles we had in Ukraine."

"There's a place in State College called Eastern European Foods that sells Russian foods," replied Olga. Her children sat quietly watching the newcomer.

"I'll have to tell Harold about this," responded Larissa.

"Yes, if he wants to come by, we can give him directions," Olga replied with a smile. "Do you miss your native foods?"

"Yes, very much." Larissa rose to leave. "Thank you so much for your time—and the food." She gave her new friend a big hug.

"No problem. Come back any time. May God be with you."

"They are a Christian family," Larissa told Harold that evening. "Olga said they go to the Brethren in Christ Church in Belleville."

"Really? Do they speak Russian?" Harold and Larissa were sitting at the table eating a snack.

"Yes, and she served me some Russian food too. It was so-o-o good." Larissa's face brightened with joy. "She said there's a place in State College where we can buy Russian foods. They will give you the address."

That weekend Harold and Larissa set out to find the store Olga had told them about. "I believe this is the place," Harold said as he turned into the parking lot. In large letters across the door was a sign saying "Eastern European Foods." Larissa's excitement grew as they walked into the store. As she browsed the shelves lined with her own familiar food, Russian music played softly in the background. It seemed almost like home. A lady behind the counter greeted them in Russian.

"These items are expensive, Harold," Larissa commented, pointing to the prices.

"Don't worry, dear. Just get what you need."

Larissa chose two kinds of salty fish, some canned fish, several bags of buckwheat, rye bread, Russian cheese, hot shredded carrots, kolbasa, Napoleon cake, and more.

That night Larissa's heart was light. It had been a wonderful day. She had gone shopping with Harold, which she always looked forward to each Friday after school. But even more important, they had found some Russian food for her and had enjoyed a wonderful supper. Now she felt relaxed and tired. "Thank you, God," she whispered as her eyes closed.

"You need to learn to relax," explained Rebecca. "That is nature's way. If you observe an animal mother you will often notice that before giving birth they find a quiet spot to lie down and relax."

The group sat around the room on mats and listened to the professional teacher give instruction. A friend had recommended attending Rebecca Lerner's birthing classes.

Now they were seated with eight other couples in a circle with Rebecca. It was a very interesting and informative study by a woman passionate about natural childbirth. She had recommended the book *Husband-Coached Childbirth,* emphasizing the need for the husband to be part of each phase of the pregnancy.

Larissa felt much better about her approaching due date since they were taking classes, and she was being taught what to expect. She could now feel the gentle kicks of the baby and loved to hear the heartbeat when she went for her checkups.

"Your iron is low, so we need to get you some iron pills," Larissa's Amish midwife said after the small instrument beeped. "If your iron count is low, there is a greater risk of hemorrhaging during childbirth."

Larissa's heart jumped at the words. She looked at Harold, who was sitting in the rocking chair waiting on her.

"But you don't have to worry," the midwife continued. "If you take a few iron pills every day and eat lots of greens, you'll be fine." She chuckled. "Eat lots of spinach."

"Harold, get up." Larissa stood beside the bed. "I have been having contractions during the night. I have been writing the times down, and I think today is the day."

Harold scrambled out of bed and ran for the telephone. He dialed Joseph Hostetler's phone number. After connecting, he let Joseph know that he could not be at school that day. Harold had asked him ahead of time if he would be willing to substitute if the birth took place during the week.

Harold then called the midwife's helper to let them know what was happening. At 11:38 a.m., a little baby boy was born.

"What is his name?" asked the midwife, handing the wailing baby to his mother.

"Dario Miguel."

Tears fell onto the little boy's cheeks as Larissa held him close. Unbidden, a prayer sprang up from the depths of her heart. "Dear God, please do not let this little boy go astray. Always keep him in your care. I want all my children to know you and love you as their Father. In Jesus' name. Amen."

As Larissa's mind traveled to her growing-up years, she felt humbled and grateful. Her life hadn't been easy. By not having a father, she had missed out on so many things. But she knew God had been with her each step of the way.

And now, she wondered, how much more could she wish for? She had a loving husband who would be a father to her children. And not only that, she had a heavenly Father who was always with her—a Father who was over all and was a Father even to the fatherless.

Epilogue

Larissa and I lived in Belleville, Pennsylvania, for almost a year before returning to Ukraine in 2007 to serve with Master's International Ministries (MIM).

When we made a trip to America the next year, we discovered that Larissa needed to live in America for a full year due to her permanent residency status. After spending another year in Belleville, we were commissioned with church leadership responsibilities and sent back to Ukraine where we served almost three more years as missionaries. Since Russian is Larissa's native tongue and I have learned to speak Russian relatively well (though not fluently), we were able to connect well with the Ukrainian people. Larissa, of course, understood her own culture and people and could give me insight into what they really meant or were thinking as we ministered.

I might clarify here that since the USSR had control of Ukraine during Soviet times, the Russian language was enforced as the primary language during that time. Since Ukraine gained its independence in 1991, the Ukrainian language is once again being taught in schools. Larissa was raised during an era of transition from Russian back to Ukrainian, so she speaks both languages fluently. The Russian and Ukrainian languages are similar to each other. They use the same Slavic alphabet and some of the same words. Maybe they could be compared to German and Pennsylvania Dutch.

Since the summer of 2011, we have lived in Belleville, Pennsylvania. We have five sons and one daughter and are expecting our seventh child in March of 2021. Larissa and I are attempting to teach our children Russian, though it's not easy while living in an English-speaking environment.

Larissa is often asked the question, "Where would you rather live, in Ukraine or in America?" Larissa responds that both countries have their strong points as well as their negative ones. She says she could enjoy living in either place, but as of now, she believes she wants her home to be in America.

Larissa and Nadia, 2011.

Larissa's mother Nadia was baptized in October of 2000. She is a member of the Mennonite church in Kiev, although she has been in America since February 2016 and rents a small house about a half mile across town from us. Nadia, who gained the nickname "Bicycle Nadia" in Ukraine, still rides her bike. She often rides her bike to our home and to the local grocery store to buy food. Nadia is in America with refugee status, and we are awaiting an update from the government regarding her future. If she is allowed to become a permanent resident in the U.S., she will likely continue to live close to us in the States. If she does not gain legal status as a permanent resident, she will be returning to Ukraine.

Larissa's half-brother Maxim is married and lives in Nadia's house in Ukraine. He has one daughter as of this writing.

Maxim with his wife and daughter.

As I dug out the details of the life Larissa and her mother experienced, I found it difficult to know what to write and what not to. I have tried by the grace of God to write the things that will give the reader an accurate picture of their lives. As you have probably detected, some of the story includes me, Larissa's husband.

Ever since we met and learned to know each other, Larissa and I have wondered how her biological father, Andre, was doing and have prayed for him. Larissa sent him an invitation to our wedding but received no response.

I will add here that Larissa's father was of the Buryat people group. The Buryat are thought to be descendants of the Mongols who moved north to escape the Mongol rule in China. The Buryat traditionally were nomadic herdsmen but have settled into permanent villages, learning farming from the Russians. Much of the area where the Buryat live is forested, so many work in the lumber industry. In 1818, the first Protestant missionary began work among the Buryat. This continued for about 20 years, but since then laborers have been few. The Bible has been translated, but there is a desperate need for an up-to-date translation of the New Testament in the Buryat language.

The population of the Buryat people is around 471,000. According to https://joshuaproject.net/people_groups/19320/RS they are an unreached people group.

Finally, in the process of writing this book, I decided to search for Larissa's father. I went online to a few Russian websites and began to request help. In January of 2019, I connected with a detective agency in Ulan-Ude where Larissa was born. The detective responded that they had found a few men by that name, but they needed more information to narrow the search.

After I gave him all the necessary information and our family photo, the detective responded that he had indeed found the family. According to Russian law, he could not give us any information until he had met with the family and obtained their permission to do so.

On February 16, 2019, I received an email from the detective saying that he had received the last positive response from Andre's daughters (Larissa's half-sisters). He said he would send us the full biological report the next day. Of course, in the process of giving Andre's daughters our information, they saw that Larissa's birthday was on Monday, February 18.

Monday morning after I came home from taking the children to school, I was planning on working in the office for the day. But upon my return, I found Larissa crying.

"What happened, dear?" I asked. Larissa couldn't speak for her deep sobbing. I held her close until she could talk.

"My sisters texted me 'Happy Birthday' this morning," she finally said. Her eyes were red from crying.

"Really?" I said. To myself I was thinking, *Shouldn't this make you happy?*

"They said my father used to talk about me. He used to tell everyone that he has a daughter in Ukraine. He was proud of that and wanted to see me." She blew her nose.

"I am so sorry," I responded. I held her close while she gained control of her emotions.

"My sisters Dasha and Lyuba have been texting me for the last fifteen minutes," Larissa said as her phone beeped again.

That day, February 18, 2019, Larissa and her two half-sisters and an older stepsister texted back and forth. They sent photos and shared about their lives.

Stepsister Nastya.

After Nadia had left Ulan-Ude, Russia, for Ukraine, Andre remarried. His second wife had a daughter named Nastya whom she brought along into the marriage with Andre. The two daughters Dasha and Lyuba were born soon after the marriage, so they are just a few years younger than Larissa.

Half-sister Dasha.

The sisters said that their father did receive the wedding invitation in 2006; they had seen it. They were not sure why he didn't respond.

Andre had a drinking problem, as can be seen from the story. He never overcame that addiction. One day while he was intoxicated, he got into a fight and was injured. He was hospitalized and soon afterwards died of head injuries. This was on September 6, 2006.

For the first years of our marriage,

Half-sister Lyuba.

Larissa struggled with forgiving her father. But God was working in her life, and eventually I could tell she had completely forgiven him. She confirmed my observation. We often prayed for Andre, not knowing of his decease.

Larissa and I are planning at some point to make a trip to Ulan-Ude, Siberia, Russia, to visit her sisters and to see the place where she spent the first three years of her life. Larissa's sisters at this point are not believers, so we ask that you join us in prayer for them.

Even though on the surface all seems well with those who have been through much difficulty, deep down inside some hurts never completely go away. Yes, by God's grace a level of healing can be experienced in this life. However, total healing and restoration will be coming in the new heavens and the new earth wherein dwells righteousness.

Larissa has encouraged me from the beginning to write this story about her and her mother, but as I finish up, she has voiced a fear of how her life will appear to those who read this book. Her desire is simply that God will receive all the glory and that readers will be inspired to trust and hope in God as a good Father.

~Harold R. Troyer

Harold, Larissa, and family in 2019.

About the Author

*H*arold Troyer lives in the charming village of Belleville in the Kishacoquillas Valley of central Pennsylvania. He, his Ukrainian wife Larissa, and six children love singing, traveling, and gardening. Harold taught junior high students for six years, bounced on a bus through Nicaragua's interior, navigated the muddy rivers of Papua New Guinea in a dugout, and stood in an unending sea of waving wheat in Ukraine. All these adventures have provided contexts for his passionate study of anthropology.

Harold has served as a foreign missionary in Central America and Eastern Europe, and has been involved in prison ministry and aftercare in the United States. Currently he serves on the Board of Directors for All-Nations Bible Translation, is a phone team member in CAM's Billboard Evangelism Program, and has a sideline construction business.

Harold desires that readers would turn their eyes on Jesus and journey further with God by reading about men and women who have fought, or are fighting, the good fight of faith. Harold would like reader comments on his book, which can be sent to htroyer@camoh.org. or by writing Christian Aid Ministries at P.O. Box 360, Berlin, OH 44610, Attn: Harold Troyer.

About Christian Aid Ministries

Christian Aid Ministries was founded in 1981 as a nonprofit, tax-exempt 501(c)(3) organization. Its primary purpose is to provide a trustworthy and efficient channel for Amish, Mennonite, and other conservative Anabaptist groups and individuals to minister to physical and spiritual needs around the world. This is in response to the command to "... do good unto all men, especially unto them who are of the household of faith" (Galatians 6:10).

Each year, CAM supporters provide 15–20 million pounds of food, clothing, medicines, seeds, Bibles, Bible story books, and other Christian literature for needy people. Most of the aid goes to orphans and Christian families. Supporters' funds also help to clean up and rebuild for natural disaster victims, put up Gospel billboards in the U.S., support several church-planting efforts, operate two medical clinics, and provide resources for needy families to make their own living. CAM's main purposes for providing aid are to help and encourage God's people and bring the Gospel to a lost and dying world.

CAM has staff, warehouses, and distribution networks in Romania, Moldova, Ukraine, Haiti, Nicaragua, Liberia, Israel, and Kenya. Aside from management, supervisory personnel, and bookkeeping operations, volunteers do most of the work at CAM locations. Each year, volunteers at our warehouses, field bases, Disaster Response Services projects, and other locations donate over 200,000 hours of work.

CAM's ultimate purpose is to glorify God and help enlarge His kingdom. ". . . whatsoever ye do, do all to the glory of God" (1 Corinthians 10:31).